A SHORT INTRODUCTION
TO THE HISTORY AND POLITICS
OF SOUTHEAST ASIA

D1716059

A SHORT INTRODUCTION TO THE HISTORY AND POLITICS OF SOUTHEAST ASIA

RICHARD ALLEN

NEW YORK
OXFORD UNIVERSITY PRESS
LONDON 1970 TORONTO

To George Taylor
In appreciation of
much wise and friendly
guidance

PREFACE

This short book is based upon material prepared for a series of lectures at Virginia Colleges given in the spring of 1968 under the auspices of the Virginia Consortium for Asian Studies. It is designed primarily for undergraduate students and the general reader. As its title indicates it has no pretentions to be more than a clear and concise survey of some of the main aspects, past and present, of an area in which the United States has assumed progressively heavier responsibilities since World War II, but with which most Americans are still only marginally familiar. For those specially interested I trust that this may be useful as a prelude to the study of particular fields in depth. The space allotted to particular countries is admittedly variable. It is in some proportion to the magnitude of the problems which they present. I assume full responsibility for any unorthodox or contentious views it may contain, so far as these did not originate elsewhere. When this is the case there is some indication in the footnotes. These have been kept to a minimum, as has the list of books at the end.

I am much indebted to the Honorable Charles F. Baldwin, former United States Ambassador to Malaysia and Diplomat in Residence at the University of Virginia, for his help and encouragement in connection with my visit to Virginia, to Dr. Kurt F.

Leidecker of Mary Washington College of the University of Virginia for the trouble he kindly took over the original version of the text, and to Mr. Arley Jonish, Librarian of Whitman College, for having generously facilitated its publication in an earlier form. I am also grateful for a number of valuable suggestions to Dr. Usha Mahajani, formerly Research Fellow at the Australian National University, Canberra, and currently Professor of Political Science at Central Washington State College, Ellensburg.

R.A.

Ellensburg
September 1969

CONTENTS

A SHORT INTRODUCTION
TO THE HISTORY AND POLITICS
OF SOUTHEAST ASIA

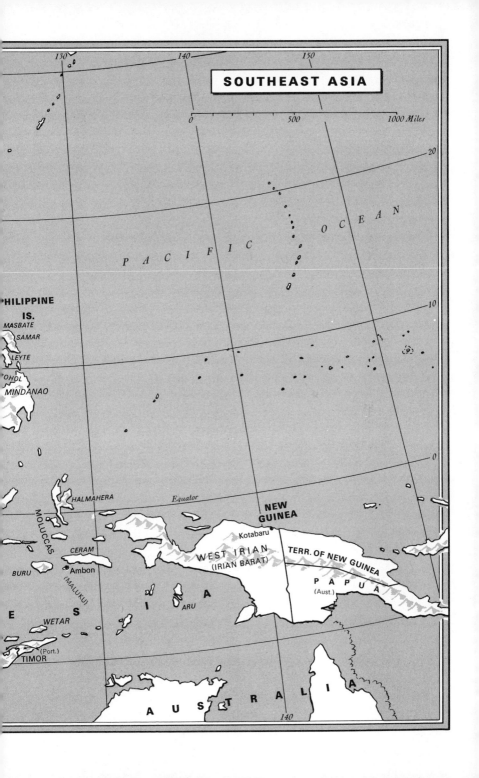

SOUTHEAST ASIA

130   140   150

0   500   1000 Miles

20

P A C I F I C   O C E A N

10

PHILIPPINE
IS.

MASBATE

SAMAR

LEYTE

BOHOL

MINDANAO

0

HALMAHERA   Equator   NEW
GUINEA

MOLUCCAS

CERAM

BURU   Ambon

(MALUKU)

E   S

WETAR

ARU

(Port.)
TIMOR

Kotabaru

WEST IRIAN
(IRIAN BARAT)

TERR. OF NEW GUINEA

P A P U A
(Aust.)

A U S T R A L I A

140

I

A FRAGMENTED REGION

The Setting

Southeast Asia is a watershed between the two great civilizations of Asia, those of India and China. Its total land area is approximately half that of the United States without Alaska, 1,600,000 square miles, with a slightly larger population than America's of some 220 million. Hence a dangerous human density in a few favored regions such as Java and the Red River delta in North Vietnam where rich soil and ample water can produce three rice crops in a year. Despite the modern specter of human multiplication, the countries of Southeast Asia are in general much less crowded than many parts of Asia and in particular than those two neighboring giants.

The Former Colonial World

There was little general interest in Southeast Asia before World War II, least of all in America, despite Washington's colonial involvement in the Philippines. The whole area except Thailand was colonial. Its lands were exotic extensions of the Great Powers. They provided many of the goods in Western stores and raw materials for industry, and it was all taken for granted. There were occasional outbursts of nationalist or communist disturbance. On the whole, however, order reigned. The subject peoples "gave little trouble" and had therefore small claim on our attention. The British, when they thought about Southeast Asia, pictured it in terms of the beachcombers or sea adventurers portrayed by Joseph Conrad (his first novel, *Almayer's Folly*, had a Southeast Asian, actually a Malayan, setting) or of the cynical sketches of colonial society in the short stories of Somerset Maugham.[1]

But Southeast Asia was also a Dutch and French colonial world and bore elsewhere the stamp of these two gifted races. This colonial world has vanished so completely that it seems a phantom. Yet independent nationhood has brought no millennium. The Voice of the People is raucous and discordant. In some areas such as Indonesia or Burma the peasants and workers may have had a more assured life materially under colonial rule than they have in the years of dissension brought by freedom. Meanwhile, America has been faced in Southeast Asia with one of the most agonizing crises in her history.

Southeast Asia: A New Concept

The term "Southeast Asia" did not gain currency until World War II. It became memorable in the first instance through the creation of the Southeast Asia Command based upon Ceylon to stem the Japanese onslaught, with Admiral Lord Mountbatten, the uncle of Queen Elizabeth's Consort, Prince Philip, as Supreme Allied Commander. Even then there was some vagueness about the exact scope

1. There is much good literature in English on Southeast Asia—and several interesting works in French, Dutch, and other languages—to be found in all well-stocked libraries, which can deepen and enhance understanding and appreciation of the area. This includes books of travel and description, folklore, memoirs, historical novels, and short stories and fiction based on personal experience. Apart from widely read writers like Conrad, Maugham, Orwell, Graham Greene, Lederer, etc., there are many others (such as Maurice Collis, Frank Swettenham, and Hugh Clifford) who have contributed significantly to this general category and who deserve to be better known.

of the term. However, it is now established that it covers Burma, Thailand, Laos, Cambodia, Vietnam, Malaysia, Singapore, Indonesia, and the Philippines. It does not cover Ceylon itself, nor Hong Kong nor Taiwan. Burma and Malaysia (which today includes most of the northern portion of the island of Borneo) were ruled by Britain; Laos, Cambodia, and Vietnam by France. The French territory was called Indochina, thus clearly indicating the dual background of the area as a whole. The huge Indonesian archipelago was ruled by the Netherlands. Thailand just escaped being a colony by nimble pliancy at critical moments and timely compromise with the exigencies of the imperialist powers. But she was not preserved from quasi-colonial subordination to the requirements of countries such as France and Britain with near-by territory. Nor of course was her vastly greater neighbor, China. America did her best to rescue them both from the diminution of their sovereignty imposed by the colonial powers.

Geography, Climate, Race

Although the definition Southeast Asia is new, this is a highly distinctive region. While most of Asia lies in continental and sub-tropical climatic zones, Southeast Asia spreads across the Equator in the stifling, humid tropics, stirred in their season by rain-bearing monsoon winds. In the north of Burma there is snow and ice, but the high northern mountain barrier in which the region culminates and which merges with the Tibetan plateau seals much of it off from the continental areas of dense population and helps to account for the general lack of human overcrowding. The mainland and the islands, deeply penetrated by gulfs and bays, are broken up by intricate and rugged mountains and are still largely covered by quasi-impenetrable jungle. At the same time Southeast Asia is a great crossroads of the sea, exposed to maritime invasion and the shifting interchange from early centuries of peoples, cultures, and religions. In a sense it can be said, as of the Greek world, that the land divides and the water unites. With ample rainfall in almost every part, Southeast Asia has fine rivers with wide and fertile deltas. The greatest is the Mekong which flows down from China through Laos, Cambodia, and South Vietnam and in part forms the border between Laos and Thailand. In Burma the country is watered by the Irrawaddy, its tributary the Chindwin, the Salween, and the Sittang. In central Thailand the principal river is the Menam Chao Praya with its delta around Bangkok. North Vietnam is threaded by the Hong (Red) and Da (Black) rivers. The country's rice bowl is their delta between Hanoi and Haiphong. In the eternal tradition of human society it is in and around these areas of easy food, the deltas and broader reaches of the main rivers, the coastal plains and the regions of rich volcanic soil such as Java, that major population centers and civilized arts and skills developed.

Southeast Asia has a remarkable diversity of peoples of whom no detailed description can be given here. It has been termed an anthropologist's paradise and was one of the homes of early man. At present the process by which this part of Asia was peopled before 2000 B.C. is being re-evaluated by archaeologists and physical anthropologists. According to traditional thinking the earliest populations entering the area were the Australoids, numbers of whom were able to make their way in prehistoric times over the land bridges linking the mainland with the Indonesian archipelago to New Guinea and on to Australia where they became the ancestors of some branches of the Australian aborigines. Again the Melanesoids were and are to be found in the eastern islands of the archipelago as well as in New Guinea.[2] Another of these simpler people are the Negritos, whose origins are unknown and subject to much speculation. It is worth noting at this point that in consequence of their relative proximity to Southeast Asia, Australia and New Zealand have found them-

2. See C. A. Fisher, *Southeast Asia, A Social, Economic and Political Geography*, London: Methuen, 1964, p. 66.

selves affected by developments there in ancient and modern times and most recently by the Japanese occupation of it in World War II. They have come to regard themselves as essentially part of Southeast Asia and destined to play a role in its affairs.

In general the trend of population movements in and through the Indochinese peninsula since pre-historic times has been from north to south from the region of what is now western China and Tibet. In the west the Mons, who later gave much of their culture to the Burmans and the Thais, seem to have moved down the Irrawaddy, Sittang, and Salween valleys, and the Tenasserim coast. Down these first two valleys came also the Burmans themselves and their predecessors, the Pyu. Another route, which seems to have been used by the Malays or Indonesians, was from the gorges of the upper Salween and Mekong to the Menam valley in central Thailand and on down the isthmus into Malaya and beyond into the Indonesian archipelago. This was also for part of the way the route for other groups of Mons and later for Shan, Lao, and Thai peoples, all the last three cousins by race. A third route, down the Mekong to its delta and westward around the Tonle Sap, the Great Lake of Cambodia, was that of the Khmer, cousins of the gifted Mons with a similar language and culture, Mongolian non-Chinese peoples who were to have a brilliant early history and a sadly reduced role in modern times. Finally, the Annamites or Vietnamese migrated into Tongking from China and gradually fought their way down the narrow strip between the Annamite cordillera and the sea toward the Mekong delta, which they eventually colonized and annexed from the Khmer. On the way southward, and in comparatively modern times, they destroyed and blotted out the Indianized kingdom of Champa which had had a long and checkered military career, thus proving that colonial oppression was neither an invention nor a monopoly of the Western nations. As these gifted races established themselves in the river basins and coastal plains the simpler peoples were driven back into the remoter jungles and mountains by the superior force and culture of the invaders.[3] Such was the fate of tribes like the Temiar of Malaya and the hill peoples generally classified as *montagnards* in Vietnam. Some of the less fortunate in this struggle for survival are still stigmatized by the dominant plains peoples with names denoting servile status, such as Sakai in Malaya, Moi and Kha in former French Indochina. There are also less backward indigenous minorities, such as the Chins and Kachins of Burma or the remote but intelligent up-country peoples of northern Borneo, which were never fully absorbed into the major states. Many of the mountain peoples tend to practice slash and burn, shifting cultivation to an extent which causes damaging erosion and ruins valuable forest resources.

The Common Characteristics of Southeast Asian Society

Rice is the central fact of life for all the peoples of Southeast Asia. Notwithstanding their differences of race, language, and religion there is an underlying cultural unity manifest in their folklore, architecture, land use, and social and political organization. There are also physical and mental resemblances. Burmans, Thais, Cambodians, Vietnamese, Malays, most Indonesians and Filipinos, all show much the same predominantly Mongoloid cast of countenance, yellow-brown skin, shortish stature, natural elegance of bearing, and an apparently innate good humor.[4] Perhaps in consequence of an enervating climate, they nearly all seem to prefer an easy pace of life to the hot pursuit of material gain, though the Chinese in their midst and the Japanese with their powerful impact in recent times seem to lose nothing of their northern toughness and dynamism and acquisitiveness in these languorous climes.

3. Rupert Emerson, *Malaysia*, Kuala Lumpur: University of Malaya Press, 1964, p. 12.
4. Fisher, op. cit., p. 7.

The Cultural Impact of India

Strangely, in view of their Mongoloid features, by far the greatest cultural influence upon these peoples historically was that of India, not China. Only the Vietnamese absorbed the culture and social structure of China and incidentally the more eclectic Mahayana form of Buddhism as distinct from the narrower and stricter Theravada or Hinayana faith which, closer to the original doctrines evolved in India and Ceylon, has been adopted by Buddhist Burma, Thailand, Laos, and Cambodia. By the early centuries of the Christian era many Indian trade centers had been established in Southeast Asia and through Indian traders and travelers first Hinduism, still the religion of Bali, and later Buddhism made converts throughout the region. In far more recent times, from the thirteenth century onward, Islam superseded but did not efface these earlier religions in Indonesia and Malaya. This too, though partly diffused from Arabia direct, came largely through early Indian converts from the region of Gujerat in northwest India. The Indians brought with them their art and architecture, their literature and philosophy, their notions of monarchy and political organization and the dynamic quality of their ideals. Yet all these Indian imports acquired a strong local character. They were transformed by the conditions of Southeast Asian society into something unique. The status of women, for example, was and is far higher and more independent in Southeast Asia than in India.

The Approaching End of Western Tutelage?

The inspiration of India led to the establishment of powerful kingdoms under monarchs with quasi-divine attributes which dominated for a time different parts of a fascinating area. But in this brief review it will be sufficient to trace these early political developments only to the extent that they are relevant to the tensions, conflicts, and ambitions which overshadow the lives of Southeast Asia's independent nations today. We have after all reached, or should shortly be reaching, a phase of history in which the West ceases to give the law to Asia as it has done for more than four hundred and fifty years, from the first landing of the Portuguese Captain Vasco da Gama in India until the establishment of Malaysia in 1963. It may well be that in the years to come the nations of Asia, including some present or potential Great Powers which have absorbed the vigorous statecraft of the West from European tutelage or example, will establish their own equilibrium and stability. Long before the arrival of the Western conqueror these nations with a far older civilization had guided their own affairs besides giving to Europe many of the basic essentials of its culture in religion, language, science, and art, much that Europeans have taken for granted as their own in a gratuitous assumption of superiority.

II

THE MAINLAND AND THE ISLANDS

The Mainland Nations

Southeast Asia falls conveniently into two halves. Long before the colonial period all these countries suffered the vicissitudes of sharply conflicting national ambitions and changes of sovereignty and power structure through savage wars, which were also characteristic of the evolution of Europe. The mainland nations constitute half of the area. With Thailand in the middle there is former British Burma to the west and former French Indochina to the east. Both Burma and Thailand have long tails stretching down into the Malay peninsula, known at its narrow point as the Isthmus of Kra, which separates the Gulf of Siam and the South China Sea from the Andaman Sea and the Bay of Bengal. The tail of Thailand reaches right down to the borders of Malaysia and contains four mainly Malay-Moslem provinces in the south. Much has been done to assimilate these by the Thais but they still constitute a kind of Malaya *irredenta* for some Malay extremists. More seriously, this jungle border is today the hideout of a well-trained hard core of communist terrorists who survived the long and bloody guerrilla war fought on Malayan soil from 1948 to 1960, a kind of preview of the Vietnam war which for various reasons had a happier conclusion. In the 1930's the isthmus was strategically significant to the Japanese. The construction of a canal was envisaged. Their plans for the domination of Eastern Asia demanded ready communication between Thailand and Burma unexposed to hostile navies or to the British naval base at Singapore. In the event, after occupying Thailand, Malaya, and Singapore, the Japanese forged their direct link at vast expense of the lives of their defeated enemies. This was the famous Railroad of Death, uneconomic and now totally abandoned, linking the Thai railway system from Kanchanaburi west of Bangkok through the Three Pagodas Pass to the Burmese system south of Moulmein.

Burma: General Background

The main area of Burma, shaped like an oyster, stretches northward well beyond the tropics to the eastern reaches of Tibet, whence many of her people came. She is the size of Texas with a population of 26.5 million and is in normal times the world's largest exporter of rice. Burma has a long border with India and East Pakistan and an even longer, thousand-mile one with India's present adversary, Communist China, mostly along the western fringes of Yunnan. Her ancient and modern history has been mainly conditioned by the movement of events toward or across these borders. By the late eighteenth century Burma had become a massive kingdom, militarily formidable by Asian standards, but this imposing structure was not the product of any assured and steady growth. It was the outcome of constant strains and clashes over eight hundred years between the different races and realms within the country, in which the Burmans eventually emerged as uncontested masters. The first major state in the Irrawaddy valley of which there is some record had a capital called Srikshetra, north of Prome. It is said to have been founded around A.D. 638 by people called the Pyu, apparently the forerunners of the Burmans and like them of partly Tibetan origin. The Pyu were for some time in conflict with a Mon kingdom based on Thaton between the Salween and the Sittang for the control of lower

Burma. Then in 850 they seem to have succumbed to a new wave from the north, that of the Burmans proper, who eventually gained control over the principal rice growing areas in upper Burma near to the Irrawaddy and its tributary the Chindwin, those of Kyaukse, Magwe-Minbu, and Shwebo. In 1044 a ruler called Anawrahta founded Burma's first national kingdom at Pagan in this upper region of the Irrawaddy. This kingdom later conquered the Mon state of southern Burma. In their long and often sanguinary co-existence with the more advanced and civilized Mons, the Burmans absorbed many of the most important elements of their culture from them, including the Mon system of writing and the orthodox form of Theravada Buddhism, which the Mons had received from Ceylon. At the end of the thirteenth century the Pagan kingdom was destroyed by the Mongol Chinese armies which had taken over Nanchao, a state east of the Irrawaddy, helped by the Thais or Shans from that general area. The Shans for a time dominated northern Burma and afterward remained in pockets around the northern zone and in strength in the eastern hill region now known as the Burmese Shan States. The Mon kingdom, which later moved its capital to Pegu, regained its independence only to lose it again in the sixteenth century when a new and powerful Burmese dynasty emerged, based on Toungoo in Burma's east-central plain, a dynasty which repeatedly invaded Thailand, imposing certain Burmese laws and the Burmese chronology on their Thai neighbors. It also for a time brought under its sway the partly Mon area of Chiengmai in what is now northern Thailand. One sign of the declining grasp of the later Burmese Toungoo kings was their decision in 1635 to transfer their capital from the conquered Mon kingdom with its ports and access to world commerce and events back to Ava near present Mandalay in the isolated and arid north. Here its rulers became, after the pattern of most long-lived Oriental dynasties, both physically and mentally inbred. In 1740, when the Toungoo dynasty was in marked decline, the Mons revolted, briefly revived their kingdom, and conquered virtually the whole of Burma, including Ava. The apparently annihilated Burmans then launched a swift and remarkable campaign of reconquest led by the son of the headman of Shwebo, north of Ava. This resistance hero raised himself to the throne as King Alaungpaya and founded the last, Konbaung, dynasty of Burmese kings, which survived until the final conquest by the British in 1885. Alaungpaya ruthlessly and permanently destroyed the Mon kingdom and gave to its southern port of Dagon, chiefly noted for its famous Golden Pagoda, the Shwe Dagon, the more familiar name of Yangon or Rangoon, meaning "End of Strife." The Mons who escaped massacre concentrated their remnants in northern Tenasserim or fled into Thailand.

In circumstances we shall be noting later, Burma came under British rule in the nineteenth century and Rangoon became the capital in place of Ava. As a British dependency she was critically exposed to the Japanese onslaught in World War II. The Burma Road into Yunnan was one of the two principal supply routes to the Japanese-beleaguered Chinese Nationalist government in Chungking, the other being that through Tongking in northern French Indochina. In 1942–45 Burma suffered terrible destruction during the two campaigns fought on her soil. The first was an Allied retreat which ended in the Japanese being halted on the Indian side of the border at Imphal and Kohima. Then the Allies returned and there was bitter fighting down Burma from the Chindwin to the south until the Japanese were decisively defeated by the British XIV Army and General Stillwell's forces.[1] Since independence in 1948 Burma has been hardly less dangerously exposed. Peking's claim to most of India's Northeast Frontier Agency threatens to bring Burma's most menacing neighbor far closer to her in the sub-Tibetan region as well as in Yunnan. Fortunately, independent India's traditional code of non-violence and neutrality and the generally sensible realism of Ayoub Khan's Pakistan have been a guarantee rather than a threat.

1. For a vivid and trenchant account of the two Burma campaigns by the general in command of the British XIV Army see Viscount Slim, *Defeat into Victory*, New York: McKay, 1961.

Burma has managed to keep good relations with them both despite the harsh treatment by her present military regime of the large Indian and Pakistani communities which had dominated much of the economic life of the country. Great numbers of these people have recently been forced to return to their already overcrowded homeland leaving their personal property behind. But Burma is also vulnerable by reason of enduring insurrections launched by her three principal minorities, the Karens, the Shans, and the Kachins, and by communist groups within the country. Situated as she is, Burma has comprehensibly adopted a strongly isolationist neutrality which has so far obviated any need for the employment of foreign troops within her borders. This has been coupled with a policy of on the whole cautious conciliation of Peking. She is well aware that China could cross her territory in a matter of days if she wished and establish a bridgehead on the Bay of Bengal far more potentially damaging to Western strategy than any communist takeover of South Vietnam. China has not in fact elected to take this step, even at moments of high tension with the West, and this may possibly show that she does not aim at moving physically into Southeast Asia but is seeking rather a protective cordon of sympathetic states around her borders, like that which Russia has managed to achieve in Europe. In any event Burma has tried to avert confrontation over a disputed frontier and sacrificed some villages to China when Peking after much stalling suddenly agreed to a not unreasonable border settlement. Characteristically, all this did not prevent a recent outburst of vituperation from Peking when Burma sternly repressed subversive agitation among students wearing pro-Mao badges.

Thailand

Thailand, with a population approaching 34 million and an export surplus of rice now exceeding that of Burma, is spared a common frontier with China by the fortunate, from this aspect, accident of colonialism which surrounded her in modern times with European dependencies. There were the British to the north, west, and south in Burma and Malaya; and the French to the northeast and southeast. The French detached Thailand's Lao cousins and former vassals while the British absorbed her other related group, the Shans, when they annexed Burma. The upper reaches of the Mekong in fact divide the former British and French territories which separate Thailand from China. This was a compromise border accepted after some dissension by both colonial powers after the incidents of 1885 when Britain moved into Upper Burma largely to prevent the French from doing the same. This area, incidentally, exemplifies the "colonial" attitudes of some Asians toward others. Prince Souvanna Phouma, the present neutralist Prime Minister of Laos, has complained bitterly that the Thais have continued to call his independent country the "Lao Province."

There are still many Thais in Yunnan, which was largely co-terminous with the ancient Thai kingdom of Nanchao, annexed in 1253 by Kublai Khan the Mongol Chinese emperor. After a slow migration southward down the river valleys the Thais were comparatively recent arrivals in the warmer regions of Southeast Asia and made vigorous impact upon all their neighbors. The first major Thai kingdom emerged about 1220 in the middle Menam valley around Sukhotai. Some fifty years later under an able ruler called Rama Khamheng the kingdom of Sukhotai extended its sway over the Khmer-dominated states of the Menam delta and the Malayan isthmus. At the end of the thirteenth century another Thai state established itself in the area of Chiengmai formerly under Mon control. Around 1350 a second and eventually more powerful Thai kingdom was founded in the southern Menam valley with its capital at Ayuthia. Only after centuries of struggle and repeated Burmese interventions was Chiengmai finally absorbed into modern Thailand.

The distribution of Thai peoples to the north, east, and west of the national borders has led some of Thailand's more ambitious leaders, and notably Field Marshal Pibun who collaborated with the Japanese during World War II, to pursue a Pan-Thai policy aimed at the incorporation under Bangkok's suzerainty of as many as possible of the peoples of Thai race. As a reward for his helpfulness in permitting the Japanese to use Thailand as a staging post for their absorption of French Indochina, Malaya, and Burma, Bangkok received back areas of Cambodia and Laos which it had dominated in the past and two of the Shan states of Burma. The Japanese also returned to temporary Thai control the four nothern states of Malaya, a somewhat shadowy suzerainty over which Thailand had been persuaded by Britain to surrender in 1909 in return for fairly valuable British concessions. After the war Thailand was compelled to restore all this Japanese-gained territory. Whatever the injustices of the colonial system, it had had one further advantage for this area. British control of Burma had put an end to the devastating wars between the rival Buddhist kingdoms of Burma and Thailand which had caused so much suffering and led to the complete destruction of Thailand's earlier capital of Ayuthia in 1767. Despite Thailand's geographic separation from China there are some three million Chinese in Thailand (strangely enough nearly ten times the number of Chinese in Burma) whom the Thais have made every effort to assimilate. Thailand being a Buddhist country, although of a different Buddhism from that of China, has greatly facilitated this assimilation, since many of the basic elements of daily life, such as the prevalence of the pig, are acceptable to both races. A similar ease of assimilation exists in the mainly Christian Philippines; and many of the elite in both countries, including the Thai royal family, are of mixed Chinese and local blood. Assimilation of the Chinese in Islamic Malaysia and Indonesia is on the other hand largely impossible because to the Muslim the pig is an unclean animal.

Former French Indochina: Laos

In former French Indochina, Laos, with the area of Britain, has only 2.75 million people; Cambodia, with the area of New York state, has 6.5 million; the two Vietnams have nearly 21 million in the north and 17.5 million in the south.

The establishment of the Thai kingdom of Ayuthia appears to have encouraged the foundation of an independent Laotian state in 1353. This was called the kingdom of Lan Ch'ang and for a period it dominated the region of Luang Prabang as well as that of Vienchang, now Vientiane. But for much of her history Laos has been divided into rival realms. Her two modern capitals, the royal capital at Luang Prabang and the administrative one at Vientiane on the Mekong border with Thailand, became at one time the centers of separate kingdoms. Other earlier semi-feudal fiefs were the principality of Xieng Khouang in the interior and the southern principality of Champassak. Laos has been subjected to the pressures and acquisitiveness of her neighbors more than almost any country of Southeast Asia. Parts have been dominated at various times not merely by the Thais but by the ancient Khmer empire of Cambodia, by Burma, and by Vietnam. Indeed at one period the Emperors of Annam exercised their influence over Xieng Khouang and the Plain of Jars much as Ho Chi Minh does today with the help of the communist Pathet Lao, led strangely enough by one of the royal princes, Souphanouvong, a half-brother of Prime Minister Souvanna Phouma. Today communist domination extends over most of the northern and northeastern belt of Laotian territory, the area bordering on China and North Vietnam. It is from here that recent assaults on Luang Prabang have been launched, and in 1954 it was just on the Tongking side of the northeastern Laotian border that the French forces were defeated by those of Hanoi at Dien Bien Phu. In contrast to this communist-dominated zone, Champassak in the south is still today a kind of hereditary fief of Prince Boun Oum, the rightist leader who enjoyed for a time the warm support of the United States. These local and personal and centrifugal forces have in fact been such throughout her history that Laos cannot really be said to have developed the fabric and spirit of a nation even in the loosely structured sense in which that term is used in modern Asia. Physically, the country consists of a head and a long trunk, the eastern backbone of which forms part of the Annamite cordillera separating the narrow coastal strip of North Vietnam and South Vietnam from the rest of Indochina. This cordillera does, however, provide a rugged form of communication from north to south conveniently inaccessible to the ineffective and fragmented Laotian authorities. This is the Ho Chi Minh Trail which has so multiplied the effectiveness both of the Vietcong guerrillas and of the battle-seasoned regular troops of Hanoi. Vo Nguyen Giap, a former schoolmaster and keen student of the campaigns of Napoleon, has been leading these with imposing tenacity and skill for well over twenty years, longer even than Napoleon commanded armies in the field. It is from supplies moving down this trail that the attacks on Allied forces in South Vietnam have drawn their strength.

Cambodia

In view of her modest size and petulant international role today it is hard to grasp that Cambodia from around A.D. 800 to the mid-fifteenth century, or the time of the fall of Constantinople, developed by far the most distinguished civilization and impressive power structure of any nation on the mainland of Southeast Asia. In this she was helped by the rich conditions for food production, especially of rice and fish, of the region of the Great Lake. The Khmer people of Cambodia were, as we saw, the cousins of the equally gifted but less fortunate Mons who helped to transmit the common culture of the two peoples to the Burmese and the Thais. Known to the Chinese as Chenla, Cambodia had earlier prevailed over its former overlord Funan in the Mekong delta. This maritime and commercial state linked with the Indonesian islands and with the China and India trade is the first major Indianized kingdom of Southeast Asia of which we have some historical record and it appears to have lasted from the first century to the sixth century A.D. Before moving to Angkor the Khmer kings had established other capitals in the general region of the Great Lake and shortly before 800 they had come temporarily under the sway of one of the major kingdoms of Java. The art and architecture of Angkor, of Hindu and Buddhist inspiration with fascinating low reliefs telling the legends of the past and the daily life of the age, are quite simply one of the wonders of the world, and it is to the eternal credit of the French colonizers that it was they who discovered and restored these monuments and gave them to the world. At the start of this period the Thais had hardly begun their movement from Nanchao southward into the Menam valley, and the Annamites or Vietnamese were only approaching the end of a thousand-year subjection to China. The Thais were a fairly primitive people in the early years of the Khmer kingdom and are depicted as semi-savages on some of the low reliefs at Angkor. They were also occasionally recruited as mercenaries by the Khmer armies. Yet during the later years of Angkor's power they had as we saw developed successively two strong kingdoms. Thus it was the ruder and more recently civilized Thais who in 1431 gave the death blow to Angkor and eventually reduced diminished Cambodia—compelled to move its capital southward to present Phnom Penh—to the rank of a vassal state.

Annam-Vietnam, Champa

Modern Vietnam has been compared to two baskets of rice slung on a pole, the "baskets" being the delta of the Red River in the north and that of the Mekong in the south, the "pole" the Annamite cordillera. Two thousand years ago, however, Vietnam (or Nam Viet, as it was then called), which was incorporated into China by the Han dynasty in B.C. 111, existed only in the north. Before its defeat by the Emperor Han Wu Ti, Nam Viet extended into what is now southern China and covered much of the province of Kwangtung. The new Chinese overlords, however, restricted it essentially to the Red River delta and the general area of Tongking and northern Annam. Indeed by excluding Nam Viet from the Kwangtung area it seems to have given the initial impulse to its southward expansion. Meanwhile, although they accepted Chinese civilization, the Vietnamese preserved their identity and tenaciously resisted assimilation as Chinese. Indeed, many of the Chinese sent to rule them adopted local loyalties. After a series of abortive revolts over the centuries a rising in A.D. 939 achieved enduring success under a leader called Ngo Quyen, who had profited by the disunity in China following the decline of the T'ang dynasty. The new governing classes of scholar-mandarin officials and remnants of the feudal aristocracy, which had been decimated in the various risings, seem by now to have found strength and support at the village level and something of an embryonic national consensus had emerged. But during the centuries of Chinese rule this "Smaller Dragon," the only sinicized part of Southeast Asia, received the indelible stamp of Mahayana Buddhism, Confucianism, Taoism, and the characteristically Chinese mandarin system.

Only once, for a period of twenty years in the fifteenth century, did China ever again manage completely to dominate Vietnam or Dai Viet, as the now autonomous country was renamed by its first firmly established rulers. Like most of the countries round China's borders, however, Dai Viet continued to acknowledge the suzerainty of Peking. During the four centuries of the Ly and Tran dynasties (1010–1400) Dai Viet or Annam (a Chinese-imposed name signifying Pacified South) affirmed and matured its national identity. After the country's temporary subjection to the Ming dynasty from 1407 to 1427 it was identified with the Le dynasty. The Le emperors were at first the actual rulers. Later they remained as symbols of authority while the country was effectively governed by two princely families, one in the north and one in the south. We shall deal later with Vietnam's temporary division and the role of these last rulers.

The fifteenth century which saw the downfall of the Angkor kingdom also saw that of the kingdom of Champa. This was a further phase in what became an implacable drive southward by the increasingly powerful Vietnamese state. The first centuries of the Christian era had been, as we saw, the period of India's civilizing influence on Southeast Asia and of the emergence of Indianized states such as Funan. Indeed while China still dominated Vietnam, the Red River delta became, up to a point, a meeting ground of the Indian and Chinese worlds. South of Vietnam the Chams, a people of Indonesian origin with little good rice land, had flourished as sailors, pirates, and fishermen. They had been little affected by the Chinese way of life and eventually became strongly Indianized. When the Han empire declined the Chams asserted their own independence in A.D. 197 and by the tenth century their kingdom dominated much of the geographical region of Annam up to and beyond the 17th parallel and stretched southward almost to the Mekong delta. For their misfortune the seafaring Chams, who had at one time sailed up the Mekong and sacked Angkor and at others had pillaged Hanoi and defeated the Chinese Mongol armies, lacked the peasant tenacity to establish their roots in the soil. This left the field free for the gradual encroachment into their region of the tough Vietnamese cultivators. Well trained in the age-old skills of Chinese agriculture these pushed ever further south, gradually taking over successive small pockets of cultivable land. During this process the balance of advantage in constant wars between these neighbors also went mostly against Champa, which shifted its capital southward, losing region after region to Vietnam. After vain attempts to recoup some of these territorial losses, Champa was decisively defeated in 1471 after more than twelve hundred years of adventurous and at times brilliant history. A broken kingdom lived on for a time in three small deltas south of Cape Varella, having lost three hundred miles of coastline to Vietnam. Finally the remnants of Champa were expunged by the Vietnamese in 1697 in an operation which can well be qualified as genocide. Today all that remains of Champa is some 30,000 Indian-featured Muslim fishermen and artisans around Phan-Rang and Phan-Ri in the general area of Camranh Bay.[2]

Having destroyed Champa, the Vietnamese continued their drive

2. Bernard B. Fall, *The Two Vietnams*, New York: Praeger, 1966, p. 13.

south, in part by planting military-agricultural colonies on the pattern of ancient Rome or modern Israel. In the late seventeenth and early eighteenth century they went on to annex the Khmer-inhabited regions of Cochinchina and the Mekong delta. These still belonged to the kingdom of Cambodia which had already lost so much to the Thais. In the nineteenth century the Vietnamese even annexed the whole southern portion of Cambodia, including its modern capital of Phnom Penh. By 1846 Cambodia had become a joint vassal of both Thailand and Annam. When the French substituted their protectorate in 1863 having taken over three provinces of Cochinchina the year before, the nineteenth-century annexations of Annam were recovered by Cambodia. In acknowledging the French protectorate, the Thais insisted on reserving as their own two of Cambodia's northern and western provinces, including the area of Angkor. But in 1907 France compelled Thailand to relinquish these also to her Cambodian protectorate.

The Sea-Girt Nations

The other half of Southeast Asia is formed by the major groups of islands and the Malay peninsula. The latter contains West Malaysia which as the Federation of Malaya obtained independence from Britain in 1957. The enlarged federation of Malaysia, constituted in 1963, includes Sabah and Sarawak in northern Borneo, and is now known as East Malaysia. Thus this new nation is in two halves like Pakistan and separated by many hundred miles of sea. The largest archipelago is that of Indonesia, for three hundred years under the Dutch, including Java (Djawa), Sumatra (Sumatera), the Celebes (Sulawesi), southern Borneo (Kalimantan), the Molucca (Maluku) spice islands, and western New Guinea (Irian Barat). Both these countries are mainly Muslim. Further north is the smaller archipelago of the Philippines, discovered by the Portuguese Magellan, Christianized by the Spaniards over more than three hundred years, and given the example and precept of democracy in some fifty years of American rule. As we have seen, the people of New Guinea are racially quite different from the Malays. So are most of the inhabitants of a flourishing enclave in the western area, the independent former British island state of Singapore. This is three-quarters Chinese although it has a quarter of a million Malays, more than in the whole of East Malaysia.

The Malay World

The population of Malaysia in round figures approaches 10.5 million; that of Singapore is two million. The population of Indonesia is that of a potential Great Power: in 1968 it was nearly 113 million and larger than that of Japan. The Philippines have nearly 36 million inhabitants. Malaysia is a multi-racial state to an exceptional degree. Barely half the population is Malay while 36 per cent is Chinese and 9 per cent Indian. Indonesia and the Philippines are mainly of Malay stock. Thus the Malay population in this southern area of Southeast Asia forms a block of some 140 million people. The six to seven million Chinese in their midst, including the sizable minorities in each of the three larger countries, are dominant in the economic field. They are, however, faced with the ultimate necessity of conforming with government policies dictated by the Malays so long, that is, as the Malay nations are in harmony with each other, which has by no means always been the case.

Early Indonesia, Malaya, and the Philippines

We have seen the links of Funan and Champa with Indonesia in the early centuries of the Christian era. This great archipelago received in full measure the sea-borne influences of India and eventually there evolved in parts of Java a highly sophisticated, artistically brilliant civilization comparable in quality with that of Angkor. It may indeed have had some influence on the marvelous art and architecture of the latter since the king who established his capital at Angkor around 800 had been a vassal of the Sailendra kings of Mataram in central Java and resident in their dominions. After the move to Angkor he seems to have declared himself independent of his Indonesian overlord.[3]

Before this, however, a powerful Indianized state had arisen in southern Sumatra with its capital at Palembang. This was Srivijaya, which endured from the seventh to the thirteenth century and seems to have extended its sway over parts of the Malay peninsula. It was essentially a maritime and commercial empire and in this the true successor to Funan which had expired in the sixth century. But Srivijaya was much better placed than Funan to play this role. Palembang was almost equidistant from the Sunda Strait, between Java and Sumatra, and the Strait of Malacca, between Sumatra and Malaya. She controlled both these vital channels through which passed nearly all the trade between Persia, India and the West, and China. And she did this at a time when the Arabs, inspired by the rise of Islam in the seventh century had overrun most of the Middle East and North Africa and had become the best navigators in this pre-European phase of Asian history. They dominated the Indian Ocean and tried to keep secret what they had learned of the monsoon winds which blew in opposite directions at different seasons. These monsoons facilitated the whole process of reliable navigation and Palembang became especially valuable as a port of call during the northeast monsoon. Yet it was not just a commercial city. According to reports from Chinese Buddhist pilgrims it seems to have been an important Buddhist center as well.

In all these ancient Indianized kingdoms a mountain, real or artificial, was its symbolic center. The Sailendras were "Kings of the Mountain" in Java and they were responsible for the splendid Bud-

3. John F. Cady, *Thailand, Burma, Laos and Cambodia*, Englewood Cliffs: Prentice-Hall, 1966, p. 49.

dhist *stupa* of Borobodur built about 772. This is a sanctuary of rising concentric terraces built over sacred relics and fully comparable in artistic greatness to the superb monuments of Angkor.

From about 850 two branches of the Sailendras seem to have ruled for a time simultaneously over central Java and Srivijaya. But by this time the Buddhist Sailendras were apparently losing their grip in Java. There was some revival of Hinduism in Mataram and it flourished in a kingdom of East Java based upon Malang. Indeed a dynasty from East Java superseded the Sailendras in central Java and constructed there in the early tenth century at Prambanan, not far from Borobodur, a complex of Hindu temples as fine in its way as the great Buddhist sanctuary.

Srivijaya seems to have been at the height of its power around 1000, by which time it had succeeded in bringing East Java under its sway. Then in 1025 it suffered a devasting blow from an attack by the Chola kingdom of South India, a strong competitor in the Asian trade. It lost East Java and never fully recovered. In the thirteenth century the center of power of this Sumatran kingdom shifted from Palembang to Jambi (Malayu) further north. Later in this century the Thai kingdom of Sukhotai subjugated much of the Malay Peninsula which Srivijaya had controlled. In 1292 the Venetian Marco Polo, who had become a trusted official of the Mongol dynasty of China and was one of the first European witnesses to ancient Asia, noted on a visit to Sumatra a new and disturbing phenomenon: people in the north of the island were becoming converted to Islam.

Meanwhile, between the eleventh century and the end of the thirteenth century much of Indianized Java was united in one kingdom under the successive dynasties of Kediri, Singosari, and Majapahit. All took their name from the capitals of the rulers which in fact fell within a small triangle of territory in eastern Java. Majapahit was the last major dynasty of pre-European Indonesia. It was founded by an ingenious prince who had outwitted in 1293 a Mongol force which had attacked Java, and it survived until the early sixteenth century.

It is said to have dominated part of the Malay peninsula as Srivijaya had before it. But it was already in decline around 1400. At this period East Java again asserted its independence and a new port-kingdom was founded at Malacca on the southwest coast of the Malay peninsula.

The founder of Malacca seems to have been a minor prince of Palembang married to a Majapahit princess who escaped from Java, temporarily established himself in Singapore and moved up the coast to escape retribution after the Thai governor of the island had been murdered. The new settlement inherited something of Srivijaya's commercial power and drew revenue from charging dues to ships passing through the Strait of Malacca. It became a wealthy entrepôt and, after the conversion of the ruler to Islam, an important center for the diffusion of the new faith throughout the Malay peninsula and the islands. By the time Majapahit fell the Muslims controlled most of the ports and coastal regions of Java. Islam had largely been brought by Muslims from northwestern India, and Indians and Javanese were highly influential in the Malacca Sultanate.

Until the rise of Malacca the small states of the Malay peninsula had to some extent been claimed as dependencies by Srivijaya, and from the thirteenth century by Thailand and Majapahit. They had been both a link and a source of conflict between the sea-girt and the mainland countries. They had responded to Indian civilization like most of the rest of the area. There was some mineral wealth, mostly tin. But the soil tended to be poor, the areas of settlement sparsely populated and separated by dense jungle. No outstanding monuments or works of art were produced. For all these reasons, before 1400 Malaya had played virtually no independent role in the history of pre-European Southeast Asia. With Malacca a minor power in its own right, all this was changed. The Sultans emancipated themselves both from Thailand and from Majapahit. In the course of a hundred years they established a dominant position in the peninsula and even over part of eastern Sumatra. As we shall see in the next chapter, Malacca acquired even greater significance in the early sixteenth century as the first point of impact of Europe upon Southeast Asia.

The smaller archipelago later called the Philippines had been little affected by the creative forces from India and China which had transformed the rest of Southeast Asia. No god-kings or extensive empires evolved there as they did in Indonesia and Cambodia. The simple village life based on subsistence cultivation along the river banks in a number of scattered islands was in complete contrast to the world to the south or on the mainland. Only in one way had the influence of Indonesia and Malaya made itself felt. Islam had spread to the southern islands of the group and by the mid-sixteenth century was beginning to take hold in the center and the north. One of the consequences of the first confrontation with Europe was as we shall see to check and restrict the Muslim advance.

The Legacy of the Past

This excursion into past history has been essential to explain the background to present-day tensions in Southeast Asia of which most Westerners are little aware. Thus the homeland of the Vietnamese is North Vietnam, which enjoys traditionally a special prestige. For the same reason the standard and generally accepted form of the Vietnamese language (as used, for example, by the British Broadcasting Corporation in its special programs) is the North Vietnamese form. Again, many of the outstanding Vietnamese leaders in the South as well as the North, including former President Diem, have been North Vietnamese. Yet the Vietnamese of both areas are emphatically one race, more similar perhaps than Americans of North and South. The South after all does not accept Yankee speech as standard American. It is true that South Vietnam was historically an area conquered from other states and races, yet it has become essentially part of a single Vietnamese nation. This sketch of the past also explains a certain cultural superiority complex on the part of Prince Sihanouk, the former king and present head of state and political leader of Cambodia, and also the bitter, prickly resentment and suspicion he often shows toward both Thailand and Vietnam. It even gives some basis for the comparative warmth of his relations with France and particularly with General de Gaulle, who has flattered and encouraged him in his cavalier attitude toward the United States and the Vietnam war. It sheds some light on the traditional dislike and suspicion between Thailand and Burma, the condescension of the former toward Laos, and the general failure of the royal Laotian government to come to terms with the critical situation it faces. Again it was on the strength of the area ruled by the ancient empires of Srivijaya and Majapahit that President Sukarno of Indonesia had ambitions to dominate Malaya and violently objected to Malaya's expansion into Malaysia by the inclusion in it of the former British Borneo territories. Indeed this was one of the basic causes of the shooting war between these two countries from 1963 to 1966, the seriousness of which Sukarno sought to mask by calling it merely "Confrontation." Finally the success of the Malacca Sultanate has been an inspiration to the Malay leadership of today. Its record and memory have dispelled the quite unwarranted doubts of some British colonial officials whether the Malays would ever be effective in governing themselves. It may further help to account for the skill and flexibility with which the Kuala Lumpur government has made of their country something of a showpiece of the new Asia.

III

THE EXPANSION OF EUROPE

The First European Incursions

These geographical, social, and cultural factors and trends of early history have helped to shape the conditions and outlook of the Southeast Asian nations today. The colonial phase which followed has also had a decisive influence. Basically, it has been the character and quality of colonial rule which has determined the extent to which Western organization and experience has been assimilated or rejected by the new Asian nations in the post-colonial era.

Marco Polo, the great Venetian, visited Southeast Asia at the end of the thirteenth century on a mission from the Mongol Emperor of China. Two hundred years later the voyages of discovery began which brought Columbus to America in 1492 and Vasco da Gama, the Portuguese captain, to India in 1498. Following Columbus's first voyage, Pope Alexander VI in effect divided the newly discovered world by a line drawn to the west of the Azores and Cape Verde Islands. Portugal could claim possession of all lands to the east of it, Spain of all to the west. Subsequently by the Treaty of Tordesillas of 1494 the line was shifted westward to bring Brazil into the Portuguese sphere. This left nearly all of Asia to the Portuguese. Only in the Philippines and the Moluccas did a dispute develop between the two Iberian powers since under the treaty both areas could be claimed by Portugal. This ceased to be relevant when the two countries were united under Philip II in 1580. Meanwhile in the early sixteenth century and within a period of about ten years Europe made its first significant contacts with Southeast Asia. In 1507 Affonso de Albuquerque had conquered Ormuz at the entrance to the Persian Gulf and three years later had made Goa the capital of the Portuguese possessions in Asia. In 1511 he attacked and captured the Malacca Sultanate and opened up communications with Thailand, the Indonesian Moluccas, and China. This last venture was to lead in 1557 to the establishment of a Portuguese settlement at Macao near Canton and the start of regular trade between Portugal and China. In Malacca, Portugal followed the example of the Sultans in trying to control the traffic through the Strait and levying profitable tolls from passing ships. According to a Portuguese chronicler of the time Malacca under Asian rule had been one of the finest ports of the world.

In 1521 another Portuguese, called Magalhaes but better known as Magellan, and working for the king of Spain, landed on the island of Cebu in the central Philippines and was shortly afterwards killed in a local fight. Not till more than forty years later, in 1564, and after a series of failures did the Spaniards manage to establish their rule in this archipelago with headquarters at Manila on the island of Luzon. Their new colony was named after Philip II, who later brought Spain and Portugal together under his rule and launched the Great Armada against England. The Spaniards were just in time to stop the spread of Islam in the central and northern islands of the group. The development of Spanish and ultimately American rule in the Philippines will be discussed in a later chapter.

The Portuguese left an imprint on Malacca which has endured. They built a massive fort, A Famosa, unforgivably destroyed by the British at the end of the eighteenth century, of which only fragments remain. Like the Spaniards, they were fierce Catholics anxious to spread the faith. But, like others who have carried Christianity to Asia, they found it hard to make converts from any of the major religions that stress the equality of men, like Islam and Bud-dhism. They had greater success with the more primitive animist spirit worshippers, and to some extent with the Hindus in India and Ceylon since conversion to Christianity offered escape to those of low caste and the outcasts from the strongly hierarchical system of their traditional faith. With all their zeal for religion they were also, like the Spaniards, eager for material wealth. They developed a profitable trade in spices between the Moluccas and Europe, not always by the gentlest and cleanest means. Lisbon prospered having become in place of Venice the principal entrepôt for the distribution of spices in Europe. But St. Francis Xavier, who acquired fame as a missionary to Japan was candid about the cruelty and corruption of which some Portuguese were guilty. He said that they had learned to conjugate the verb "to rape" in all its tenses.[1]

The Dutch Contest with Portugal, Spain, and England

Unfortunately for the Portuguese, their absorption by Spain brought down Spain's enemies upon them. The toughest of these were the Dutch. The Netherlands, indeed all of Flanders, had been a Spanish dependency but the Dutch rebelled against Spanish rule in 1580 and from then on were grimly fighting both Iberian nations for their freedom. Their independence was not officially recognized until the Peace of Westphalia in 1648. They were already the leading maritime and commercial and financial people of northern Europe and at that time well ahead of the English. They had acquired from the Portuguese many of the navigational skills which the latter had learned from the Arabs and developed these with Nordic persistence and efficiency to even greater purpose. They were determined to carry their war of independence from Europe to Southeast Asia and the Far East and in the process to break Lisbon's quasi-monopoly as

1. D. G. E. Hall, A History of Southeast Asia, London: Macmillan, and New York: St. Martins, 1968, p. 244.

middleman for the spice trade. They would try to develop this fabu-
lously rewarding business direct. As it happens they embarked on
this new course at roughly the same time as England, which was
prompted by the same motives. The two countries soon found
themselves in deadly rivalry in Southeast Asia.

An English East India Company was founded in 1600. It was to
organize trading expeditions to the East Indies and was granted a
monopoly of trade in the whole region between the Cape of Good
Hope and the Strait of Magellan. It thus covered in principle the entire Indian Ocean and the Pacific. But "East Indies" was an ambiguous term. The main objective of the company was not India as such
—there were as yet no English settlements on the Indian mainland
—but the Indonesian spice trade; and England's Southeast Asian
ventures antedated the successful establishment of any American
colonies. The Dutch founded their own United East India Company in 1602 with similar objectives. In both cases there had been a
number of earlier unregulated exploratory voyages. Among those undertaken by English adventurers the most famous name was Sir
Francis Drake. He had acquired spices in the Moluccas during his
voyage of circumnavigation of the world in 1572. Of the two organizations the Netherlands company was more solidly organized in the
early stages than its English rival. It disposed of more capital and
ships.

The Dutch soon won a decided advantage over the Portuguese in
Southeast Asia and eventually over the British too. They believed
that the strength and prosperity of their country depended upon acquiring an absolute monopoly of the spice trade with the Indonesian
Moluccas and set themselves with ruthless determination to achieve
this. The English were not struggling for their national existence
and quite apart from their relative weakness in ships and money had
no interest in prolonging their already long fight with Spain and Portugal. They would have been content to acquire a share of the spice
trade by doing a deal with Madrid. The Dutch on the other hand
contended that with their bigger and stronger fleets they were bear-

ing the main burden of opening up the spice trade. The British were just moving in their wake and seeking to profit by their efforts and sacrifices. Matters came to a head after the end in 1619 of a ten years' truce between the Netherlands and Spain. An agreement to share the trade was actually reached in Europe between England and Holland but was in effect sabotaged by the forceful Dutch Governor-General in the field. Ugly clashes and the execution by the Dutch of most of the members of the English trading post on Amboyna in the Moluccas contributed to the withdrawal of the British from most of Indonesia. They still maintained trading stations at Makassar in the Celebes and Bantam in West Java until the latter part of the seventeenth century. Then they were evicted by the Dutch from these as well. The English retired to Bencoolen (Bengkulu) on the west coast of Sumatra, one of the centers of the pepper trade, where the Netherlands company had not yet established its grip. The Dutch made their headquarters in Indonesia at Djakarta in Java, which they renamed Batavia. This city has now reverted to its original name as the capital of the Republic of Indonesia. In 1641 they captured Malacca from the Portuguese but the trade of this once flourishing port was then subordinated to the interests of Batavia as was all Dutch enterprise in this profitable area. It is one of the ironies of history that if the Dutch had been willing to share the Indonesian spice trade with the English the latter might never have felt moved to concentrate as they did on building up their stake on the Indian mainland; and there might never have been a British Indian Empire. As we shall see, Britain succeeded in making something of a comeback in Southeast Asia in the nineteenth century. For Portugal no such revival was in store. All that remains today of the gallant adventures in the region of this once dynamic small nation is her colony occupying half of the Indonesian island of Timor and the charming Iberian patina of countenance and customs, and some monuments and inscriptions in Malacca.

The Dutch made a deeper, more widespread, and enduring mark in what became the Netherlands East Indies. In the process the Indies made them rich. The golden age of Dutch society, art, and scholarship in the first half of the seventeenth century reflected something of this wealth. They had gone to Indonesia with no deliberate imperialist intentions. The English also had no such intentions when they first went to India. The idea was to trade profitably from coastal settlements and to become as little involved as possible in all the complexities and cost of annexing and administering Asian territories and peoples. Yet both Holland and eventually England were overtaken by the fate which seems to await all peoples who seek their fortune at the expense of less developed, or differently developed, nations. To shape things to their will, to stop the chaos or subversion which threatened their profitable undertakings, they were drawn into a process of ever more extensive territorial intervention with all the military, political, and administrative burdens this involved. And this in time swallowed up most if not all of the profitable advantages which had originally been invoked to justify the intervention.

Thus, to enforce their spice monopoly and make it pay, the Dutch had to impose a new regime upon the Moluccas. The islanders were forbidden to sell their spices to others, and, to keep prices up, production was restricted under official supervision. In recalcitrant areas whole populations were removed and other more amenable people brought in from elsewhere. But Makassar in the southern Celebes was a breach in the system. Through this port the English and others were still able to obtain spices which had been smuggled out from the Moluccas. So in 1667 the Dutch had to fight hard to conquer and take over this new area. The same objective dictated further efforts to control some of the main pepper ports of Sumatra. The stake of the Dutch in Indonesia became progressively more elaborate and demanding. Java was the center of their empire. They had to fight for complete control there too, to suppress local opposition, command the food supplies required, and grow the valuable cash crops for which the island was particularly suited. But not until 1772, after three expensive wars, did the Dutch become complete

masters of Java with two vassal Sultanates at Jogjakarta and Sura-
karta. Not long before they had also taken over the Sultanate of
Banjermasin in southern Borneo.

By this time the Dutch East India Company was running a heavy
deficit which for reasons of credit and prestige was temporarily kept
from the public. Another contributing factor was the proliferation of
trade in breach of their restrictions stimulated by the buccaneering
activities of the fiercer islanders, such as the Bugis from Makassar
and the Illanos from the Sulu archipelago. This had also helped Holland's rivals, such as France and Britain, to secure specimens that enabled them to grow spices in their own territories. Finally Holland's
alliance with the American colonies in the war of the American Revolution exposed her to severe retaliation from Britain, by now the
strongest maritime and commercial power. Holland's monopoly system was largely broken and replaced by free trade. By 1800 the
Dutch East India Company was bankrupt, the Netherlands had
been invaded by French revolutionary forces, and the Dutch empire
in Southeast Asia taken over by the Netherlands government.

The British Return to Southeast Asia

By 1780 Britain had established a triangular framework of power in
India based upon Madras, Bombay, and Calcutta, the seat of government. Despite the set-backs of the American war, her fortunes were
saved and indeed improved in India by a Governor-General of outstanding quality, Warren Hastings. Shortly after he left in 1785 the
lessons of the war induced the British to return to Southeast Asia.
During their struggles with the French their navy had been closely
pressed by the enemy on India's eastern, Coromandel, coast where
there were no good harbors. This was partly because the French kept
a dockyard on the eastern side of the Bay of Bengal at the Burmese
port of Syriam opposite Rangoon, while British warships were compelled to make the long voyage round to Bombay to refit. This

prompted the British in 1786 to take up an offer from a Malay ruler, the Sultan of Kedah, to cede to them his island of Penang at the northern entrance to the Strait of Malacca if Britain would help him against his enemies. The Sultan envisaged trouble both from the south and the north. Throughout history there have been movements of population between the Indonesian islands and the Malay peninsula so that a substantial part of the population of Malaya was and is of Indonesian origin. This had been especially the case in the eighteenth century when many Indonesians were emancipating themselves from Dutch control. Not content with their exploits on the sea, numbers of Makassar Bugis settled more or less permanently in some of the southern and western Malay states. Indeed they acquired a dominant position in Johore and Selangor and were threatening Kedah. The Sultan's other fear was the Thais who still claimed suzerainty over much of the Malay peninsula. After their defeat by the Burmese they had made a remarkable recovery and might, it seemed, be planning to convert their pretentions to overlordship into effective domination.

The British occupied Penang and their intermediary with the Sultan, a merchant captain named Light, was made superintendent of the settlement. Their attempts to grow spices were not very successful. Penang was also disappointing as a shipyard in view of the quality of the local timber. But British protection and the lack of special restraints on trade such as the Dutch had sought to impose in their areas attracted numbers of Chinese, Malays, and southern Indians. The Chinese with their keen business instincts soon became the dominant community. In moving into Penang the British had ignored the condition of reciprocal assistance to the ruler of Kedah which had been the basis of the original cession. The sultan attempted to retake his island but was beaten off by the British forces. The British ultimately persuaded him to cede to them a strip of the mainland opposite the island as a source of food supply and this was called Province Wellesley after the Governor-General of India at the time. They gave him a financial allowance to cover both their acquisitions. Later Kedah was invaded by the Thais and the unfortunate ruler became for years a refugee and pensioner in his own former island. In 1795 Malacca too fell into British hands. Holland had, as we saw, been invaded by the French with whom Britain had resumed war and once again the Dutch colonial empire was vulnerable to British expansion. In 1810 the British occupied Java until the end of the Napoleonic wars. As Lieutenant-Governor they appointed an imaginative civil servant, Thomas Stamford Raffles, who had steeped himself in the culture and traditions of the Malay peoples and who published after he left what is usually regarded as the first scholarly history of Java. His period of rule, for which he was criticized by the British East India Company since it was not economically profitable, has been regarded even by modern Indonesians as signifying a liberalization of some of the harsher aspects of Dutch rule. On the other hand the policies he pursued—many of them subsequently reversed —were in part those which the more enlightened Dutch administrators had themselves wanted to apply. He sought among other things to substitute a land rent for the heavy burden of contributions in kind by the local cultivators. He diminished the feudal powers of the Javanese aristocracy and aimed at some initial introduction of a money economy into the static traditional pattern of Javanese village life.

Raffles and Singapore

At the same time Raffles was ambitious for his country. He believed unhesitatingly in the superior benefits of British rule, had visions of adding Indonesia permanently to his country's dominions, and was bitterly disappointed when for reasons of European politics the London Cabinet decided after 1815 to restore these important dependencies to the Dutch. In 1819, with the hesitating acquiescence of the British Governor-General of India, and to the fury of the Dutch, Raffles established a British foothold on Singapore. This island at the tip of the Malay peninsula was regarded as coming within the sphere of the Netherlands-protected Sultanate of Johore, a state which had gained some of the prestige of the earlier Sultanate of Malacca and covered the present Malay Sultanates of Johore and Pahang, the neighboring Riow archipelago, and the island of Lingga. Despite Dutch protests and after some wavering, both London and Calcutta decided to retain Singapore. Before his early death, Raffles strongly insisted that it should have free trade and freedom from racial discrimination in economic matters; and that piracy should be stopped. Singapore soon became a major trading center and a predominantly Chinese city. The policies of Raffles, exceptionally convenient entrepôt facilities, and an ideal location at the junction of the Strait of Malacca and the South China Sea, eventually made of it one of the world's greatest ports. When it became clear that the stronger British had no intention of abandoning their prize the hard-headed Dutch came to terms with the situation. By the Treaty of London of 1824 they definitively surrendered Malacca and recognized the whole of the Malay peninsula and Singapore as a British sphere of influence, while Britain relinquished her last foothold in Indonesia, at Bencoolen in Sumatra, and recognized the archipelago as the exclusive sphere of the Dutch. The three British port dependencies in or adjacent to the Malay peninsula were subsequently grouped together as the Straits Settlements, of which Singapore became the capital in 1832.

France and Southern Asia

The French gave serious attention to southern Asia later than the British and, from one aspect, in quite a different manner. As a Catholic power France was known as the "elder daughter of the Church" and a belief in her mission to spread the Catholic faith loomed large in her earlier Asian policies, as it had in those of Portugal and Spain. The Protestant nations such as Holland and Britain were more bluntly materialistic. Proselytizing and conversion were not envisaged as a sacred duty and they had no compunction in seeking an alliance with Muslims to destroy their fellow Christian Catholics, as the Dutch had done in attacking Portuguese Malacca. But the Catholic powers were also, as we saw, in quest of wealth and in 1664 a French East India Company was revived based on Pondicherry in southeastern India, the efforts of which were to be co-ordinated with France's more spiritual endeavors. This was in the reign of Louis XIV when France had emerged as the leading nation of Europe and her power and prestige were jealously promoted by her royal master. The French secured papal support for their claim to assume authority over Catholic missionary work in the Orient in place of the now feeble Portuguese and appointed French Vicars-Apostolic for various Asian countries. In 1663 the Paris Seminary for Oriental Languages was expanded into the Society for Foreign Missions and a French Bishop was sent out to work in China or alternatively Annam. After being shipwrecked in the Gulf of Siam, the bishop returned to Ayuthia and set about making Thailand the headquarters of these Catholic missionary efforts which, from the 1670's, expanded into Cambodia and Vietnam. At the same juncture the Thai King, dissatisfied with the performance of the Dutch and English East India companies in his dominions, encouraged as a counterweight the commercial activities of the French East India Company. The Jesuits, regarding themselves as the elite forces of the Church, were not content to leave the Catholic effort to the Society for Foreign Missions. They had strong influence over the French King and, outbidding their rivals, promoted a plan to establish not only French religious influence but French political hegemony in Thailand. For this purpose they ingratiated themselves with a Greek adventurer, Constantine Phaulkon, who, starting as a cabin boy in the service of the English East India Company, had become first an interpreter at court and eventually controller of Thailand's foreign trade. But the French overplayed their hand. They asked eventually for concessions so sweeping that they aroused Thai suspicion and resentment. In

1688 King Narai, Phaulkon's protector, died. Many were jealous of and hostile to Phaulkon. He was arrested and executed, and from the time of his downfall the Thai rulers were convinced of the danger of intriguing Europeans and isolated their country from most Western contacts for over a hundred and fifty years, until the mid-nineteenth century when King Mongkut welcomed and inaugurated modern reform.

Yet even during this period of political isolation from the West the Kings of Thailand permitted the continued if somewhat checkered operation of French Catholic missions which, even more importantly than their East India Company, laid, as we shall see, the foundations for the future French presence in Indochina. Meanwhile, during the same period the Burmese, as we saw, destroyed Ayuthia in 1767 and the Thais subjugated Kedah in 1821 in a drive to reinvigorate their nominal authority in at least the northern half of the Malay peninsula. The isolation of the Thais was in fact never as complete as, say, that of Japan before the arrival of Commodore Perry. Among other things, they continued to appreciate the importance of trade far more keenly than did the Burmese. Hence their decision to place their new capital, Bangkok, nearer to the sea. Although its observance was less than perfect, the Thais in 1826 concluded a commercial agreement with the British who, having brought much of India under their control, were now the dominant power in Asia. But it was not only in India that British imperialism had progressed. By the mid-1820's another part of Southeast Asia had just become a British dependency, namely, the western and southern area of Burma.

Britain and Burma

Once the British had become masters of the Madras Presidency, Bombay, and Bengal, there were bound to be factors allegedly requiring or justifying their further expansion into rich, fragmented Southeast Asia, lying immediately to the east. Among these were ri-

valry and clashes with the French. Another factor was the growing importance of the China trade now that Britain had become the world's foremost maritime and commercial nation. We
have seen the naval and economic reasons prompting Britain to
acquire the island of Penang off the Malay coast, and subsequently
Malacca and Singapore. But by the late eighteenth century neighboring Burma had herself pursued imperialist expansion. The war in
which she destroyed Ayuthia had led to her permanent acquisition
of the area of Mergui in southern Tenasserim, formerly Thailand's
principal western port of entry. More importantly from the standpoint of her relations with Britain, in 1784 she had also annexed the
kingdom of Arakan. This gave her a low-lying land frontier with
Bengal which could easily be crossed and led to serious friction. In a
mood of military arrogance Burmese forces had also traversed the
mountain barriers which normally insulated her from British India
and temporarily imposed their will on the Indian border states of
Assam and Manipur.

During Burma's earlier periods of growth and internal struggle the
British had had only desultory and generally inauspicious contacts
with her rulers. They had developed some trade, mostly with discouraging results, and they had operated for a time a British shipyard at Syriam where, as we saw, the French installed one too. In
1753, the year of Alaungpaya's triumph over the Mons, the British
occupied the island of Negrais near Bassein in the Irrawaddy delta,
with some encouragement from the King who hoped to acquire
through this new European trading post imports that he badly
needed, particularly artillery. After six years, however, and heavy loss
from disease, the British decided to pull out and withdrew their
main garrison. Those who remained were massacred by Alaungpaya's
forces, partly because he suspected that they had been intriguing
with the Mons and partly because a letter on gold leaf ornamented
with rubies which he had sent to King George II had never been
answered. In their arrogant and pedestrian fashion the British of the
time expected minor Asian monarchs to deal with and through the

East India Company. To Asian rulers who looked down on commerce and saw in the Company a purely trading organization this was an insufferable insult. It was Alaungpaya's successors who pursued Burma's imperialist drive marked by the destruction of Ayuthia, the annexation of southern Tenasserim and Arakan, and the assaults on Assam and Manipur. The British sent two missions to Ava to promote peaceful relations and conclude a commercial treaty, but both were abortive. The climax of a rebellion in Arakan and Burmese pursuit of the rebels across the Bengal border was the outbreak of the first Anglo-Burmese war in 1824. Despite characteristic mismanagement in the early stages of the British campaign the superiority of European armament was conclusive. British and Indian forces, still clad in the stifling uniforms of Waterloo, captured Rangoon and encamped in the sacred precincts of the Golden Pagoda. They then pursued the enemy up-country to the approaches of Ava, killing their leading general on the way. Here a humiliating peace was dictated to the King of Burma by the East India Company, involving the surrender of Arakan and Tenasserim and the payment of an indemnity of one million pounds.

Understandably, this turn of events did not reduce the xenophobia of the Burmese kings. It seemed to confirm them in their arrogant aversion to foreign contacts. In 1840 the king repudiated the treaty forced upon Burma by the British, and diplomatic relations were broken off. Ava continued to resist commercial arrangements and dealings on equal terms with the outside world at a time when even China, its nominal suzerain, was being compelled by the so-called Opium War in 1842 to accept such arrangements. This attitude, which Thailand wisely avoided, was bound to involve disastrous risks in an age when the Western nations were increasingly conscious of their power and convinced of their manifest destiny to bring progress and enlightenment to a supposedly backward Asia. In 1852 a trivial clash of interests in Rangoon was allowed to develop into a second Anglo-Burmese war. In this, after further defeats, Burma lost her remaining coastline and the fertile central southern zone including the Irrawaddy delta. In the final stages of the war a prince came to the throne as King Mindon and proved to be the finest and most constructive of Burma's modern rulers with qualities similar to those of his contemporary, King Mongkut of Thailand. Sadly for his country, however, his efforts to achieve reform on the Western pattern, to communicate and come to terms with the modern world, were bedevilled by entrenched reactionaries at home and by misplaced British masterfulness deriving from a long tradition of authoritative dealings with princes in and on the borders of India. Mindon was chivalrous enough to create no difficulties for Britain when she was dangerously extended in the Crimean War and the Indian Mutiny. The British nevertheless presumed to treat Burma, much of whose territory had already been incorporated in their Indian dominions, somewhat like an Indian dependency and to control her foreign relations. This attitude logically provoked the king into seeking the support of other Western powers, notably of France. This nation had by now established itself in the Mekong delta, had imposed its protection on Annam and Cambodia, and was preparing to take over Tongking. Through Tongking, France was seeking to secure access to Yunnan and Kwangsi. She also aimed, like Britain, at establishing a direct route to China from Burma through the western border of Yunnan. Mindon, who died in 1878, was succeeded by a sadistic weakling, King Thibaw, who was supported by the reactionary faction. Determination to forestall the French coupled with punitive tax demands upon a British timber company were the cause of Britain's third move against Ava. In 1885 troops sent by steamship up the Irrawaddy brought a swift capitulation. Burma with nine hundred years of proud and frequently imposing independence was reduced to the status of a minor province of Britain's Indian Empire. Her national identity was further effaced by the abolition of her monarchy, a fate which even the Indian dependent states had not suffered since the Mutiny. Deep resentment of this last major act of British aggrandizement in Asia produced a long and bitter guerrilla war in Upper Burma. After periods of happier and relatively constructive adjustment between Burmese nationalism and the British system, these resentments have gained new strength in recent years under a military dictatorship which has reverted to some of the less enlightened attitudes of the Burmese kings.

IV

FRANCE AND INDOCHINA

Early French Expansion into Indochina

In Annam and other parts of Indochina the French Catholic missionaries based in Thailand and intermittently supported by their East India Company managed in the seventeenth and eighteenth century to continue the work of the Church. This had been started by the Portuguese Jesuits based on Macao and by other priests forced to leave Japan and China when the rulers of both countries turned against Christianity. In this period one of the pioneers of the French presence in their future colony, Alexander of Rhodes from Avignon, the papal enclave in France, compiled the first map of Vietnam and the first dictionary of Vietnamese. His works were published by the Vatican's missionary organization, the Propaganda Fide, which also encouraged the training of native priests. The French missionary drive in this early period was by no means exclusively nationalist. Exercising France's new pre-eminence in the diffusion of Catholicism in Asia, in 1674 the French Vicar-Apostolic in Thailand appointed a Christian Chinese from the Philippines as Vicar-Apostolic to China. This was resented by the Spanish Dominicans, who had become the dominant religious order there and had acquired in the process some of the largest agricultural plantations. At the time this Franco-Spanish dispute was resolved by the assignment to the Spanish Dominicans in 1693, as a kind of compensation, of the Vicariate-General of Tongking. Thus the Spaniards from their base in the Philippines became marginally involved in the affairs of Indochina.

The Rival Dynasties of Annam

In the eighteenth century the French missionaries concentrated their efforts mainly in and around Hue, which had become one of the two principal centers of Vietnam. This division was the result of a long triangular civil war following the decline of the dynasty of Le Emperors around 1500. Two out of the three leaders in this struggle emerged as effective rulers of the northern and southern areas of the country, respectively, and set themselves up as kings who still for a time acknowledged the overlordship of a puppet Le Emperor. The two dynasties were those of the Trinh in the north and the Nguyen in the south, and it was the latter whom the French found more receptive to their enterprises. By one of the strange coincidences of history, in the 1630's the Nguyen built two great walls across the narrow waist of the country near Dong Hoi, only a few miles north of the present Demilitarized Zone, to keep their northern rivals out. It is tempting to conclude from this that there is some basic and fundamental difference between what is once again North and South Vietnam. But this would be quite fallacious. The earlier division resulted simply from a rivalry between rulers of the same race. Both regimes were virtually identical [1] and a truce between them was effective for a hundred years, from 1673 to 1774. But although the northern kingdom had at one time four-fifths of the population of all Vietnam it never succeeded in overcoming the Nguyen and was itself displaced at the end of the eighteenth century. It is paradoxical that this should have occurred, especially in view of the fact that the North favored the Manchu dynasty which was in the ascendant in

1. Fall, op. cit. (*The Two Vietnams*), p. 18.

China, while the South helped refugees from the deposed Ming dynasty. The balance of power shifted eventually in favor of the South; partly, it seems, because the economy of the North was static, its trade dead, and corruption widespread. Wealth was concentrated in the hands of a few mandarins, and the country was plagued by peasant rebellions. Another source of strength for the Nguyen was that they were conducting a campaign of colonization which gave them an elastic frontier and permitted the movement of population and economic expansion. Many from the more overcrowded north, hungry for land, flocked southward where there was plenty of it, especially in the rich Mekong delta. In the setting of an ancient rather than a new land the process was not dissimilar to the opening up of the American West. But whereas the latter tended to minimize social differences and democratize the structure of society, in Vietnam tradition and vested interests were too strong. One leading authority suggests that the great landowners did not permit Vietnam's economy to rise above the village level, despite the country's fantastic growth, because they feared that economic undertakings not rooted in the village, such as the creation of a rich merchant class and urban centers of political power, would threaten their position and strengthen that of the central government. They knew that their privileges and power would be more secure if the existing order remained unchanged. Hence Vietnam's continuing semi-feudal, bureaucratic, ideological stagnation and impotence in the struggle against the West. These upper classes split the country and delayed the development of a unified national community while the central authorities gave them a free hand to exploit the peasants. Yet it was the peasants who achieved territorial expansion and the preservation of national unity.[2] Against this it can be argued that skilled and intelligent leadership was fundamental to the development of national greatness—and indeed for all the major measures essential to the agricultural and administrative organization of the new areas—and

2. Joseph Buttinger, *Vietnam: A Political History*, New York: Praeger, 1968, pp. 52, 53.

that this normally emerged among the educated classes. The same author admits that the initially successful peasant rebellion of the late eighteenth century caused no change in the country's social structure.[3]

Fresh Opportunities for France

During the truce between the North and the South, in 1749–50, the French East India Company, invigorated by their great empire-builder Dupleix, sent a mission to Hue to conclude a commercial treaty. Again, however, their forward movement failed. The mission incautiously gave offense by abducting an interpreter, and this led to the expulsion of French missionaries. Dupleix was recalled, and in 1769 the French East India Company shut down for the second time. Yet a new turn of events soon gave fresh opportunities to the French.

Vietnam's expansion into Cambodia in the 1770's, in competition with Thailand, was checked by a rebellion of three peasant brothers from the village of Tay Son in Cochinchina. While the Nguyen forces were defending Saigon the Trinh forces marched south and occupied Hue but were dislodged by the Tay Son brothers. Having eliminated the Nguyen in the South and killed off nearly all the family, the rebels invaded the North. They captured Hanoi in 1786 and not only disposed of the Trinh but also terminated the shadowy Le empire which had continued to be recognized as an ultimate symbol of authority. They thus reunited a country which now stretched from the borders of Yunnan and Kwangsi to the Ca Mau peninsula. One young prince of sixteen, Nguyen Anh, a nephew of the last southern king, managed to escape from the massacre of his family to an island in the Gulf of Siam. A French bishop, Pigneau de Behaine, who had been head of a seminary in Ha Tien province near the Cambodian border, had saved the boy's life by hiding him

3. Buttinger, op. cit., p. 72.

and helping him to the island. This began a friendship and association which were to have significant consequences.

The prince's rescue occurred in 1777. Subsequently he made two attempts to recover his country, having raised forces with the help of the Bishop. He even managed to reoccupy Saigon and to rule in Cochinchina for some four years. Defeat followed, and in 1784 he became a refugee in Thailand. After some thought apparently of turning to the British, the Dutch, the Portuguese, or the Spaniards he was persuaded by Bishop Pigneau to ask for French support. This energetic prelate then did his best to interest the French authorities in Pondicherry in sending help. Having failed there, he returned to France, taking with him Nguyen Anh's small son, where he urged his case upon the government of Louis XVI in those fatal years just before the French Revolution. Here he was more successful. He returned as a Royal Commissioner to Pondicherry, with a treaty of alliance promising military aid in return for France's being given exclusive trading privileges in Vietnam and the cession of Condore Island (Poulo Condore) off the Mekong delta and the harbor of Tourane (now Da Nang), south of Hue. The French government, however, had independently authorized the Governor of Pondicherry to decide whether the expedition should in fact take place, and official support was eventually withdrawn in April 1789. The Bishop, however, by his own efforts raised a small force of some 300 volunteers and somehow found the money, ships, and guns to make them effective. But by the time Bishop Pigneau was able to rejoin the Prince it was July 1789, the very month of the fall of the Bastille and the beginning of the French Revolution. Meanwhile Nguyen Anh had made considerable progress by his own efforts. He had received Thai help in return for help the Vietnamese had earlier given the Thais against the Burmese. Once again he had reoccupied Saigon and the southern provinces of Cochinchina. By now the Tay Son were losing ground and he was gaining popular support. Nevertheless the French military and administrative help and French supplies were still in time to be of value. With this aid Nguyen Anh was able conclusively to defeat his rivals and unify the whole country. French advisers and technicians then helped to organize the Vietnamese Navy, fortifications and arsenal, and the new administration. The Bishop served his former protégé as Foreign Minister before his death in 1799. In 1802, after Nguyen Anh had conquered Hanoi as well as Hue, he was proclaimed emperor of Annam under the title of Gia Long.

After Gia Long's death a nationalist and anti-Christian trend set in among his successors, who, unlike him, owed nothing special to the French. The Vietnamese monarchs displayed the xenophobic tendencies characteristic at one time or another of most Southeast Asian rulers. They declined to recognize a French Consul or to have dealings with the English East India Company, though they were alarmed by the Company's easy victory in the first Burmese war and by the humiliation of China in the so-called Opium War of 1839–42. In 1825 Gia Long's successor had pronounced Christianity the perverse religion of the European which corrupted men's hearts, and in the 1830's seven missionaries were executed. Despite this, French missionary activity in Vietnam continued to expand. The last Emperor of independent and united Vietnam, Tu Duc, reigned from 1847 to 1883. His year of accession saw the first concerted French attack upon his country; the year of his death the treaty which virtually ended Vietnam's freedom.

The French Colony in Indochina

As usual in such cases, France's acquisition of Vietnam and other parts of Indochina was the upshot of varying motives and a rather confused chain of events. The quest for prestige seems to have been the dominant consideration rather than economic profit. Woven into this was the continuing zeal for the promotion of the Catholic religion under the patronage of France, fortified by a strong Catholic revival in Europe in the early and middle years of the nineteenth century and the characteristic faith of this period in the West's mission to bring progress to the supposedly backward non-Western lands. Yet France's imperial enterprises were sometimes ill-judged and mismanaged. She had failed to secure the concessions stipulated in return for her original help to Gia Long, and in 1844–45 French forces tried unsuccessfully to establish a base on Basilan Island in the Sulu archipelago of the southern Philippines in place of Poulo Condore off Vietnam.

In 1847 a French Admiral bombarded Tourane and destroyed its forts and the Vietnamese Navy, after having failed to receive the assurance that the persecution of missionaries would cease. This only led to the murder of Europeans, and in 1851 and 1852 four more French missionaries, including two bishops, were executed. By this time another revolution had brought Napoleon III to the French throne. To enhance his acceptability as the representative of an upstart dynasty the new ruler had to outbid his more legitimate predecessors in zeal for the Church, which urged intervention in Indochina. An Anglo-French force had been sent in 1858 to impose Western policies on China in the aftermath of the Taiping rebellion. Napoleon III decided to take advantage of this enterprise to press forward in Indochina. In view of their missionary interests in Tongking, the Spaniards helped the French to make a fresh assault on Tourane, which failed through dissension and mismanagement. The expedition, commanded by Admiral Rigault de Genouilly, then moved south to the area of the Mekong delta, and in 1859 captured Saigon and the key points in three provinces of Cochinchina with the help of fresh troops evacuated from China. In July 1861 the French Commander announced the annexation to France of Saigon and the surrounding territory. The Spaniards insisted that they must have a comparable foothold in Tongking, but their claims were ignored. In 1862 Vietnam was compelled to sign a treaty giving France control of the three provinces of Cochinchina she had occupied and the island of Poulo Condore. An indemnity was to be paid, there was to be freedom of religion in Vietnam and the French were to have priority in case of any future alienation of the nation's territory. It had been a tragedy for Vietnam that Gia Long's successors, unlike himself, had isolated themselves from knowledge of the West. They had spiritually and physically shut themselves away, as the Burmese kings had done. When the West knocked on the door they had neither the armed strength nor the pragmatic statesmanship to compromise with some of their principles, as Thailand and Japan had done, in order that their country should survive as an independent state. As in China, the Emperor was surrounded by ignorant and arrogant mandarins who gave him no inkling of the true state of affairs.

The French Protectorate Over Cambodia

The next French move was, as we saw, into Cambodia in 1863, King Norodom being eventually forced by a French naval officer at pistol point to accept France's terms. After this unceremonious start to their relations, Cambodia found that she could accept French tutelage with good grace since it freed her from far more arbitrary vassalage to Thailand and Annam. In 1867 the French moved into the rest of Cochinchina. This new aggression, regrettably for Vietnam, gave fresh power to the conservative mandarins at Hue, who were able to stifle the reform movement urged by some progressives. Such a movement might have preserved the country's independence as similar reforms had done in Thailand and Japan.

The French Annex Tongking

The defeat of the French by Prussia in 1870 did not check their colonial expansion. Indeed the German victors rather encouraged this in order to distract France's attention from any obsession with recovering her European losses. Adventurous Frenchmen explored the possibilities of taking over Tongking. In 1873 the French Governor at Saigon tried to seize Hanoi on his own initiative and failed. The French did, however, manage to extract from the weakened Emperor of Annam recognition of French sovereignty over the whole of Cochinchina and agreement to the opening to trade of the Red River in Tongking, the most convenient channel of entry into Yunnan. In an attempt to check French moves in the North the Emperor at this juncture sent tribute missions to Peking in acknowledgment of China's suzerainty, and some Chinese troops moved into Tongking. In 1882 the French sent a military mission, ostensibly to expel these Chinese "intruders." It seized Hanoi and the coastal province with its valuable anthracite deposits near Haiphong. In 1885 China agreed to French claims to establish a protectorate over the whole of Vietnam and to French commercial access to Yunnan. We have seen that this was the year in which the British moved into Upper Burma, largely for fear of further French expansion in that direction. For twelve years, from 1885 to 1897, the French had to fight rebellion in Tongking. Fifty years later this phase of history was to repeat itself in far grimmer and more enduring form.

Thailand Surrenders Laos and Northern Malaya

In 1893 the French moved into Laos also. Laos had had, as we saw, a long history of fragmentation, and at the end of the seventeenth century it had broken up into three parts: the center had come under the suzerainty of the rising power of the Nguyen in South Vietnam; those in the North and South, that is, in the Luang Prabang and Champassak areas, were nominally under Thai suzerainty. In 1778 Vientiane accepted Thai suzerainty as well as Vietnamese. Finally in 1836 the whole of Laos was annexed to Thailand. With Thai permission a French consulate was established at Luang Prabang, and this development implied recognition by France that Laos was Thai territory. But this Consul, who was subsequently appointed French Minister at Bangkok, encouraged anti-Thai and pro-French feeling in Laos. Then the expulsion of two French agents from Thailand was used as a pretext for demanding all of Laos beyond the Mekong. Britain had been consulted beforehand and advised Thailand to accept these demands, which were emphasized by the despatch of French gunboats to Bangkok. In 1907 France insisted, as we saw, on the surrender by Thailand of the two Cambodian provinces which she had recognized to be Thai as the condition of Bangkok's acceptance of the French protectorate over Cambodia, and also of more Lao territory on the right bank of the Mekong. In 1909 a further somewhat nominal sacrifice was extracted from Thailand by Britain. This was the surrender by Bangkok of its by now rather shadowy suzerainty over the four northern states of Malaya some of which already had British advisers functioning with the approval of the Thai King. In return Britain abandoned the extraterritorial status of its nationals in Thailand and furnished a loan to facilitate the construction of a railway through southern Thailand to link up with the Malayan rail system.

The Modernization of Thailand

As we saw, Thailand at the end of the seventeenth century had entered a period of isolation from the West after France's abortive attempt to dominate the country. The partly Chinese Chakri dynasty, which came to the throne in 1782 after the period of recovery following the Burmese invasions, was to play through many vicissitudes the decisive role in Thailand's survival as an independent state in the heyday of European imperialism in Asia. Despite loss of autocratic power the kings have remained a deeply respected and stabilizing symbol of authority in Thailand to this day. This is due in large measure to the outstanding personality of two monarchs who drastically reformed their country in the late nineteenth and early twentieth century.

Under the first three kings of the dynasty, however, Thailand's cautious avoidance of adjustment to the modern world might have prepared her for the fate of lands, like Burma and Vietnam, which became dependencies of Europe. The British Burney mission in 1821, in quest of a commercial treaty, was rebuffed and the Crawfurd mission of 1826, after the first Anglo-Burmese war, only secured an emasculated agreement. An incipient new phase was, however, a pact of 1833 with the United States permitting the appointment of an American Consul and the operation of American Protestant missionaries and, in principle, American trade. Meanwhile the removal of the threat of Burmese invasion as a result of Britain's annexation of Tenasserim enabled King Rama III to complete the annexation of Laos, to reassert Thai authority in the northern Malay states, and by making the Phnom Penh ruler a vassal of both countries, to counter-balance the predominance of Vietnam in Cambodia. But, to the end of his reign, Thailand was only open in a very minor way to trade in Western vessels. Thailand's foreign commerce, including that with Singapore, was largely carried in Chinese ships. The Chinese were favored partly because they also functioned as the country's tax farmers and customs collectors and they were determined as far as possible to maintain their privileges. In the later years of his reign Rama III turned against Western missionaries and refused to liberalize Thailand's trade system as the British and Americans would have liked.

All this was changed with the accession of his half-brother, Prince Mongkut. The new King had been only nineteen when his father died in 1824. He was then eliminated in favor of Prince Thap, the future Rama III, who had in some respects weaker claims. He became a monk for twenty-seven years, a scholar in the Buddhist sacred texts, and an influential reformer. He was also strongly interested in the West and received instruction from a French Catholic Bishop and American Protestant missionaries. From this time the Americans had a specially important modernizing influence through their concentration on such fields as science, medicine, hygiene, and practical education. King Mongkut positively encouraged contacts with the West. He engaged numbers of foreign advisers and technicians and Western ladies to teach English and be governesses to his eventually numerous offspring. Among the latter was an English widow from Singapore, Anna Leonowens, an opinionated and imaginative lady whose views on the monarch and his times have been travestied, to the resentment of the Thais, in the well-known musical *The King and I*. A man of great moral and intellectual gifts, he proved to be one of the most intelligent of benevolent despots. He had insisted that his more Westernized brother Prince Itsarate should be "Second King" in accordance with Thai tradition, and the influence of the latter on Mongkut was considerable.[4]

One of Mongkut's first acts was to conclude a treaty with Britain granting sweeping concessions to Western demands, which became the model for a whole series of similar treaties with the United States and the European powers. These liberalized trade, established extraterritorial rights for foreigners, including even their Asian subjects, foreign representation in the country, and free access for foreign ships to Thai ports. Mongkut also employed some eighty foreign advisers in the main fields of government. Englishmen organized the police and ports and to some extent decided economic policy through their financial adviser. Under his influence Thailand pursued free trade, with high reserves to back the currency and a favorable balance of trade. Some United States authorities suggest, perhaps unfairly, that this held back the economic development of the country in the interests of Burma and easy access for British manufactures.[5] Meanwhile the French trained the army, an American ran the customs, and another American became head of the first government school for the aristocracy.

All this had meant the acceptance by Thailand in the interests of saving her national sovereignty not only of special privileges for for-

4. Hall, op. cit. (*A History of Southeast Asia*), p. 667.
5. See John F. Cady, *Southeast Asia: Its Historical Development*, New York: McGraw-Hill, 1964, p. 494.

eigners but of limitations on her fiscal and judicial autonomy, a customs tariff of only 3 per cent, free access to the interior for traders
and missionaries, and restriction on the taxation of tangible foreign-
owned assets. But the resulting progress was real and on the whole
durable. It is regrettable that in Asia so few nations have had, like
Thailand, the adroitness to accept an adaptable synthesis of old and
new, and even substantial sacrifices, in order to escape alien rule.

One of Mrs. Leonowens's most gifted pupils was Prince Chulalongkorn, who later reigned from 1868 to 1910 and proved to be
even more progressive and emancipated from tradition than his father. Between them they transformed a medieval Oriental autocracy,
in which everything flowed from and was for the benefit of a god-
king, into a relatively modern state which nevertheless retained a
style of Asian splendor and much that was Asian in thought and
outlook. King Chulalongkorn abolished slavery, introduced councils
with advisory and legislative powers, a modern cabinet, religious tol-
eration, freedom of the press, modern medical practices. The scope
of the British advisers was extended to cover education, land survey,
and mining. The Belgians and then the Americans were advisers on
foreign affairs. The Belgians and French improved judicial procedure. With some pressure from the United States, Thailand's unequal treaties were revised in 1926. Under Chulalongkorn's successors,
Rama VI and Rama VII, further progress had been made with the
modernization of the country along the lines initiated by the two
great reformers. Rama VI, a vigorous character educated abroad,
stirred the patriotism of the Thais and tackled the assimilation of
the Chinese as well as the final reform of the legal system. Rama
VII, shyer and more cautious, was faced in 1932 with a revolution en-
gineered by a Westernized group. This was led by a lawyer, Nai
Pridi Panamyong, but included among its military elements an ambitious young officer, Colonel, afterwards Field Marshal, Pibun
Songgram. A new and ostensibly democratic constitution was introduced, making the king a constitutional monarch, but half of the
parliament was to be nominated so that the executive retained effec-

tive control. The king abdicated three years later and was succeeded by a minor. Pridi, having displayed disturbingly left-wing tendencies, especially in economic planning, was briefly forced into exile. He returned in 1938 and negotiated new treaties giving Thailand complete sovereignty and equality with the West. But in the same year he was displaced by Pibun, who then sought to enhance the greatness of his nation in a regime with "many of the trappings if not the substance of fascism." [6]

6. David A. Wilson, *Politics in Thailand*, Ithaca: Cornell University Press, 1962, p. 19.

V

THE PHILIPPINES UNDER TWO RULES

The Philippines Under Spain

Spanish rule and American rule in the Philippines were a complete contrast. Indeed some wit suggested that the Filipinos had spent three hundred years in a Spanish convent and fifty in Hollywood. In many ways the Spanish system was intolerably harsh for the people of the country. Yet in the first self-righteous flush of victory in 1898 many Americans were perhaps too ready to condemn everything about it. It was in general similar to the feudal paternalism of Spanish rule in Latin America, for example, that of Peru under the Spanish viceroys, about which the American Thornton Wilder wrote with such nostalgia in *The Bridge of San Luis Rey*. In one or two respects Spanish rule in the Philippines was slightly less onerous and more humane than that in Latin America. And its very inefficiency to some extent lightened the burden of exploitation. At some moments, for example, when island populations in the Moluccas were uprooted or during the nineteenth century Culture System in Java, the far more precisely and thoroughly organized Dutch rule in Indonesia may have borne even more hardly upon the local peoples. In any event Spanish rule, both in America and the Far East, had about it a certain dignity and style, and a fatalistic and not entirely unattractive gift for accommodating itself to human weaknesses.

The Spaniards had small difficulty in establishing their regime. Later they proved to be the only European colonizers who succeeded in Christianizing a whole region of Asia. But these successes can hardly be ascribed to the strength and determination of the Spanish assault, which was carried out with relatively few men. It was rather due to the simplicity, fragmentation, and consequent permeability of Philippine society for the reasons indicated in Chapter II (p. 28). Except to some extent in the Muslim-penetrated South there were no kingdoms bearing the imprint of Indian or Chinese civilization and no major political or military organizations capable of resisting the invader. The Filipinos lived in widely scattered and largely isolated villages bordering on jungle or mountain. They were predominantly of Malay stock having migrated earlier from Indonesia or Malaysia. Their small settlements were mostly kinship groups in which a chief, the *datu*, wielded some authority. These were known as *barangay*, after the name of the boats which had brought them from overseas. Again (save in the south) they had acquired no major religion, such as Hinduism, Buddhism or Islam, inspiring them to resist the at least formal and superficial acceptance of Christianity. They were animists, believers in spirits like so many other of the simpler peoples of Southeast Asia. But in the Philippines their spirit worship was reconciled with belief in a Supreme Being or Deity and in an after life, and this again smoothed the path for their absorption of two fundamental doctrines of Christianity.

Thus the Spanish occupation of the archipelago was relatively bloodless. Philip II seems in fact to have been concerned that the conquest should be less cruel than that of Peru and Mexico. The king had appointed a friar as joint commander with Miguel Lopez de Legaspi, the founder of the colony in 1564, and the Catholic clergy showed at least in the initial stages some zeal for the protection of their Filipino converts from exploitation by the colonists.[1] Fortunately for them, Islam had barely touched the central and northern islands and they were able, as we saw, to confine the Mus-

1. Hall, op. cit. (*A History of Southeast Asia*), p. 248.

lims to parts of Mindanao and the Sulu archipelago. Even by 1898 the "Moros" (as the Spaniards called them in memory of their historic wars against the Moors in Spain) had not been completely subdued and the Americans had to fight them to complete the task. Muslim integration into the national community on a basis of full equality is at last being achieved under independence.

To gain a share in the spice trade was even more important to Spain than religious conversion. But the Philippines produced no spices and the Moluccas were only open to the Spaniards after their absorption of Portugal in 1580. A generation later the Dutch appeared there in force. Eventually, as we saw, they almost completely drove Portugal, Spain, and England out of this region and until the mid-seventeenth century even strove to take over the Philippines as well. A further goal which Spain also failed to achieve was to use the Philippines as a base for the conversion of China and Japan, but both countries took steps against this western penetration.

Christianization of the Philippines went hand in hand with the establishment of autocratic civilian rule. Conversion was achieved primarily by bringing the people "within the sound of the Church bells." The Spaniards gathered their scattered settlements, the *barangays*, into large villages or *pueblos* in which the *barangays* became the different quarters, each with Philippine headmen who together formed the *principalía* or principal people of the locality. Each of these *pueblos* had massive churches with their bells and priests and there were usually near-by religious corporations controlling large estates. The church authorities thus literally dominated the local scene. The Catholicism accepted by the Filipinos was often richly mixed with inherited pagan cults. They may have acquired little understanding of its finer doctrinal points. They often mocked and cheated and resented Spanish officialdom and the powerful friars. Yet it can hardly be disputed that there was some value in the basic Christian ethic instilled by a Church which upheld the equality of all men whatever their color or condition in the sight of God and fought to render slavery and oppression of the darker races less onerous than it was in some Protestant lands. The Spaniards also established in 1611 what became the first European university in the Far East, the Dominican College of Santo Tomás at Manila, which predates Harvard by twenty-five years.

Selected leaders of the *principalía*—"little governors" as the Spaniards called them—were entrusted with minor administrative responsibilities. The *principalía* were in a sense political shock absorbers and cultural middlemen.[2] They transmitted the Spanish demands for taxes and labor to their countrymen and interceded with the friars and Spanish officials to mitigate their severity. The Spaniards resigned themselves to the fact that they could not obtain all they wanted. Thus the "colonial equilibrium" was established which operated without major protest until the eighteenth century. The Spanish kings, impressed with the hardship inflicted on the natives in their American possessions through the abuse of Indian labor in mines and plantations, forbade mining operations in the Philippines and also, until the eighteenth century, the residence of Spaniards in the provinces apart from officials and priests. At the same time foreigners were forbidden to own land.

Although there were never very many individual Spanish estates, nevertheless Spain was responsible for the growth of the large scale landlordism which became a prominent factor in the Philippines in the nineteenth century and has remained so to this day. Indeed some of the social injustices it produced have survived and contributed in recent years to the Hukbalahap insurrection. *Encomiendas* —theoretically leaseholds—were granted to certain colonists. This gave them the right to collect tribute, sometimes in the form of labor services, from the Filipinos on their estates in return for protecting them and ensuring their conversion. The system was abused, the Church complained of illegal exactions, but in practice the *encomenderos* treated the land as their own property. Again in a society where landowning had been communal the Spaniards introduced

2. Onofre D. Corpuz, *The Philippines*, Englewood Cliffs: Prentice-Hall, 1965, p. 28.

the notion of ownership. Property in the *barangay* land was assumed by the chiefs and much of it sold to the religious corporations who also received land grants from the Spanish crown. These religious estates became the largest of their kind and covered some of the most fertile areas,[3] although the bulk of all cultivable land remained in possession of the Filipinos. Nevertheless the peasants were exploited, sometimes in conditions of semi-slavery, not only by the friars and civilian authorities for whom directly or indirectly they worked, but also by their own chiefs.[4] The large estates were not necessarily worked by the friars or lay landlords themselves. They would rent them out to the more enterprising natives or those of mixed blood, the mestizos, who as tenants or *inquilinos* often became prosperous by exploiting the *kasama* or peasants who did the actual cultivation. Indeed, much of the Filipino land gradually came into the hands of the mestizos, usually children of Chinese fathers and Filipino mothers who inherited their fathers' keen business instincts. In view of this Chinese admixture and the relatively small number of Spaniards in the Philippines the mestizos there were often of a more energetic quality than those of Latin America where most were of Spanish and local Indian blood. Another difference was that whereas in the Spanish colonies of Latin America Spanish came to be generally spoken this was by no means the case in the Philippines. In spite of the injunctions of the Spanish governors the teaching of Spanish to the natives was sabotaged by the priests who learned the local dialects and preferred to keep their flock in ignorance of the subversive doctrines they might absorb from knowledge of a European language. Yet another was the fact that the Philippines was not governed directly from Madrid but from Spain's major colony of Mexico. For that reason the quality of Spanish officials in Manila was on the whole lower than in the American possessions.

In the Philippines as in France before 1789 it was not so much

3. The friars owned over 420,000 acres of land with some 60,000 Filipino tenants. I am indebted for these figures to Dr. Usha Mahajani, whose *Philippine Nationalism* will shortly be published by the Queensland University Press, Australia.
4. Hall, op. cit., p. 252.

poverty and oppression which produced the revolutionary explosion. When this came to a head towards the end of the nineteenth century it was chiefly because of the emergence of a relatively prosperous local middle class which was not prepared to tolerate any longer the injustices which their forefathers had accepted.

This prosperity had come slowly and only after a long period of relative stagnation in which even the big estates produced little more than was needed for the immediate consumption of the locality. The sophisticated needs of the colony were mostly supplied by the visit of one galleon from Acapulco every year which the British frequently sought to capture during their many wars with Spain. On its return the galleon loaded luxuries from China. These were bought by exporting large quantities of Mexican silver dollars. As late as the 1930's these were still common currency in China.

In the mid-eighteenth century King Charles III of Spain's French Bourbon dynasty made a serious attempt to improve conditions under the influence of the French Enlightenment. A more decisive factor was the British capture of Manila in the Seven Years War. The British with their vast responsibilities had no desire to take the Philippines over. But their temporary intervention gave rise to a demand in Europe for profitable local products. The growing of cash crops such as tobacco, sugar, and abaca for Manila hemp was greatly stimulated. Trade with Manila was partly freed in 1789 and completely in the 1830's. Later it increased as elsewhere with the opening of the Suez Canal. The friars, who taught the Filipinos modern methods of cultivation, helped to launch the commercial plantation agriculture which is still the main support of the Philippine economy.

The Nationalist Revolution and American Intervention

The capture of Manila proved the vulnerability of the Spanish regime and had consequences in the political sphere. As commercial agriculture prospered a Filipino middle class started, as we saw, to emerge, mainly from people like the *inquilinos* and members of the *principalía.* When these could afford higher education for their children, often by sending them abroad, their descendants became the *ilustrados,* the Filipino elite of today. It was the latter who produced most of the leaders of Filipino nationalism which from small, mostly local and abortive beginnings in the eighteenth century became a general movement toward the end of the nineteenth. One of the significant factors stimulating this later movement had been the liberalizing Spanish revolution of 1868 which removed Queen Isabella II and briefly permitted a much freer regime in the Philippines, followed by a wave of reaction and oppression. By this time the intellectuals who spearheaded the nationalist cause were only articulating grievances which were widely felt by the masses of the people. At first the leaders were behind the led. They had to create within themselves as well as without, the concept of a Filipino nation where formerly there had been only a pattern of fragmented and disparate racial groups. It was in fact a laborer and self-educated man, steeped in the traditions of the French Revolution, Andrés Bonifacio, who in 1892 founded a secret group the *Katipunan* (Society of the Sons of the People) which launched the first Asian revolution against a colonial power. The *Katipunan* was rapidly successful and by mid-1896 when the Philippine revolution started, both the elite and the masses were united in their view of a Filipino nation. The attack on the friars in Marcelo del Pilar's *La Soberanía Monacal,* and his periodical, *La Solidaridad,* helped to fortify this consensus.

The national hero of the Philippines has become José Rizal. His books, *Noli Me Tangere* and *El Filibusterismo,* with their criticism of abuses, were an inspiration to many. Founder of the Liga Filipina, also in 1892, he was essentially a scholar who only sought reform although his second book, with the name given by the Spaniards to their enemies, envisages an ultimate transition to violence. Yet Rizal was never a leader of the masses and was against the revolution at the time it was unleashed by the *Katipunan* because he felt that the latter did not have enough arms and that an ill-prepared uprising would only lead to the annihilation of the Filipinos. Unjustly and foolishly the Spaniards arrested and executed in December 1896 this moderate nationalist who presented no immediate threat to their regime and prepared the path for a more ruthless and implacable leadership. For the time being, Bonifacio remained at the head of the *Katipunan*. But Emilio Aguinaldo had dominated one faction of the association. The initial stages of the fighting, unsuccessful though they were for the rebels, showed him to be a better military commander than Bonifacio and in March 1897 a revolutionary convention meeting at Tejeros elected Aguinaldo President of a Philippine Republic. Bonifacio tried to set up a rival government but was caught and executed on Aguinaldo's orders. In view of their setbacks the rebel leaders compromised with the Spanish authorities and Aguinaldo and other leaders went into exile in Hong Kong.

Four months later the Spanish-American war had broken out, involving both Cuba and the Philippines, for reasons it is unnecessary to record in any detail here. The sinking of the U.S. battleship *Maine* in Havana harbor, an incident which Spain had offered to submit to inquiry on Washington's own terms, had aroused American emotions in a way which played into the hands of the sensational press. By the end of 1898 the mood of some Americans like Theodore Roosevelt was strangely comparable to that of the British imperialists inspired by Kipling's vision of "The White Man's Burden" which happened to be published in America at this juncture. Others were strongly opposed to this concept and all that it implied. On May 1, 1898, Commodore Dewey, in command of an American naval squadron, destroyed most of the Spanish fleet in Manila Bay. Dewey then enlisted the support of Aguinaldo and brought him back from Hong Kong to head another nationalist insurrection, promising him the independence of the Philippines. The Filipino forces took over most of Luzon except Manila and in June 1898 Philippine independence was formally declared at Aguinaldo's headquarters. But he did not manage to capture Manila. This was achieved by the Americans in August after they had received reinforcements and by what is alleged to have been a prearranged deal with the Spaniards to keep the Filipino army out of the city. At the end of the war in December 1898 Spain ceded the Philippines to the United States and the claim of the Philippines to independence was rejected by Washington. In defiance, the constitution of the Philippine Republic was promulgated in January 1899 and Aguinaldo was formally sworn in as President. There was bitter fighting between Filipino and American forces for some two years until Aguinaldo's capture in 1901. It was regarded by many in the United States as a deplorable paradox that the imperialist urges of some American leaders should have led their country temporarily to negate the democratic process for which America had always stood. But there was one qualifying factor. This was the high noon of European imperialism in Asia, and the Germans in particular were on Dewey's heels with a fleet of their own. It is almost certain that the Philippines would have fallen into the hands of other less enlightened colonialists if the United States had held back.

The United States, the Commonwealth, and Independence

In 1899 the Schurman Commission, headed by the president of Cornell, checked the situation on the spot. It declared the Filipinos to be unanimous for independence but as yet incapable of governing themselves. A second commission arrived in July 1901 when military rule ended. This was headed by William Howard Taft, the future President and Chief Justice of the United States, who afterwards became the first Governor-General. The Taft regime implemented the various measures approved by the McKinley government, including the creation of a legislature under a Philippine Organic Act of 1902, the reform of the legal system and the introduction of a U.S. type of Supreme Court. They also instituted new systems of provincial and municipal government, and of civic education, and effected a thorough administrative reorganization with particular emphasis on health and hygiene measures as well as a sweeping educational campaign in English, led by American teachers and missionaries. Private as well as official Americans embarked on dynamic reconstruction in nearly every field. Businessmen and technicians from the United States made it their task to develop the economic resources and communications of the country.

But Philippine nationalist agitation smoldered, and in 1901, a year in which Aguinaldo was still fighting, a Sedition Act was passed which forbade all advocacy of Philippine independence. Yet soon moderate nationalism prevailed. This was in part a general response to the liberal policy of the United States. More particularly it was because the Filipino elite was co-opted into the colonial regime. Those who had prospered under the Spaniards gradually became the governing classes under the Americans. The new rulers thus successfully moved Philippine nationalism into conservative and constitutional channels so that ultimately the nationalists compromised with rather than rejected the colonial system. But the basic social structure was not altered. The landlords and *ilustrados* remained broadly in command even after independence. Little was done about land reform. All too often the place of the friars was taken by absentee owners and grave injustices persisted for the peasant masses, who were by no means assured of a fair return for their labor. The large estates admittedly facilitated commercial agriculture but a drastic and honest reform redistributing part of them could have produced that invaluable base of social stability, a really widespread class of peasant proprietors. In fact the number of such proprietors, too small under the Spaniards, declined under the Americans. The efforts of the latter to ensure that the friar lands which the U.S. government had bought were taken up by the small cultivators were stultified by landlord pressure on the Filipino administrators of the scheme.[5] Other social maladjustments flowed from the continued domination of the traditional upper classes. Only in the 1960's, with

5. Hall, op. cit., p. 774.

the rise of new elements from below, does there seem to be some prospect of a change.[6]

In the early years of the occupation the mood of mutual comprehension between the Filipino elite and the Americans went so far that some wealthy Filipinos formed a Federal Party advocating annexation of the Philippines as a state of the Union. But in 1907 the new legislative system began to function. The ban on advocating independence was lifted. A Nationalist Party swept the board under the leadership of Sergio Osmeña and Manuel Quezón. This party in effect remained dominant until independence in 1946. Despite their platform of "immediate" independence the relations of the Nationalists with the American rulers were hardly less friendly and constructive than those of the Federalists. They accepted an ever greater participation in the colonial government, a process which was accelerated after President Wilson took office in 1913. Imperialism had less appeal for the Democrats than for the Republicans. The new administration sent out a remarkable Governor-General, Francis Burton Harrison, who not only implemented the Filipinization program but advanced the cause of national integration between Christian and Muslim Filipinos. In the aura of mutual trust he created, the American army was completely withdrawn from the Philippines during World War I. The Jones Law was passed, giving the Filipinos with certain reservations complete control over their own internal affairs. It also announced the intention of granting independence as soon as a stable government could be established in Manila. But the Republican government of 1921 declared that immediate independence would be a "betrayal of the Filipino people" who needed a further period of apprenticeship.

Not until the 1930's, when the Democrats were again in power under President Franklin Roosevelt, did another significantly progressive measure gain the approval of Congress, the administration, and the legislature in Manila. This was the Tydings-McDuffie Act of March, 1934. It provided for freedom in 1946 after a ten-year

6. Corpuz, op. cit. (*The Philippines*), p. 107.

transitional period in which the Philippines became a Commonwealth in association with the United States. The Act limited Philippine immigration into America and set quotas for the duty free entry of Philippine sugar, copra, and hempen cord. Between 1941 and 1946 the duties on Philippine imports would rise from zero by 5 per cent a year until they reached 25 per cent. Meanwhile U.S. goods would enter the Philippines duty free. Later the ending of U.S. trade preferences was set for 1960 instead of 1946. The Commonwealth was formally inaugurated in November 1935, with Quezón as President and Osmeña as Vice-President. By now the process of Americanization had been at least superficially far-reaching. The constitution adopted, like that which came into force on independence, was closely modeled on the United States Constitution, with the ultimate addition of an item veto for the President.

Meanwhile General MacArthur, one of the Americans most respected in the Philippines and perhaps the greatest strategist of World War II, ably organized their armed forces. He led both the retreat from and the reconquest of the islands during the Japanese occupation. In 1943 the Japanese established a puppet Republic under the Presidency of José Laurel. One of the other prominent collaborators, Manuel Roxas, afterward became President on independence. None of the major collaborators was convicted. Philippine resistance to the Japanese was strong and toward the end they only controlled twelve out of forty-eight provinces. In Luzon the Hukbalahaps (People's Army against Japan) were particularly effective. Before the war they had attacked the entrenched landlords and had done some redistribution of land. After the war their leaders were first imprisoned, then released and elected to Congress but denied their seats. Finally Luis Taruc was allowed to take his seat. But he soon quit, admitted his communist affiliations, and resumed the guerrilla war which the Huks had conducted intermittently since the Japanese departure. Eventually after 1950 Ramon Magsaysay, Minister for Defense under President Quirino and later President himself, achieved remarkable success against the Huks by genuinely trying to improve the harsh conditions of the peasants. But neither the abuses embittering the peasants nor the Huk movement have been finally eliminated.

Independence on July 4, 1946, was an occasion of warm goodwill toward America with a few disturbing reservations in the background. Two parties, the Liberal and the Nationalist, developed out of the original Nationalist Party and alternated in the operation of the spoils system while their candidates not infrequently changed from one to the other. But for some years no political leader of either party who hoped to get elected could afford to proclaim anti-American policies. Two main irritants between Manila and Washington, which in time emerged more acutely, were the Philippine Trade (Bell) Act and the Philippine Rehabilitation (Tydings) Act, both of 1946. A third was the American bases. The Filipinos were of course aware that the grant of independence was dictated by American self-interest as well as idealism. American labor wanted to deny right of entry to the United States of cheap Philippine labor. American business wished to exclude imports of Philippine sugar and copra competitive with their own and other sources of supply. The Philippines wanted economic as well as political independence but could not afford to lose the American market too soon. The Bell Act was an elaboration of the economic provisions of the earlier Tydings-McDuffie Act. Until 1954 the Philippines would have eight years of duty free imports into the United States subject to quotas. Then between 1954 and 1974 there would be a graduated rise in duty until the full American tariff was reached in the latter year. Meanwhile, American goods would enter the Philippines free and Americans would have equal rights with Filipinos in the latter's country. In connection with rehabilitation no war damage payments above $500 would be made until the Bell Act had been accepted. A 1947 agreement gave the United States ninety-nine-year leases of twenty-three bases with full legal jurisdiction including, in the case of many offenses, jurisdiction over Filipinos as well as their own people. Inevitably, Philippine pride was hurt by provisions in these

measures which went far further than anything that other former colonial powers had sought or obtained from their former colonies.
Yet the Bell Act was accepted at the instance of the Filipino sugar
interests and its termination in so few years casts a cloud of anxiety
and doubt over the future. Meanwhile all these sources of discord
between themselves and their former protectors have turned the
thoughts of the Philippine leaders toward closer association with
their fellow Asians and particularly with the neighboring countries
of Malay race. After Magsaysay's tragic death in an air crash in 1957
this new trend was emphasized, as we shall see, in the policies of his
successors, Presidents Garcia, Macapagal, and Marcos.

VI

THE DUTCH AND BRITISH
EXTEND THEIR CONTROL

The Netherlands East Indies in the Modern Age

The Philippines has significant mineral resources as well as profitable cash crops. So in even greater degree do Indonesia and Malaysia. Malaysia produces about half of the world's natural rubber and nearly 40 per cent of the world's tin. The Philippines and Malaysia are today the most prosperous countries of Southeast Asia. Indonesia under Dutch rule was richer still, but its economy declined disastrously under the capricious rule of the now deposed President Sukarno. In his day, Indonesia, like Burma under its present military regime, was obsessed with destroying its colonial heritage. The severe paternalism of Dutch rule, more efficient, careful, and exacting than British rule, contributed to this extremist attitude. So, in the case of Burma, did mistakes of British policy, such as the incorporation of the country in India and the abolition of the monarchy. From the standpoint of modern economics both countries lost materially by this process of rejection. From this same standpoint the Philippines and Malaysia, which on the whole assimilated the colonial system and built on its foundations, have been more wealthy and successful.

The so-called Culture System introduced by the Netherlands Indies authorities for Java in the 1830's was an inauspicious example of

Dutch efficiency. It required the compulsory and intensive cultivation by the Javanese peasants of cash crops such as coffee, sugar, indigo, tea, tobacco, pepper, cinnamon, cinchona, oil palm, cotton, and cochineal and their sale at a low price to the Dutch authorities. It was an economic monopoly run by the king and government. The system produced massive profits sufficient to pay off the Dutch public debt and build the Netherlands railways. It was operated through the traditional Javanese chieftains who were allowed to make a profit out of it themselves and for that reason were prone to exact even higher production than that demanded by the Dutch authorities who prescribed what crops should be grown. These special crops were to be raised on one-fifth of the cultivated land of each village and no more labor was supposed to be required of the peasants than that needed to grow rice on the same area. But the profits were so tempting that there was an excessive diversion of land and labor from rice cultivation. Starvation ensued in some areas where the population had sharply increased in consequence of the improved organization and stability introduced by the Dutch.

The government monopoly was abolished after 1848 in favor of private enterprise. This actually produced far greater profits and led to the settlement in Indonesia of numerous Dutch planters and businessmen, amounting to some 67,000 by 1900. The Dutch in Indonesia did not have the *apartheid* complex which their descendants exhibit in South Africa. Legitimately or illegitimately they begot many children of Indonesian mothers. These Eurasians were identified in status with the Dutch and enjoyed the privileges of the ruling class. Their prominence in official jobs came to be much resented by the Indonesians. This group was eliminated from the public service after independence, many being turned out of the country in 1957 together with most of the residents of pure Dutch origin.

Dutch plantations and mining enterprises were progressively extended in the later nineteenth and twentieth centuries to Sumatra and the other Outer Islands, such as Borneo and the Celebes. In the two former, oil was discovered in important quantities. There were also considerable resources of tin on islands such as Bangka, and the Netherlands Indies eventually outstripped Malaya in the production of rubber. But most if not all of the profits derived by the Netherlands from their Indies were swallowed up for a time by military expenditure which tends, as we saw, to be one of the inevitable penalties of colonial rule. In 1873 the Dutch felt impelled to start a campaign for the subjugation of the North Sumatran Sultanate of Acheh which dragged on for some thirty years. It proved the futility of the hopes of those earlier British and Dutch colonizers who had favored simply port settlements for trading with no involvements in the interior. A similar though less burdensome commitment was undertaken by the British in Malaya only two years after the start of the Dutch Sumatran campaign.

In the 1860's the Culture System had been strongly attacked by the liberals in the Netherlands because of its harsh impact on the natives, and it was gradually abolished. One consequence of this attitude was a new solicitude for the welfare of the Indonesians. This was encouraged by the Dutch authorities in the 1890's and led to the adoption of their Ethical Policy. Strong pressure developed in the Netherlands after 1900 for increased educational facilities in the Indies, the improvement of social services, and the inclusion of Indonesians in the senior posts of the administration. The Netherlands government took a number of useful and progressive steps. They reformed the labor system and improved agriculture and education. They protected native industries and raised the standard of housing. They promoted irrigation, public credit facilities, co-operatives, and debtor relief. But the broader scope of the Ethical Policy was defeated by the obstinate resistance of the European business community which wanted to restrict the role of the Dutch government in the Indies and have a bigger share in making policy and running the administration themselves. They denounced the new liberalism and particularly the plan to have Indonesians in responsible government jobs. They argued that this would lower efficiency just when higher standards were necessary. This attitude was also characteristic of the French in Indochina.

In India the British faced similar opposition from their business communities. But they nevertheless persisted in responding to nationalist pressure, in particular after 1909, for devolution of responsibility to the people of the country, however gradual in practice they strove to make this process. The result was that just before independence there were only a handful of British civilian officials left in responsible positions in India. In their particular response to Asian nationalist demands the British may have been unconsciously motivated by the salutary shock of the American revolution which attuned them to the ultimate and inevitable separation of their dependent territories. In the absence of any such constructively humiliating experience in their own colonial histories neither the Dutch nor the French seem to have contemplated before it was forced upon them actual and complete withdrawal. They found it hard to take seriously the rebellious motions and grandiloquent rhetoric of the nationalist leaders whom some of them seem to have assessed as fractious and ungrateful children. In 1936, only six years before the downfall of their regime, the Dutch Governor-General declared "We have ruled here for 300 years with the whip and the club and we shall still be doing it in another 300 years." [1]

Despite the high culture of many areas of Indonesia in the past, this was a country no less fragmented than the Philippines. The vision of an Indonesian nation was the product of varying trends and factors in the modern age. Aside from the devout *santri* the observance of Islam was on the whole more relaxed and accommodating than in the fiercely orthodox countries of the Near East. Yet it had always been a strong force and in the twentieth century a modernized concept of Islam, influenced by Western education, served the nationalist cause by challenging Dutch rule. But the Islamic nation-

1. Sutan Sjahrir, *Out of Exile*, New York, John Day, 1949, p. 112; see Herbert Feith, *Indonesia* in *Governments and Politics of Southeast Asia*, ed. G. McTurnan Kahin, Ithaca: Cornell University Press, 1964, p. 195.

alists looked to the ultimate establishment of an Islamic state and were to some extent suspicious of the liberal, secular, nationalist movements which were also a twentieth-century product of Western education.[2] Meanwhile the Dutch attempted with some success to seek the friendship of certain Muslim groups.

The first nationalist organization as such was Budi Otomo (Noble Endeavor) established in 1908. It aimed rather after the manner of Japan at strengthening and rejuvenating certain aspects of the national culture—in this case traditional Javanese culture—to enable it to face up to the modern world and stem Western control. It appealed to young radical intellectuals favoring reform. Although it was never a mass movement it was in this group that communist spokesmen first gained a hearing. By this time it had antagonized the Dutch and offended the Islamic elements. Its leadership was exiled in 1913.[3]

Meanwhile, in 1912, an Islamic Association, Sarekat Islam, came to the fore with definite political objectives. It had a wider appeal and more dramatic impact. Organized in part by Arab and Sumatran merchants against their Chinese rivals in the *batik* cloth trade of Java and also against the Dutch, it had a membership of some hundreds of thousands by 1916. It represented on the one hand peasant rejection of increasingly rapid economic and social change. On the other hand it demonstrated through urban leadership its ability to channel discontent.[4] It was given legal recognition in 1916 and for a time served a useful purpose in uncovering grievances, some of which were righted by the Dutch. But part of it became infiltrated by the Marxists and in 1920 this last group turned itself into a Communist Party and was separated from the Association. A further contributory cause of the disintegration of Sarekat Islam was its launching of an avalanche of demands in 1917 which alarmed the Dutch and discredited their Ethical Policy. Yet another factor was the de-

2. J. D. Legge, *Indonesia*, Englewood Cliffs: Prentice-Hall, 1964, p. 122.
3. Cady, op. cit. (*Southeast Asia: Its Historical Development*), pp. 377, 378.
4. Feith: Kahin, op. cit., p. 194.

sertion of the merchants and the Association's acceptance of protection money from the Chinese. The last is a characteristic device of this wealthy and subtle race. Today as in the past they find it convenient to smooth their path in this manner by conciliating their opponents or bringing under an obligation those who might be useful to them. After the decline of Sarekat Islam, Muslim nationalism tended to be channeled through more specifically religious organizations. One of these was the mainly urban Islamic reform movement *Muhammadijah* which favored a Back-to-the-Prophet concept coupled with the assimilation of Western science and history and the rejection of Indian cultural survivals and traditional law (*adat*). Another with a more rural background was the Muslim teachers' organization, the Nahdatul Ulama.

The measures taken by the Dutch to meet the growing wave of nationalism were cautious and partial. As we saw they supported Islam to some extent and cultivated the modernized Muslim Indonesian elite. They permitted Indonesian participation in local advisory councils, but these were usually controlled by Europeans with Indonesian membership confined to officials. In 1918 they established a Volksraad or People's Council for the Netherlands Indies and in the following year completely banned forced labor. But the First World War inevitably gave external stimulus to the nationalist movement in Indonesia as elsewhere. The white man's image was already tarnished in Asia by Japan's victory over Russia in 1905–06. Although Holland was not herself involved, the image was further discredited in the world war by the spectacle of the white races ruthlessly destroying each other. Nevertheless Indonesia reached a very high level of prosperity during the war, and after, with economic expansion greater in the Outer Islands than in over-populated Java. The state played a larger part than would have been normal in Europe. Private enterprise co-operated with it in such fields as irrigation and agricultural experiment. Most of the tin mines and two-thirds of the coal mines were state operated or under state control. Meanwhile investment by Western enterprises only increased the gap between the indigenous and the modern sector. And in the Outer Islands the break with traditional life was accentuated by a labor force often of migrants from Java or China. The boom years to 1930 seemed to the Indonesians to entrench Dutch interests more firmly than ever.

The Emergence of Indonesian Nationalist Leadership

The facilities for Western education established by the Dutch in Indonesia were painfully limited. As late as 1939 secondary graduates in any given year averaged around 800 only, while the total attendance at university level was about 1100, including many non-Indonesians. During the same period out of 3039 higher civil service positions only 221 were held by Indonesians.[5] Most of the advanced educational facilities were vocational and in fields such as agriculture, technology, law, and medicine.[6] Some Indonesians, however, were educated in Europe and a number joined the nationalist Indonesian Association in the Netherlands. By the 1920's Western education had helped to create a minority dedicated to the overthrow of the existing order. The Dutch were faced in those years with active subversion and went over to strong repressive action. Nationalist and communist defiance were bound to seem to them more closely linked than in fact they were. In 1926 a section of the Communist Party launched a revolt in West Java and Central Sumatra, the first of three which were to occur within forty years, and in mid-1927 a group of students and graduates from Bandung headed by Sukarno, then a young engineer, established the Indonesian Nationalist Party (PNI). Stirred by Sukarno's oratory they demanded complete independence but the government arrested the leaders in 1929. Associated with Sukarno were two leaders of the Indonesian Association recently returned from the Netherlands, Sutan Sjahrir and Moham-

5. Feith: Kahin, op. cit., p. 197.
6. Cady, op. cit. (*Southeast Asia: Its Historical Development*), p. 538.

med Hatta, both of whom had studied in the Netherlands. The former was the future founder of the Indonesian Socialist Party (PSI) and Prime Minister of Indonesia from 1945 to 1947. The latter was to be for a time Vice-President under Sukarno's post-war Presidency. After the banning of the PNI they concentrated on training other nationalist groups. Finally, the Dutch turned decisively against the whole nationalist movement. In 1934 all three were banished to remote islands. They were not released until the Japanese invasion of 1942.

By this time the prospects for Indonesian nationalism had been further advanced by the world economic slump which had led the Dutch to encourage the manufacture of cheap consumer goods in the Indies and to treat Indonesia to some extent as a self-contained economic unit. The separate status of Indonesia was subsequently enforced by the early events of World War II. Holland was occupied by the Germans in 1940 and the Dutch in Southeast Asia were cut off from their home base. This war later saw the resounding defeat of the white colonial powers in Asia by an Asian nation. It thus decisively helped the Asian peoples to their goal of freedom. Yet the inter-war and second-war period had another far-reaching consequence which has deeply disturbed and painfully involved both the old colonialists and the new nations. This was the strengthening of communism as a world force. In the 1920's the new Soviet Union had repudiated and exposed the imperialism of the Czars who had seized most of central and northern Asia. It had denounced all "unequal treaties," and especially those forced on China. It had proclaimed itself the champion of oppressed colonial peoples. In all these ways communism won innumerable followers despite Moscow's post-war prosecution of a new imperialism in eastern Europe and elsewhere. When it triumphed in China too it seemed to some of its followers and enemies that it might be on the verge of taking over much of the world.

British Intervention in the Malay States

The mid-nineteenth century was a period of relative inactivity for Britain in Malaya. Some action was taken to limit Thai pretentions to suzerainty except over the northern states. In 1842, Bangkok was persuaded to restore the Sultan of Kedah, though his territory was reduced by the loss of a small northern area which became the separate state of Perlis. Harsh conditions in southern China resulting from the Taiping rebellion brought an influx of Chinese. Many of them, using the Straits Settlements as a base, moved into the interior of the peninsula to intensify the production of tin which their countrymen had exploited there for centuries. As in Singapore, there were some sanguinary feuds between Chinese secret societies which the British tried to stop. This was particularly the case in the tin mining area of Perak around Larut. Conditions in this state were further complicated by a three-way dispute over the succession to the throne. Quite a different dispute had meanwhile developed between the Straits Settlements and the British authorities in India by whom they were controlled. The official and mercantile communities—both British and Asian—increasingly objected to being treated as a minor outpost of an Indian empire with only limited understanding of their essentially different problems. Resentment came to a head when Calcutta suggested imposing the Indian currency and customs duties and taxes in violation of the free trade principles laid down by Raffles. The communities were also disturbed by the interest shown by France and Germany in the peninsula, their natural hinterland. They had prospered by trading from the Settlements. They were impressed with the riches in tin which the Chinese managed to extract from the western Sultanates of the peninsula and particularly those of Perak and Selangor, despite constant insecurity and lack of good government, enhanced by Malay dynastic feuds. Apart from tin they foresaw a big future for modern plantations.

They counted on larger profits if the British government would bring order into the interior and thus facilitate their operations there without making them meet the cost. After many vicissitudes this is generally what occurred.

The Straits merchants had a useful lobby in London and in 1867 they scored a first success. The Settlements were removed from the jurisdiction of India and made into a separate Crown Colony directly under London. Seven years later Sir Andrew Clarke, the second Governor of the new colony, started intervention in the Malay states. The British government had long discouraged anything of the kind, but by now they had begun to yield to pressure from various quarters. Clarke was given careful and contradictory instructions stating that London had no desire to interfere but proposed to rescue Malaya if possible from the ruin which must befall her if the disorders there continued unchecked. Would the appointment of a resident British officer help to solve the problem? Clarke decided that this was too cautious. One of the claimants to the Perak throne said (with some prompting) that he would welcome British protection and a British resident. The Governor summoned as many as possible of the Malay dignitaries concerned—and the quarrelling Chinese—to a conference on an offshore island. The Chinese agreed to peace between themselves. In the absence of the two other candidates the prince who wanted British protection was recognized as Sultan of Perak and a senior British official, James Birch, appointed as Resident to the state. Birch was a tactless and impatient Victorian. His zeal for swift reform, especially of the finances, made the local chiefs fear the loss of their traditional revenues. Finally he was murdered with the encouragement of the Sultan who had asked for his services. This did not deter the British from their new course. They sent a punitive military expedition, and substituted a Sultan of a different stamp. They installed a fresh Resident, Hugh Low, who managed through quiet persuasion to win the confidence and co-operation of the new ruler. In his twelve years there he changed the state's deficit into a flourishing credit balance while the population rose more than two and a half times. His methods and achievements became a model for similar Residential arrangements in three more of the Malay states by now outside the orbit of Thailand, namely, Selangor and Negri Sembilan on the west coast, and Pahang in the center and east. Selangor had been one of the principal centers of Bugis power in the eighteenth century and Negri Sembilan had been strengthened by settlers from the pepper areas of Sumatra, the Minangkabaus, who had a matrilineal structure of society. Pahang was the largest, wildest, and least populated of the Malay states. In 1896 these three states along with Perak were induced to enter a federation which established a centralized administration based on Kuala Lumpur. This had been a small tin mining settlement created by the Chinese, which eventually became the capital of the whole country. The federation substituted quasi-direct rule for the original largely indirect Residential system. Port Swettenham, the harbor of Selangor, still today commemorates Sir Frank Swettenham who carried through the scheme.

The White Rajahs of Sarawak

In the middle and later years of the nineteenth century the British also became involved in northern Borneo. In December 1838, an adventurous Englishman of private means, James Brooke, sailed for Borneo in his yacht. In a previous announcement he echoed some of the attitudes and policies of Raffles. He sharply criticized the Dutch, whose domination of Indonesia was due to British "vacillation and weakness." His voyage would be partly for scientific exploration but also to see if another British settlement could be founded in an area which the Dutch had not yet penetrated.[7] He was encouraged by the authorities and business community of Singapore. In August 1839 he landed in Sarawak, then a small area around Kuching. Up-

7. Steven Runciman: *The White Rajahs*, Cambridge: Cambridge University Press, 1960, p. 53.

country there were gold and antimony mines which had attracted numbers of Chinese with their invariably keen eye for gain. Sarawak was the western province of northern Borneo, which was all that remained to the Sultans of Brunei of their seventeenth-century dominions. Then they had ruled the whole of Borneo and their suzerainty extended over the Sulu archipelago in the southern Philippines. In its decline, however, Brunei had had to cede the northernmost tip of Borneo to the Sultans of Sulu and this was to lead to major complications in the modern age.

Piracy and subversion flourished and when Brooke reached Sarawak, the Malays and Land Dayaks there had revolted and the Sultan's uncle had come to crush the rebellion. He enlisted Brooke's help and their efforts were eventually effective. In return for this service Brooke was offered and accepted the position of Rajah and Governor of Sarawak under the Sultan, and was formally installed as such in November 1841. The Dutch were seriously disturbed for they were far from having established themselves in the main part of Borneo. In the eighteenth century they had only extended their influence to some isolated coastal areas such as the Sultanate of Banjermasin in the south. They protested that Brooke's action was a breach of the Anglo-Dutch treaty of 1824 which generally excluded Britain from Indonesia. Eventually, however, the validity of this new British intervention was accepted on the grounds that it occurred north and not south of the Equator. But it aroused the Dutch into adopting a more energetic policy. Soon after the Brooke incident they annexed Banjermasin and intervened in Sambas and Pontianak in the west and Kutei in the east. Meanwhile, James Brooke had founded a dynasty known as the White Rajahs which lasted for a hundred years, until just after the Second World War. During that time they absorbed most of the territory up to and around Brunei itself of the Sultan to whom they owed allegiance.

The first Rajah had essentially a dual role. He had become an Oriental prince in his own right in an area which was not yet British. But he also functioned for a time as the agent of the British Government and received from it some help and recognition. He was involved for years in fighting the local tribes and especially the fierce unruly Sea Dayaks or Ibans. His success against them and against hostile intrigues at the Sultan's court was ensured by the support of the Royal Navy. In 1846 Brooke persuaded the Sultan to cede to Britain his offshore island of Labuan, valuable as a coaling station for ships sailing to the Far East. In 1847 the Sultan was further induced to conclude a treaty with Britain "for the furtherance of commercial relations and the mutual suppression of piracy." This provided for extraterritorial jurisdiction over British subjects and precluded the Sultan from ceding territory to any other nation or national without the consent of Britain. After these arrangements there gradually developed a regular movement of trade and navigation between Singapore and Malaya, the north coast of Borneo, China, and eventually Japan.

The British Government then made Brooke Governor of Labuan and British Consul-General in Brunei. He was knighted and was for a time in high favor with British ruling circles and society. But he was no easy character. He had the uncompromising intensity of the Victorians and he remained a hot-tempered, life-long bachelor. He incurred the enmity of a former business agent. He was accused in British quarters of unwarrantable harshness in his suppression of local rebels and had to answer to a court of enquiry in Singapore. Although this acquitted him he was regarded by local Asians as having ceased to enjoy the support and approval of the British authorities. The Chinese who resented the river tolls he had introduced attacked Kuching in force and Brooke only narrowly escaped. Once again, however, he succeeded in restoring his position and eventually in widening his dominions at Brunei's expense. When he died in 1868, Sarawak extended to Bintulu, almost halfway to Brunei itself. James was succeeded by his nephew, Charles Johnston, who had served under him and who adopted his name. Equally forceful in character, Rajah Charles was perhaps even more domineering and seriously tenacious than his uncle. Under him the frontiers of Sarawak were extended considerably further. Until the later years of the third Rajah, the Brookes ruled as benevolent autocrats mostly through British and Malay officials. Except for the permitted activity of the Borneo Company, the Rajah's bankers, the Brookes set their face against economic exploitation of the country by outside business interests. Sarawak was in any event a poor land. Mineral resources were very limited and the soil depleted by too much monsoon drenching. Rubber, tolerant of the poor soil, and pepper, were developed as smallholder crops, while big plantations were discouraged. But there were severe limitations on the acquisition of land and the land hunger of the Chinese smallholders has produced grave political and social problems in our day. The Brookes judged that the primitive but gifted native peoples would be happier preserving their traditional ways and as far as possible avoiding contact with European civilization. Any land which they had once used was reserved for them. But for the Ibans and Land Dayaks, the Kenyahs, Kayans, and others this meant in practice a minimum of education, of medical facilities, and of participation in running the country. There was widespread illiteracy and until well into the twentieth century messages to Dayak headmen were often conveyed by pieces of knotted string.[8]

British North Borneo

Meanwhile American citizens were showing an interest in the Pacific and in Southeast Asia. In 1865 a former American seaman called Lee Moses, who set himself up as United States Consul, persuaded the Sultan of Brunei to grant him a concession covering North Borneo, that is the area north and east of the city of Brunei extending

8. See Richard Allen, *Malaysia: Prospect and Retrospect*, London: Oxford University Press, 1968, pp. 40, 41, 67, 68.

to the Sulu Sea. Certain sums were promised to the Sultan and his heir which were never paid.[9] Moses promptly sold his concession to two American merchants in Hong Kong, Joseph Torrey and Thomas Harris, and their Chinese partners. They formed the American Trading Company of Borneo with a capital of only $7000. Torrey, like Brooke, was made Rajah and Governor and he and his companions started a settlement at the mouth of the Kimanis River. After some land had been cleared and planted the settlement failed, chiefly through lack of money and food. In 1866 Torrey tried to interest the U.S. Government in the concession but was told that Moses had acted on his own authority in obtaining it. Finally, in 1875 Torrey managed to sell his rights to a German, Baron von Overbeck, who was Austrian Consul-General in Hong Kong. Having failed to interest the Austrian or German Governments or business circles in Vienna in pursuing this venture, Overbeck went into partnership with a young Englishman, Alfred Dent, of Dent Brothers in London. The Sultan now received his first payment and the Brunei lease was renewed. To ensure the validity of the title the Sultan of Sulu was then also approached. The British administrator of Labuan and a British businessman called Cowie who had become a trading partner of the Sultan of Sulu helped to persuade the latter to cede to Overbeck and Dent the area he claimed, in return for an annual payment.

Objections to this new British expansion were raised from three quarters. The Spaniards, having just conquered the Suluks, claimed all the territories which had been subject to them. But they abandoned their Borneo claims in 1885 in return for British recognition

9. Lee Moses has been variously evaluated. K. G. Tregonning in A *History of Modern Sabah*, Singapore: University of Malaya Press, 1965, p. 5 describes him as "The American Consul"; Cady, op. cit. (*Southeast Asia, Its Historical Development*), p. 441, calls him "an ex-naval officer and pretended U.S. Consul"; Runciman, op. cit., p. 178, says ". . . Moses appeared in Brunei with documents announcing him to be Consul for the United States . . . How Moses, who was a cashiered seaman from the American Navy, had obtained his papers is unknown. He had borrowed money in Singapore to pay for his passage to Brunei . . ."

of their sovereignty over the Sulu Archipelago. Much later, by an Anglo-American convention of 1930, the U.S. government recognized North Borneo as being under British protection. After independence, however, the Philippines took a different course and the deal with the Sultan of Sulu forms the basis of their present claim to North Borneo, or Sabah as it is now called. This claim was sponsored by Senator, later President, Macapagal and presented to Britain in 1962. The conflict is now with the federation of Malaysia which we shall be describing later. The Dutch objected too, perfunctorily. Finally Rajah Charles Brooke strongly resented a "set of mercantile adventurers" establishing themselves in a region on which he might have had eventual designs himself. He set out to advise the natives to resist and was told by the British authorities that as a Brunei Rajah he had no right to incite these people to disobey the orders of his suzerain, the Sultan.[10] More valid was his objection that under Brunei's treaty with Britain of 1847 it was only with special British permission that the Sultan could cede any part of his territory to someone not British. This point was met when Overbeck sold out to Dent, who formed the British North Borneo Provisional Association in 1878. This later became the British North Borneo Company which received a Charter from Queen Victoria in 1881. British protection was extended to Brunei, Sarawak, and North Borneo in 1888.

In each territory, government evolved on very different lines. The local Malays, prominent in Brunei itself, had to some extent a privileged position in them all. Yet they were not necessarily of Malay stock. Virtually any native person could qualify as a Malay by embracing Islam. Those who did so, such as the Melanaus, Kedayans, Illanuns, Suluks, and Bajaus usually came from the islands or the more accessible areas in contrast to the remote up-country tribes. These lived lives apart, most of them in long houses, and tended to straddle the mountainous frontier region between the British and Dutch areas. Brunei was eventually reduced to a small neglected en-

10. Tregonning, op. cit., p. 16.

clave in Sarawak in which little changed despite the presence of a British Consul-General and later Resident. Yet her poverty became affluence through the discovery of an oilfield in 1929. Meanwhile, the austerely conservative Sarawak regime was changed under the third Rajah, Vyner Brooke. In September 1941, for the dynasty's centenary he promulgated a progressive constitution under which his powers could only be used with advice and consent. But the Japanese occupation followed in three months. North Borneo was governed by officials from Malaya hampered by dictation from the Company in London, especially after Cowie became its dominant figure. Though there were bad miscalculations, the economy was run on the whole on modern business lines and this does not seem to have prejudiced the natives any more than the conservatism of Sarawak. But the country lacked labor and much had to be recruited from outside. It had some rich volcanic soil and much excellent timber. It produced first rate tobacco until the industry was killed by a U.S. protective tariff. The edible birds' nests so prized by the Chinese were one of its economic staples.

Expansion and Completion of British Malaya

The federation of the four central Malay states was not popular with the Malays. It emasculated the State Councils and the Sultans' prestige and authority. Although a Conference of Malay Rulers was started in 1897, in practice decisions were taken by the central administration and passed on to the State Councils for action. It was not in fact a real federation since it largely abolished state autonomy in favor of administrative co-ordination. Supposedly indirect rule had become almost indistinguishable from direct rule. In any event, little administrative responsibility was given to the Malays and they resented it. The commercial, mining, and planting communities also objected to this centralization. The establishment in 1909 of a consultative Federal Council presided over by the British Governor (who was concurrently High Commissioner for the Malay States), with the Sultans as passive members, did not improve matters. The authority of the Rulers was again diminished. It is thus hardly surprising that when in the same year Thailand renounced her suzerainty over Kedah, Perlis, Kelantan, and Trengganu their rulers declined to join the federation. They were supported in this by Johore which had always had its own special relationship with Singapore. The British authorities accepted these objections. The five states were allowed to retain a wider autonomy as the Unfederated Malay States. British Advisers, not Residents, were appointed. They made courteous suggestions to the Rulers but no more. This had advantages for the future, since in the unfederated states Malays occupied most of the responsible posts and this was a useful training for self-government. The future Prime Minister of independent Malaya, himself half-Thai, was to be a prince of the Royal House of Kedah.

In view of the attitude of the unfederated states, the British to some extent decentralized the structure of the federation in the 1920's and 1930's thus hoping to attract the former into membership. The federated states were given back control over agriculture, health, and public works and again became responsible for legislation. Up to the outbreak of the Second World War British rule in Malaya continued to develop in this haphazard and rather untidy fashion. Yet despite some obvious flaws in the system which the Malays were entitled to dislike, the country was run with reasonable efficiency, and prosperity blunted the edge of discontent. For in the twentieth century Malaya learned to exploit a source of wealth even more profitable than tin. This was rubber. Seeds of the wild rubber tree were smuggled out of Brazil in 1877. They were planted first in the botanical gardens at Kew near London and then in those at Singapore. For long, Malayan planters (chiefly of coffee) took little interest. By 1910, however, the automobile industry had stimulated a boom. Ten years later Malaya exported more than half the world's production of natural rubber and, as we saw, her production approaches this figure today. The expanding demand for labor on the rubber estates was met by the recruitment of Indian laborers, mostly Tamils from the south. Initially much of this labor was introduced under a system of indentures which at worst was extremely harsh. Objections in India led to the adoption by Malaya of an amended Labor Code in 1923 and to the appointment in the same year of an agent of the Indian government in the Federated Malay States to supervise the working conditions, wages, and other matters affecting Indian labor.[11] Eventually the indenture system was abandoned. Indian labor conditions, however, continued to be unsatisfactory. But there was a rigorous campaign to improve them after the Second World War by a strong National Union of Plantation Workers under a dynamic South Indian Secretary-General. Meanwhile Indian immigration had introduced fresh human problems into what was already a multi-racial society.

In the special circumstances of Malaya there was virtually no national movement directed against Britain before World War II. One paradoxical reason for this phenomenon may have been that in Malaya as in India and Pakistan the British, however involuntarily, were creating the structure of a nation in territories which had always suffered from political fragmentation. But in Malaya, unlike India, there was little articulate opposition to their methods. They had left the Sultans as the visible rulers of a number of states which had long been united by language, religion, and custom but which found themselves in constructive co-operation for the first time.[12] It is said that on being asked by a visitor, "Don't you want your freedom?", one of the Sultans replied: "Freedom? What do you think we pay the British for?" But the very readiness of Britain to accommodate herself to the varying demands of two groups of Malay States and the exigencies of differing racial communities meant that the country was far less tightly knit together than it should have been in the moment of trial. There were three different regimes in

11. Usha Mahajani, *The Role of Indian Minorities in Burma and Malaya* (issued under the auspices of the Institute of Pacific Relations) Bombay: Vora, 1960, p. 98.
12. Allen, op. cit., p. 63.

Malaya when the Japanese attacked, that of the Straits Settlements and those of the Federated and Unfederated Malay States. This divided structure and lack of co-ordination, which Britain sought to correct after the war, greatly facilitated the enemy's task. The Japanese achieved surprise by landing at Kota Bharu in Kelantan on December 8 but two hours before Pearl Harbor from bases they had established in Thailand with the consent of Prime Minister Pibun. They were well prepared to move through the jungle where the defenders did not expect them. Being sensibly equipped with bicycles they were able between battles to roll down the excellent roads the British had built and attack the great naval base of Singapore from the rear where there were virtually no defenses. The surrender of Singapore occurred even more swiftly than that of the bravely defended American outposts of Bataan and Corregidor in the Philippines.

VII

BRITAIN AND BURMA

Burmese Nationalism and British Rule

Britain gave Burma a government which was on the whole just, orderly, and materially most successful in developing a land of substantial mineral wealth and great agricultural resources. This profited the foreign investor, but it also produced a prosperity, now vanished, which was of general benefit to the Burmese. Yet institutions like the British parliamentary system, the rule of law, a free press, impartial administration, and the influences of European liberalism never took firm root in Burma as to some extent they did in India where indigenous traditions of democracy could be traced back to ancient times.[1] But although British rule in India lasted more than three times as long as in Burma, independent India made only a selective adoption of the British system. Cabinet government was retained, as were the powerful Indian Civil Service and certain formal and ceremonial elements in the British style of rule which had evoked some response from Indians possibly because of their many ethnic affinities with Europe. But monarchy was rejected, despite the many examples of it in the Indian princely states. So was the overriding sovereignty of Parliament as it exists today in Britain. Instead India,

1. A. L. Basham, *The Wonder That Was India*, New York: Grove Press (Evergreen Edition), 1959, pp. 82, 96, 97.

following the example of the United States, adopted a bill of fundamental rights and gave its independent judiciary the power to determine the constitutionality of any legislation. But although Burma long functioned as part of India after the British conquest, neither the British system of rule nor the features in the American constitution which interested the Indians evoked any deep response from the Burmese. Some of the British system naturally survived during the first phase of independence, but such survivals have since been almost totally effaced.

The abolition of the monarchy and Burma's incorporation into India meant the gratuitous humiliation of a proud nation with a long tradition of masterful achievement. The first step had not originally been Britain's intention. The Viceroy of India at the time favored making Burma a protectorate under its own kings on the pattern of the princely states of India or of the French in Indochina. But the country was thoroughly disorganized. After Thibaw's reign, the governing council, the *Hlutdaw*, was discredited and no suitable candidate for the throne survived who would in British judgment have been able to maintain himself without their troops.[2] But any ingenuous European notion that the Burmese would welcome the removal of a sanguinary tyrant and the advent of more just and efficient rule was soon dispelled. Upper Burma was Burma's homeland and the spirit of the people there was quite different from that in the outlying regions which Britain had formerly annexed. The Burmese army, the local notables, and a number of princes refused to surrender. They carried on a fierce guerrilla war for five years that required some 40,000 troops and military police to suppress. In the case of their first annexations, such as that of Tenasserim, the British administrators, who knew little about Burma, had been told to govern according to local law and custom but to introduce liberal principles where possible. Some of them came from the Straits Settlements and had little experience of the Indian system. But as time

2. D. G. E. Hall, *Burma*, London: Hutchinson's University Library, 1956, p. 142.

went by more and more officers with an Indian background were transferred to Burma and these progressively applied Indian codes and methods which were quite alien to the Burmese, for example, judgment by fixed legal principles instead of by the kind of arbitration procedure familiar to Burmese legal practice.

The local administration was also transformed with unhappy results. Traditionally the country was divided into circles under dignitaries known as *thugyis,* who arbitrated local disputes according to custom. But many of the *thugyis* had been implicated in the rebellion. The circles were broken up and the villages made into administrative units on the lines of those in India. The villagers and their headmen were now supposed to maintain order and collect revenue. Then many villages were amalgamated and the number of headmen reduced so that those who remained should have adequate salaries. The amalgamated villages thus finally became artificial administrative units while the rigid British-Indian legal system replaced the flexible and familiar customary judgments of the traditional local authorities. Even more serious was the British failure to ensure any system of authority or discipline over the *Sangha,* the Buddhist monastic order. This had been controlled by the king through a senior abbot and an ecclesiastical and lay council which he appointed. These had powers of discipline and managed endowments though much autonomy was left to the monasteries. The village pagodas and monasteries with their schools had produced a high degree of literacy. But the British felt themselves precluded from officially supporting the traditional system by their undertaking after the Indian Mutiny not to interfere with religion. They were prepared to recognize an ecclesiastical superior but would not invest him with any legal powers. This meant that ecclesiastical cases came in time before the civil courts, and a stable, customary system for regulating admission to and conduct within the order disappeared. With disintegrating discipline the monks, once cultural leaders, tended to become ignorant and subversive.[3] Sometimes actual criminals took refuge in the yellow robe.

3. Hall, op. cit. (*Burma*), pp. 137, 145, 146.

Subversion was also bred by other factors. During the whole colonial period the Burmese with their past military renown strongly resented being, as they put it, "kept down by Indian troops." In spite of the vital elements in their civilization which they owed to India, the Burmese of the nineteenth and twentieth centuries had only a moderate regard for their darker-complexioned neighbors. Self-satisfied in a rich uncrowded land with more than enough food for all, the Burmese in an essentially Buddhist tradition of indifference to material gain had been content to take life at an easy pace. They tended to despise the restless exertions of the Indians dictated by the struggle for survival in their overpopulated world. Indians became numerous in Burma in the wake of the British conquest and the annexation of the country to India. The small town of Rangoon, the capital of British Burma in place of Mandalay, the capital of the kings, was developed as an essentially British-Indian city. Eventually its *lingua franca* became Hindustani and in the new capital of Burma there were more Indians than Burmese. Indian moneylenders, merchants big and small, clerks, and officials were allowed into Burma sometimes with British encouragement as a hard-working and convenient prop for a regime which could by no means always count on Burmese co-operation. In addition Indian labor, as in Malaya, was often brought in under a system of indentures which sometimes involved serious exploitation. The assignment of such labor to lowly tasks which no Burmese would touch, such as the cleaning of public and private conveniences, contributed to the lofty and critical attitude of the local citizens. As we saw, these resentments have come to a tragic climax in recent years. Large numbers of Indians and Pakistanis in Burma have been deprived of their livelihood and forced out of the country.

A special cause of resentment for many Burmans of the former master race was that as inhabitants of an Indian province they found themselves denied both scope and identity. They seemed to have become just one community among many in their native land and with the most limited chances of employment. Europeans held most of the higher posts. The middle and lower ones were largely in Indian, Chinese, or Eurasian hands or in those of some of their more dynamic countrymen such as the Arakanese, the Mons, and the Karens. The Burmans were also handicapped in seeking to enter the Indian Civil Service by their generally modest level of intellectual achievement. The British in fact lowered the standards of government examinations to ensure that a fair number of Burmese did enter the public service and there was eventually a distinguished Burmese elite in responsible posts, especially in the judiciary. But the grievance of the Indian connection never ceased to rankle. The Burmese saw their affairs handled as minor problems in the backwash of Indian political and administrative reforms.[4] Yet it was just this link with India, where the movement toward independence swiftly advanced between the wars, which by 1941 had made Burma a largely self-governing country and had placed her far ahead of the rest of Southeast Asia, except the Philippines. She had also secured from 1937 one capital objective, namely, separation from India. But the path to these advances was slow and controversial.

With its agricultural and mineral wealth Burma was one of the richest areas of British India and made an impressive contribution to the central government's revenues. Yet the administrative hierarchy set up in this ancient kingdom was at first not even that of a full-fledged Indian province. From a career standpoint it was regarded as a backwater. Until 1897 Burma was governed merely by a Chief Commissioner; after that, a Lieutenant Governor was appointed. Only in 1923 did the country become a regular Governor's Province. Apart from municipal committees set up in 1874, the Burmese had virtually no representation in the government. Even these committees eventually met with Burmese apathy, partly because urban areas had four separate communities with differing interests, Burmese, Indian, Chinese, and European, and partly through fear that the committees might be used to increase taxation. District

4. An excellent account of the initially casual neglect of Burma's aspirations to resume a national identity after the introduction of the Montagu-Chelmsford dyarchy reforms in India in 1919 will be found in Hugh Tinker, *The Union of Burma*, London: Oxford University Press, 1957, pp. 1–3.

Councils in the rural areas were on the whole even less successful, due to the frequent transfers of the district officers who had to supervise them, save in those communities where there was some racial homogeneity and tradition of common action.

The Lieutenant Governor was given a Legislative Council but it consisted entirely of officials and nominated non-officials. In India, after the Morley-Minto Reforms of 1909, the provinces included a sizable elected element. In Burma, however, although the Legislative Council was enlarged from nine to seventeen, only one of these was elected and that by the Burma Chamber of Commerce which was entirely European. When the legislature was further enlarged to thirty in 1915 there were still only two elected members, the second of these being chosen by the Rangoon Trades Association. The Council thus remained almost entirely a forum for British officials and businessmen, while the districts were administered with paternalistic autocracy by British officers.[5] The usual rather ponderous departmental organization of British India was set up in Rangoon in a massive Secretariat of surpassing Oriental-Victorian hideousness. Around and after the turn of the century a department of Jails and Hospitals, a Chief Court of Judicature with a Judicial Service, a Commissioner of Land Revenue, a Chief Conservator of Forests, a Director of Agriculture, an Excise Commissioner and a Public Health Department were established. State education was extended after 1900. Meanwhile, even before the annexation of Upper Burma, the introduction by the British of scientific irrigation in the Irrawaddy delta and the abundance of cultivable land there had attracted a flow of Burmese from the north. The impressive development of this and other areas for rice cultivation which ensued was due to the hard work of the Burmese, this being a field in which they were keenly interested, and it did much to belie their normal reputation for only moderate exertion. Unfortunately, the need for capital for this development was to some extent exploited by the Indian and other money-lenders who offered loans on comparatively

5. Tinker, op. cit., p. 1.

easy terms but charged, as is customary in the Orient, rates of interest rarely lower than 25 per cent and far in excess of anything admissible in Western practice. The result was a disastrous growth of rural indebtedness in the rice-growing areas with frequent alienations of land to the moneylenders and a large scale breakdown of peasant proprietorship. The attempts of the government to encourage credit arrangements at lower interest were less successful than they should have been due to the stricter conditions they demanded.

During World War I the Young Men's Buddhist Association, founded in 1908 on the lines of the Y.M.C.A., acquired political significance as a channel for the tentative expression of nationalist goals. A more decisive nationalist trend emerged with the announcement in 1917 of the Montagu-Chelmsford Reforms promising the gradual introduction of responsible self-government for India, in the first instance through a system of concurrent Indian and British rule known as dyarchy. This plan was later implemented by the Government of India Act of 1919. The Burmese were incensed that the Committee which framed this plan did not visit Burma, apparently on the assumption that the Burmese, despite their long history of independent and effective nationhood, would be unequal to operating a constitution of the Western democratic type. The General Council of Burmese Associations which had superseded the Y.M.B.A. as a politically articulate body now advocated home rule through agitation. The new Rangoon University, under official control, was partly boycotted and numbers of independent National Schools set up by the protesting Burmese. The nationalists won their point and in 1921 special legislation for Burma led to the establishment of dyarchy there also and the placing of the country on the same footing as the other provinces of India. The Shan states, however, and certain other hill areas were excluded from the operation of the new scheme. A greatly enlarged Legislative Council with procedure modeled on the British House of Commons now had a big majority of members elected on a surprisingly wide franchise. The Governor retained responsibility for so-called reserved subjects. They were the vital ones of defense, law and order, and finance and revenue. Other subjects, known as transferred, were handled by Burmese Ministers responsible to the legislature whose advice the Governor was in principle bound to accept. Among the latter were education, public health, forests, and excise. The dominant opposition party was on the whole moderate. It demanded for example better education, quick Burmanization of the public services, more indigenous economic development, and less "foreign exploitation." Despite some good progress in education and public health the dyarchy experiment was condemned by a noted British official of liberal views. According to him "the new constitution undermined village administration . . . without providing any substitute . . . the public in general took little interest in the proceedings in the [Legislative] Council [which] . . . had no root among the people . . . it represented only the western superstructure divorced from national life . . . The condition of the cultivators deteriorated, racial tension became more acute, crime increased and disaffection spread." [6] Yet, another leading authority with practical experience of Burma says "dyarchy was by no means a facade; there were men of goodwill on both sides who aimed at making it a real step forward in the political education of the people." [7] Nevertheless, dissent was a real factor. Nineteen thirty saw serious communal rioting against Indians in Rangoon and at the end of the year a medieval type of rebellion under a fanatic called Saya San. Two extreme nationalists who defended some of the rebels in court, U Saw and Dr. Ba Maw, later had notorious careers.

Responsible Government and the Stress of War

When the next stage of constitutional progress was considered by the British authorities in 1928 the Burmese demanded separation

6. J. S. Furnivall, *Colonial Policy and Practice*, New York: New York University Press, 1956, pp. 162, 163, 165.
7. Hall, op. cit. (*Burma*), p. 152.

from India. This was precipitated by the progress of Indian self-government. The number of Indians in Burma had steadily increased and the Burmese feared that they might one day become a subordinate fraction of a vast country ruled by Indians. But when separation was strongly supported by the British, the Burmese became suspicious and many temporarily reversed their stand. Eventually, however, opinion swung back and separation under a more advanced constitution became effective on April 1, 1937. The new constitution, drawn up in 1935, was similar in most respects to that of the Indian provinces. It introduced almost complete responsible government. Burma came directly under London where a separate Burma Office dealt with her affairs. The Governor had responsibility only for external and internal defense, monetary policy, currency and coinage, and the still excluded hill areas; with certain special emergency powers to ensure internal peace and the protection of minorities, and to prevent unfair discrimination against the British. There was a Senate and House of Representatives, half of the former being elected by the House and half nominated by the Governor. Most of the House members were elected by territorial constituencies; the remainder represented communal and other special interests. There was a Burmese Prime Minister with his own cabinet, responsible to parliament. The Burmese were thus placed in control of practically all their internal affairs. It was further provided that the Governor's reserve powers would be progressively restricted and that his emergency powers would be held in abeyance as far as possible.

One of the first acts of the new government was legislation for the protection of tenants, which was strongly opposed by the *chettyar* moneylenders. Unfortunately, despite some useful measures of this kind, the nationalist leaders, knowing that Britain was still ultimately in charge, often behaved with an irresponsibility which they might not have shown had they themselves been completely in control. Furthermore, the system had little time to give experience of responsibility before the two campaigns of the Japanese war caused such destruction and disorder that the country has never fully recovered. The Burmese of today, like the Vietnamese, have never known stability. Only a small minority have any memory or appreciation of the degree to which Burma had acquired self-rule under the British. Among the Prime Ministers under the new constitution were Dr. Ba Maw and U Saw. The first was eventually arrested by the Governor; the second was detained early in 1942 on a charge of contact with the Japanese. It was not, however, with these old guard politicians that the future lay. In the 1930's a group of students at Rangoon University launched the *Thakin* movement. They insisted that Burmese should be addressed by this term of courtesy mostly reserved for Europeans and be treated in all respects on the same footing as their rulers. Among them were a former school superintendent called Nu; the Secretary of the Student Union, Aung San; the future founders of the Socialist Party, Kyaw Nyein and Ba Swe; and Raschid, a Burmese patriot of Indian-Muslim antecedents. The Japanese, seeking out all subversive groups also contacted the Thakins. They inspired them to raise a group of thirty (later known as the "Thirty Heroes") for Japanese military training and a force called the Burma Independence Army. Among them Thakin Shu Maung, who assumed the name Ne Win, was later to play a decisive role.

When the Japanese invaded Burma with the help of the B.I.A., the considerably weaker British forces, supported by Chinese troops under General Stilwell, were forced into a long but on the whole skillful retreat. This eventually brought them battered but still in being as an army across the Indian border to Manipur. Here new Allied forces were assembled which checked and eventually defeated a strong Japanese thrust in the region of Imphal which was to be the prelude to the invasion of India.[8] Meanwhile, the Governor of Burma with some of his collaborators established an administration in exile at the Indian hill station of Simla.

In Burma as elsewhere the Japanese soon squandered the credit they had earned as Asian conquerors of the white imperialists by

8. See Slim, op. cit., Chapter VI. His account of the aftermath of, and reasons for, the defeat is particularly significant.

their offensive disregard of the susceptibilities of the fellow Asians they had nominally freed. In organizing their Japanese-dominated regime in Burma they needed more experienced co-operation than that of the young Thakins, and Dr. Ba Maw became their tool. In 1943 they set up the ostensibly independent Republic of Burma with Ba Maw as head of state with the title of *Adipati* giving him the status of a fascist leader. Aung San and U Nu [9] became respectively Ministers for Defense and Foreign Affairs. The Burma Independence Army which had got out of hand was dissolved and another force organized under close Japanese supervision as the Burma National Army. Meanwhile, the Burmese nationalists became increasingly restive under an occupation regime ever more clearly intent on exploiting Burma rather than ensuring its genuine independence. A change of course became imminent in early 1945 when the British-Indian XIV Army, with General Stilwell's Chinese, drove the Japanese out of Upper Burma. The B.N.A. marched out of Rangoon ostensibly to fight for the Japanese. Instead they joined the British. Rangoon was captured in April toward the end of a mainland military campaign in which the Japanese were conclusively beaten months before their final surrender.

In the later stages of the war and immediately after it there were divergencies in British policy. Some authorities, including Lord Mountbatten, had in effect accepted Aung San as the prospective leader of the country. Others thought he should be treated as a traitor. Somewhere in between was an unimaginative London decision to send back the former Governor and temporarily suspend the 1935 Constitution. Behind this was the sensible thought that it would be best for Britain to retain control and delay full independence until the chaos and destruction of the war had been made good, and orderly government restored. But it should have been possible to foresee the resentment aroused by this decision after Burma had enjoyed

9. Since the war he has been universally known as U Nu, just as his former information secretary, now Secretary-General of the United Nations, is always known as U Thant. The U—literally Uncle—is a term of courtesy used in Burma in referring to others of equal or higher status.

for a time at least nominal independence under the Japanese. The nationalists now sought to sabotage the machinery of government and to discredit the system inherited from the British and the Burmese officials trained in British ways. They insisted on immediate independence and soon Britain's post-war Labour government decided, as they were already deciding in the case of India, that it would be best to grant it with the least possible delay. Years later the nationalists had reason to repent that Britain's hand was forced so quickly. In 1961 the Rangoon Prime Minister declared that the British had given Burma her independence a year too soon. They should first have ensured that all the arms scattered around the country were collected and removed.[10]

In January 1947 Aung San and other leaders, including U Saw, went to London for negotiations in which, to their surprise, they were given virtually everything they wanted. There would be full independence within a year, a Constituent Assembly, and the recognition of Aung San's cabinet as an interim government. A new Governor had been appointed who was to implement these decisions. The agreement was rejected by U Saw, intensely jealous of the position which the young Aung San had acquired. During the next six months, attempts were made to solve the various internal dissensions and notably those of the communists and the hill peoples. One section of the communists, the so-called Red Flags, had gone underground in July 1946. The other, later known as the White Flags, was led by Aung San's brother-in-law, Than Tun, who had been given prominent positions during and just after the war. His insistent demands led to his expulsion and that of the communists from the nationalist coalition, the Anti-Fascist Peoples' Freedom League. This larger communist group later joined in a long term anti-government insurrection which has continued to this day.

As we saw, Burma like Malaya was a multi-racial country. The Burmans who largely monopolized the nationalist movement were

10. This was stated by U Nu during his last period in office in a personal interview with the writer.

little more than half the population. The hill peoples, on the whole reliable supporters of the British, had themselves suffered at the hands of the Burmans. They were understandably disturbed that they had not been represented on Aung San's mission to London, and that there had been no reference to their aspirations in the agreement with the British. These minorities included the gifted Karens in the mountains bordering on Thailand and the Irrawaddy delta (many of whom had been converted by the American Baptist Judson), the Shan cousins of the Thais, the Kachins, and the Chins. To counterbalance the recalcitrant Burmans, reluctant to fight for the country which had suppressed their freedom, the British had extensively recruited the hill races into their armed forces. This was another grievance which the eventually Burman-dominated army was determined to redress. But at this initial stage the Burman leaders sought, if in somewhat cavalier fashion, to unify the frontier areas with the rest of Burma. In February 1947 a meeting was held in the Shan States attended by representatives of the Shans, Kachins, and Chins. The Karens were already split between pro- and anti-government factions and looked to a measure of real autonomy. They only sent observers and claimed that they were not consulted. These Panglong negotiations and the subsequent enquiry by a Frontier Areas Committee seem in fact to have been strongly weighted in favor of the AFPFL. So were the elections to the Constituent Assembly. Ultimately, all these transactions for the hill peoples were essentially unreal. Shan, Kachin, Kayah, and eventually Karen states were created, and a Chin Special Division. The minorities were encouraged by these ostensibly federal provisions which even embodied for some of them a theoretical right of secession after a period of years. Yet in practice Burma remained a unitary state with the decisions made in Rangoon. There were no state legislatures, only councils consisting of state members from the central parliament.[11]

11. Tinker, op. cit., p. 30.

Independence and After

In July, Aung San was tragically murdered with nearly all his government team. The crime was traced to the former Prime Minister U Saw, who was ultimately tried and hanged. From this time Aung San was honored as the national hero. To fill his place the Governor turned to the other outstanding nationalist, U Nu, then President of the Constituent Assembly. A fresh agreement with London was concluded and on January 4, 1948, U Nu became the first Prime Minister of independent Burma. He retained the leadership for nearly all of the ensuing ten years, displaying a fascinating blend of gentleness and piety, laxity and suspicion, humility and self-confidence, shrewdness and statesmanship which placed their stamp upon the Burma of his day and saved her new government from what seemed at times imminent downfall.

Unlike India, Burma left the British Commonwealth though Britain still accorded her imperial tariff preference. Most of her new political leaders had too little experience of the outside world to realize that countries like Australia and Canada were just as free as Britain herself or the United States. Burma's Constitution of 1947 had a parliamentary system broadly of the Westminster type. The lower house was similar to the House of Commons. The upper house, the Chamber of Nationalities, in which the Burmans were in a minority, was designed to reassure the minorities, at least in form. The President had essentially ceremonial powers. Fiery Marxist slogans were often uttered by the new leaders without any very clear understanding of all that they implied. But during this period Burma, though officially neutral, was, in practice, on excellent terms with Britain and the West. In the economic field she pursued the brand of socialism favored by the British Labour Party. On the one hand the goal was the *Pyidawtha*, the welfare state. On the other, nationalization or partial nationalization was invoked to avert the recurrence of exploitation by Western business even though this supposedly evil process had opened up the country's wealth. Thus rice marketing was nationalized and the government profited by the margin between the modest price paid for rice to the peasants (a source of dangerous discontent) and the price at which they sold it on the world market. For the rich lead and silver and tungsten mines and the oil industry a system of joint ventures between Western management and the Burma Government operated reasonably well. The government engaged American financial and technical advisers. Although at one point U.S. government aid was declined for fear of possible strings attached, private and foundation aid was welcomed.

After this fair start Burma was soon in the grip of a multiple insurrection which engulfed most of the country. These first massive uprisings were, as we saw, in part communist. There were also the *Mujahids*, Muslim marauders from northern Arakan, and Aung San's private army, the People's Volunteer Organization. Far more serious was a revolt of the Karens, including their regiments in the Burmese army. This implicated the Karen Commander-in-Chief and he was replaced by Ne Win. In due course the army leadership was largely Burmanized and its new commander became potentially the most powerful man in the country. After the insurgents had occupied nine-tenths of the country the tide was gradually turned with the help of the Chin and Kachin units. U Nu took credit for the fact that by the end of his time only one-tenth of Burma remained in insurgent hands. Unfortunately a further international complication emerged at the end of 1949 when defeated Kuomintang troops took refuge in the border country between Burma, Thailand, and Laos and eluded all efforts to wipe them out.

In 1956 Nu was briefly replaced at his own wish by the leader of the Socialist Party, Ba Swe, who had been Deputy Prime Minister and Minister for Defense. Otherwise he remained in power until the AFPFL split in April 1958. This was largely due to the Socialists' jealousy of Nu's long tenure of office and particularly that of Kyaw Nyein, their other leader who had been in charge of economic affairs. With reduced backing, Nu was forced to turn for support to the communist-influenced National United Front and for the next six months his government was notably less effective. This aroused the resentment and ambitions of the army leaders. In October Nu was forced to invite General Ne Win to become Prime Minister. The army accused the civilian politicians of corruption and inefficiency and this was not entirely false. Many ill-qualified persons had been made ministers in an absurdly swollen cabinet for having been political supporters of the AFPFL. It demonstrated its own efficiency by an eighteen-month period of brisk and disciplined rule during which the constitution was scrupulously preserved. The ministers in a greatly reduced cabinet were mostly trained officials. But in each ministry army officers were installed who in effect watched and controlled its work. The armed forces also set up business organizations of their own and took the initial steps to force foreign interests out of the export trade. But early in 1960, to the dismay of some of his officers, General Ne Win insisted on holding elections and on reinstating U Nu when the latter triumphed at the polls. Unfortunately, after resuming power Nu seemed recklessly indifferent to the risk of antagonizing the military again. He insisted on making Buddhism the state religion in fulfillment of an election pledge, thus upsetting the non-Buddhists. Then he inserted guarantees for the latter which led to damaging demonstrations by the Buddhist monks. He permitted irresponsible talk by the hill peoples of seceding from Burma. He even allowed them to meet in conference in Rangoon to discuss such matters, clearly with the idea of letting them blow off steam. All this led General Ne Win to believe that the country was seriously threatened. On March 2, 1962, in a sudden night action the military took over the government of Burma again.

This time the armed forces made a clean sweep of most existing institutions including the constitution and parliamentary government. All foreign firms and banks and all larger Burmese firms were nationalized. Income tax was raised to 99 per cent on higher incomes and the managerial elements, which were becoming a reasonably prosperous middle class, now faced destitution. There followed a drive to eliminate all private enterprise, and set up a communist-style economic system. Even rice is now rationed, although Burma is a large surplus producer, and everyday necessities are frugally dispensed in Soviet-style People's Stores. Most of the politicians and top civilians and Shan chieftains were imprisoned and have only recently been released. Only one civilian, the Foreign Minister, has remained in the government, now a Revolutionary Council of officers under the General's chairmanship. Since 1962 this Council has been implementing a program called The Burmese Way to Socialism which declares that capitalism has no place in the new Burma. Progress has been made toward establishing a single political party and trade union organization, again on the Soviet pattern. This has the obvious risk that the well-organized communist elements might seize control, though this has hitherto been prevented. Foreign firms have been squeezed out and Indians and Pakistanis victimized. All private Western aid has been cancelled and government aid, now again permitted, greatly reduced and precisely balanced against that from the communist bloc, as have scholarship programs for both groups of countries. The only major work still undertaken in Burma by capitalist enterprise is that financed by Japanese reparations. Communist China, which extended an $84 million interest free loan, was the most favored source of technical aid (followed by the Russians) until China's recent condemnation of Ne Win led to cancellation of the loan payments.

Although local pro-communist elements are sometimes consulted, Burma's revolutionary leaders are by no means wedded to communism or the communist bloc. They are strongly chauvinistic and isolationist. "All we want is to be left alone," is one of their stock phrases. Their self-centered suspicion of the outside world and of private enterprise, and their occasional ruthlessness, seem in many ways to reflect the attitudes of the Burmese kings. But this posture of effacement at least does not drive the Eastern and Western Powers to fight out their differences on Burmese soil. Meanwhile insur-

gency is still serious. The government has brought over one group of
Karen rebels and the communists in the field have dwindled but
Shan and Kachin insurrections have broken out and the attitude of
the peasants and monks is uncertain. Some feel that the army could
have put down these recent insurrections (which cannot be compared to those in Malaya and Vietnam) but their continuance is a
pretext for the army's dominant role and generous share of the
budget.

Burma has now almost totally eradicated the colonial system and
this necessarily gives her neutrality some anti-Western bias. There is
little overt opposition to the military regime but the kind of discipline it imposes is not calculated to appeal to the Burmese people
who do not love regimentation. In any event, the revolutionary program having achieved no great popular support, something of an im-
passe has been reached. There are rumors of negotiations between
the military and the released politicians. This would be logical, since
the sudden disappearance of General Ne Win, whose health is not
strong and who has some determined enemies, would leave a critical
power vacuum. In such an event the local communists would make
a bid for the succession but would be unlikely to succeed. None of
the officers now serving seems qualified to fill the General's place,
yet the army will not be easily turned out. If there is to be a resumption of civilian rule with a phased reversion of the armed forces to
their proper tasks the lead will have to be taken by someone with
high credit in military and political circles. One possible future
leader would be a man of both worlds who temporarily headed the
revolutionary government some years back. This is ex-Brigadier
Aung Gyi, a former Joint Secretary-General of the Socialist Party
who subsequently joined the army and came to be regarded as the
General's heir apparent. Later he was removed and arrested. Should
a vacancy in leadership permit him to join forces with his former socialist colleagues, this could be a significant step toward the restoration of normal rule.

Relations with China remain, of course, a capital issue. However correct her earlier relations with Peking, Burma did not hesitate to close down, with the others, two Communist Chinese banks which in the interests of communism used to finance small capitalism by helping local Chinese extend their businesses, thus securing their co-operation. She also cracked down on pro-Peking demonstrations. In the present mood of anger with Ne Win, China has called for his overthrow as Moscow once called for that of Tito. Yet Peking has gone no further than vituperation and it is doubtful whether China has plans to pursue with her own forces another challenge to the West beyond her borders.

VIII

THE FRENCH REGIME
AND ITS ENEMIES

French Colonial Rule in Indochina

Whatever failings the French regime in Indochina may have had, American views on the French colonial record have on the whole been resolutely adverse. Some seem to betray a certain lack of appreciation of the Gallic temperament and genius not uncommon in America. This is in strong contrast to the admiration for French civilization common to all European nations, including Britain, which has been France's adversary for most of her history. Thus President Franklin Roosevelt freely denounced France's exploitation of her colony and was so strangely unperceptive as to offer General de Gaulle at one point the loan of Filipinos to show him how France's task should be performed. In any event, short though it was, France's administration of Vietnam was to be as fateful for that country as its earlier thousand years under China.[1]

1. Fall, op. cit., p. 25. Fall's vivid and vigorous writing—that of a man equally at home in the French world as in that of Central Europe and the United States —is refreshingly corrective of the strong critical trend of most American writing on the French record in Indochina. It is a curious fact, perhaps attributable to racial and linguistic affinities, that American criticism of British colonization in Asia has on the whole been less severe even when the British record was ostensibly no less "imperialistic" than that of France. It is also strange that although the United States was far less conscious and deliberate than France in trying to spread its civilization, "so strong were the cultural forces emanating

French colonization of this area seems to have been chiefly a matter of prestige. There was a conscious and deliberate drive, in the Roman tradition, to project the metropolitan civilization overseas.[2] This was far less conspicuous in the case of the British and the Dutch. One reason is that France laid the foundations of her nineteenth-century colonial empire in North Africa near to her shores and tended to regard her colonies as limbs or extensions of France. Their economies "must be intimately related to that of the mother country and . . . the colonies should produce not whatever paid best (like those of Britain under *laissez faire*) but rather such commodities as were specifically needed by . . . France, for whose exports they should in return provide a privileged and closely controlled market." [3] In fact this goal was not achieved until the twentieth century and then only in part. In the early years there were many divergent voices in France, including those who urged at least a partial withdrawal in view of the burden of the long campaign of pacification in Tongking. Others oscillated between faith in the kind of direct rule applied in Algeria and indirect rule in "association" with the native governing classes. Some authorities suggest that had these last methods been genuinely carried through the history of Vietnam under French guidance could have been far happier.[4]

All this revealed a curious lack of clear design on the part of so logical a nation. Indeed, apart from emphasis on France's civilizing mission (in a country with a civilization no less old than her own) the French performance in Indochina was somewhat like British imperialism, a medley of haphazard and contradictory moves. It

from American rule that in certain respects the results were not very different from France's policy of cultural assimilation in Indochina. . . Of all the countries of Southeast Asia subject to colonial rule, none afford more obvious evidence of the imprint of metropolitan cultural and social influence than do the Philippines and Indochina." (John Bastin and Harry J. Benda, A *History of Modern Southeast Asia*, Englewood Cliffs: Prentice-Hall, 1968, pp. 56, 57.)
2. Fisher, op. cit., p. 538.
3. Ibid., p. 538.
4. Chester A. Bain, *Vietnam: The Roots of Conflict*, Englewood Cliffs: Prentice-Hall, 1967, pp. 91, 92.

never inspired much enthusiasm in the French people. This was in part because France between 1860 and 1890 had wasted so much treasure on other enterprises, such as the Mexican adventure in support of Emperor Maximilian and the vain attempt to construct the Panama Canal. Further terrible losses had been incurred in the Franco-Prussian War of 1870. Yet these reverses had also produced a contrary impulse. At a time when from France's standpoint the Anglo-Saxon countries were doing altogether too well, the French government was spurred to seek glory and achievement in new fields. But there was at first hardly any French capital keen on investing in Indochina and for some years the administrative deficits had to be met reluctantly by the home government. Initially there were irregularities and some ugly profiteering in land. The French Navy was at times rash and bungling. From 1879, however, the Colonial Ministry took over and the administration became rather more systematic and efficient. Cochinchina and Tourane (Da Nang), Haiphong and Hanoi came under direct rule as a French colony. The protectorates over Annam and Tongking were ruled in principle by a native mandarinate under the formal supervision of the Emperor at Hue. But in practice the imperial administration was closely supervised by French Residents-General who decided all matters of importance. Like the Federated Malay States a system of nominally indirect rule had been changed into one of virtually direct rule.

In 1895 the Governor-General, Paul-Armand Rousseau, insisted on effective steps to end more than thirty years of costly improvisation. It was too late now for France to draw back and he insisted on a settlement of the debts incurred in Tongking, a loan for public works, and more extensive administrative powers. He won his point but died before his reforms could be carried out. In his place Paris appointed Paul Doumer, the Minister for Finance in a recently defeated cabinet, who was deeply interested in Indochina though he had never been there and had no experience of colonial administration. Despite some important mistakes it was Doumer who by the early twentieth century had made Indochina into France's richest colony. But vested interests at first made his task extremely difficult in Vietnam, especially in Cochinchina. Here the French had created a system essentially their own. The first Governor-General would have preferred to work through the local authorities but these vanished removing their records, evidently with the secret encouragement of Hue. They had to be replaced by French inspectors of native affairs who were given wide powers but had at first no knowledge of the country. By the time the French had taken over Annam and Tongking the attitude of the mandarins and the emperor had changed in respect to those areas. They realized that non-co-operation had gained them nothing in Cochinchina, and in the protectorates they settled for the kind of unreal collaboration inherent in the French concept of indirect rule. Meanwhile in Cochinchina French economic interests had gained in strength in conjunction with French officialdom and resisted schemes for the benefit of all parts of French Indochina. Paradoxically the Governor-General's powers were thus extremely limited in that part of France's new dominion where French rule was most direct.[5]

In Cochinchina, the French first developed the almost virgin plains west and south of the Bassac River joining Phnom Penh with the Mekong delta, which was the effective limit of Vietnamese settlement at the time of the occupation. They developed rice production as the British had done in the Irrawaddy delta of Burma. But unlike the British who promoted peasant proprietorship (although the moneylender often stepped into the peasant's shoes) the French established a system of relatively large estates based on scientific irrigation and drainage and worked by tenant farmers who normally paid 40 per cent of their crop as rent. This was in marked contrast to the smallholdings of 2 to 12 acres in the area settled before the advent of the French. These large estates in the newly cultivated areas did not produce yields as high as the smallholdings and they helped to create the major problem of landlordism in South Viet-

5. See Joseph Buttinger, *Vietnam: A Dragon Embattled*, New York: Praeger, 1967, Vol. I, p. 12.

nam today. For apart from a few French owners most of the big rice estates were acquired in time by South Vietnamese. Concurrently, the transport, milling, and marketing of rice became, as in Thailand, almost a monopoly of the Chinese who were largely concentrated in Cholon across the river from Saigon.[6] Both these groups had benefited by, and were responsive to, the new economic regime, and local vested interests supported those of the French. In 1880, before France controlled Annam and Tongking, a Colonial Council had been set up in Cochinchina. This became the instrument of the French establishment there at a time when 2000 Frenchmen in the region sent a deputy to the French parliament. Of these 1500 were alleged to be on the government payroll while the remaining 500 were linked with it in some way.

Doumer's first task after he arrived in 1897 was to break the power of the Council in order to introduce general services, and in particular a general budget, for the whole of Indochina. The Council resisted but in 1898 was overridden by Paris. A Superior Council for Indochina was set up which eventually included the *Résidents Supérieurs* of Tongking, Annam, Cambodia, and Laos, the Lieutenant-Governor of Cochinchina, the army and navy commanders, the presidents of the chambers of agriculture and commerce, the directors of the General Services, and two mandarins. Doumer was at last able effectively to launch his reforms. He stayed in office till 1902 and during his remaining four years concentrated on building up the public finances through a proper system of taxation and making Indochina independent of grants by the home government. He introduced the French legal system. He specially promoted improved communications such as roads, canals, port installations, and railways. He reorganized the finances so that the state budgets received their funds from direct and personal taxes, and the general budget from customs duties and indirect taxation, the revenue from which was raised by the introduction of state monopolies for opium, alcohol, and salt. These measures were a swift success. By 1900 all five

6. Fisher, op. cit., pp. 539–541.

territories had balanced budgets and were contributing to the public works program. The colony was even able to pay part of its military budget, and a large loan was raised in France for railway construction. Doumer had the illusion that railways would be a sure key to future wealth.[7] Two main lines were built where they seemed likely to be most profitable, one from Hanoi to Saigon and the other from Haiphong to Hanoi, then on to the Chinese border at Lao Cai, and eventually to Yunnanfu (Kunming). Unfortunately the expected volume of freight did not materialize and the railways never paid their way. In spite of this misjudgment, considerable economic progress was made under Doumer's rule. The commerce of Indochina more than doubled and trade with France trebled. Rice exports became important. Agriculture was diversified by the cultivation, as in Indonesia and Malaya, of valuable cash crops such as tea, rubber, coffee, and sugar cane in scientifically run plantations.

Doumer's reforms extended to all parts of the country. Modern agriculture was developed wherever conditions were favorable. So were scientific services in the fields of geography, geology, archaeology, meteorology, statistics, and medicine. In the political field Doumer further emasculated the imperial authority in Vietnam. In 1887 the Emperor's theoretical prerogatives over Tongking had been transferred to a French-picked and French-controlled Vietnamese Viceroy in Hanoi. Doumer abolished the Viceroy and substituted a French Résident Supérieur. In Annam until 1897 the Emperor had governed within the limits of French control through a privy council or cabinet. Doumer replaced this by a new council presided over by the French Résident Supérieur instead of the Emperor. In this council every Vietnamese minister was given a French counterpart. The French also took over the collection of taxes and the mandarins became in effect French-paid officials.[8]

In Cambodia, however, the Royal Government was left relatively intact, subject to the abolition of slavery and other traditional

7. Buttinger, op. cit., Vol. I, p. 28.
8. Buttinger, op. cit., Vol. I, pp. 14, 15.

abuses. It was in this country, moreover, that the French did some of their finest work in discovering, restoring, and studying the incomparable monuments of Angkor.. This was one of the main undertakings of the *École Française d'Extrème Orient* (French Institute of the Far East), an outstanding example of European scholarship in Asia. Its foundation in Hanoi, as the center of French cultural work, was probably Doumer's most valuable initiative. In Laos the French recognized only one local ruler, the King of Luang Prabang, who eventually became King of Laos. The other parts of the country, including Champassak, Vientiane, and Xieng Khouang, became virtually French provinces. The French *Résident Supérieur* at Vientiane directly controlled eight of the provinces of Laos and indirectly controlled the kingdom of Luang Prabang. Like the Cambodians, most Laotians found nothing special to resent in the substitution for the somewhat archaic and arbitrary dominance of an Asian suzerain of the more progressive rule of a European power. This brought the abolition of slavery and better finances, health, and education. At the same time France respected local custom and supported the local chiefs and the king. Laos, like Cambodia, had suffered at the hands of Vietnam. It had another form of religion and different traditions. While Vietnam became the center of resistance to colonial rule, both these smaller countries retained a certain regard for France.

Mercantilist Trends in the French Economic System

As we saw, France tended to regard her more distant colonies in the same light as her North African dependencies. Hence certain mercantilist objectives in the economic field at a time when mercantilism had been largely discredited as a doctrine. In pursuance of such goals economic links with France were developed in a manner which benefited the mother country while Indochina's natural trade links with neighboring Asian countries were neglected. But

France only set up an effective system of tariff protection after World War I. Between 1901 and 1910 foreign imports and exports were greater than those of France in Indochina and other French colonial territories. Moreover, in Indochina foreign countries made good profits without having the large expenditure with which France was faced. The experience of Indochina has again proved how rarely colonies are a direct source of profit to the governing power except for occasional limited periods as during the Dutch Culture System. Vietnam was never, in fact, an exclusive economic preserve of France.[9]

If France's economic policy was in some respects illiberal this was because of jealousy on the part of vested interests in France and in Indochina (as was the case to some extent with American business in the Philippines). On the whole the French preferred to treat Indochina essentially as a source of raw materials and limited the establishment even of medium and light industry, though the country with its important resources of anthracite coal (in Tongking) and iron would have been well suited for this purpose. In fact silk mills, distilleries, cement works, and hydroelectric power did make their contribution to local prosperity. With the more important growth of plantation industry large capitalism became dominant. Although there was a considerable degree of peasant proprietorship of land in North Vietnam little progress was made, as we saw, with developing Indochinese proprietorship of land in the South. French citizens owned an increasing number of plantations while the local moneylenders played their usual role and often acquired land through foreclosure on unpaid debts. All too often the Vietnamese peasant had little prospect in life except that of being a laborer or tenant farmer. With the tremendous population pressures (as high as 3800 per square mile in one province of the Red River delta) hunger, the eternal seed-bed of communism, was a constant specter.

As the twentieth century progressed the French taxpayer insisted on Indochina's paying its way and on largely monopolizing the colo-

9. Fall, op. cit., p. 29.

nial market, excluding other capital than French. Yet in contrast to U.S. policy in the Philippines no reciprocal advantage was accorded to Indochinese products in French markets.

Political Instability and Bureaucratic Elaboration

Despite some illiberal economic trends the main failings of the French system were in the political field. One weakness was instability. For most of the colonial period the French rulers changed with the same bewildering rapidity as the governments in Paris. There were twenty-three Governors-General in forty-three years. One reason for the lack of a consistent colonial policy was that Napoleon III had simply laid it down that "colonies will be ruled by decree . . ." So decisions regarding Indochina remained essentially the affair of the ministers in Paris and governors in the field and were not subjected to any close scrutiny by the French parliament. Another defect was an over-elaborate bureaucracy. A plethora of French officials deprived the Vietnamese of many of the minor jobs which they were perfectly capable of filling and which were in fact filled by local people in other European dependencies. Thus, apart from the armed forces which were the decisive factor in both territories, in 1925 some 325 million Indians were governed by fewer than 5000 British civilian officials while Indochina employed the same number of French officials for only 30 million people. Again the Vietnamese who were in minor jobs saw Frenchmen in the same or lower rank paid two or three times as much. One crowning absurdity was that the French janitor at the University of Hanoi received more than a Vietnamese with a Ph.D. from Paris. This problem of the "small whites" was peculiar to the French colonial system, and the spectacle of men of the ruling race doing menial jobs was inevitably damaging to the prestige of the colonizers.

Yet France did send some first-rate men to govern Indochina. One of these, of comparable quality to Doumer, was Albert Sarraut.

Notable progress was made during his period in office from 1911 to 1917. When he arrived he found that nine-tenths of the French officials could not speak the local languages. He insisted on this being put right and saw to it that Vietnamese were taken into the junior ranks of the government service. In this and other directions he ended some of the bureaucratic blight.[10] He and Doumer are commemorated today even in communist Hanoi, which still has a Pont Doumer and a Lycée Albert Sarraut. Eventually, though comparatively late in the colonial period, Vietnamese and French with comparable academic records were admitted on an equal footing to executive posts. A less prudent French policy which helped to keep alive tensions between Vietnam and both Cambodia and Laos was that of giving high posts to Vietnamese in the two latter countries where they had lorded it in the past. But it must be recognized that the French did a creditable job in reducing illiteracy and that their health services, with a network of Pasteur Institutes, were among the best in Asia. Their labor system was also in the long run progressive. From 1935 the Popular Front government in France liberalized the regime in Indochina and introduced advanced labor legislation. In 1937 the International Labor Office found labor conditions in Indochina better than anywhere else in the Far East. In the light of all the controversy about the French record it is noteworthy that an eminent Indian scholar who had no cause to flatter a colonial regime should in spite of everything have given the French credit for the efficiency of their administration, their network of communications, their cultural work, and various economic measures for the general benefit.[11]

Yet, undeniably, advanced educational facilities were sadly inadequate and access to the top elite was severely restricted for Indochinese. The privilege of naturalization as French citizens was only for those who spoke French, who had been in government service

10. Cady, op. cit. (Southeast Asia: Its Historical Development), p. 431.
11. K. M. Panikkar, Asia and Western Dominance, New York: Collier Books 1969, p. 168.

for ten years or in the army, had married French wives, or received the Legion of Honor. Only a couple of thousand were in fact able to acquire French citizenship as assimilated persons. As we saw, nearly absolute control was imposed by French Chiefs of Province in the Colony and French Residents in the Protectorates despite the nominally advisory status of the latter. For example, the most that the Emperor's War Minister at Hue was allowed to do was to command the Palace Guard. Above all it was the lack of an outlet for local opinion, the absence of a truly representative assembly, which rankled most. The delegate to the Paris parliament from Cochinchina only represented the French and the small group of naturalized Vietnamese. There were, it is true, elective village councils and regional advisory assemblies in which the Vietnamese were represented. These had a French preponderance in Cochinchina but a Vietnamese preponderance in Annam and Tongking. There was also a Colonial Council, like the Dutch Volksraad, set up after World War I, but of its twenty-four members only ten were Asians and its decisions could anyway be annulled by the Governor-General's Privy Council of twelve which contained only two Asians. What was in principle a legislature for the whole of Indochina was created in 1928 and called the Great Council of Financial and Economic Interests. This could decide on such questions as loans and indirect taxes. Nevertheless out of fifty-one members only eighteen were Vietnamese. There were in addition five members from Laos and Cambodia.

Vietnamese Nationalism

There had been strong nationalist resistance from the moment the French established themselves in Cochinchina. A mandarin protest known as the Scholars' Revolt dominated the situation at Hue after the Emperor Tu Duc's death in 1883, eliminating three of his successors deemed to be too ready to compromise with the invader.

This and other movements of armed resistance of a more or less traditional kind kept the French forces fighting until 1913. Meanwhile in the early twentieth century nationalism in Indochina as elsewhere was stimulated, not only by Japan's victory over Russia in 1904–05, but also by the overthrow of the Chinese empire in 1911. One of Vietnam's outstanding nationalists emerged during this period. This was Phan Boi Chau, who had rejected a French offer to enter the administration, put his faith in both Japan and China and hoped that the former would help the Vietnamese to modernize their country as a preliminary to successful revolution. He was arrested by the French in 1925. It was alleged that the communist leaders had betrayed him in exchange for money from the French but the circumstances are disputed.[12] After a commuted sentence he was kept under house arrest at Hue until his death in 1940. He was an obvious inspiration to the future nationalist leader of our day, Ngo Dinh Diem, who frequently corresponded with him. Another more moderate nationalist, the journalist Pham Quynh, urged reform under French protection. He gained the support of the Emperor Khai Dinh who died in 1925. The latter's son and successor, Emperor Bao Dai, shared these views and he was also to play an important role in our time. Bao Dai returned to Vietnam in 1932 after two years of subversion and severe French repression. He nevertheless hoped to secure a genuine protectorate from the French by putting his house in order. In the following year he called on Ngo Dinh Diem, then a young liberal mandarin, to become Minister for the Interior and lead a reform commission, while Pham Quynh was appointed Minister for Education. After a few months Diem resigned, finding he was making no progress. He blamed Quynh for being too conservative, and the old mandarins and French officials who were opposed to change. Meanwhile revolutionary nationalism had, as we saw, continued its subver-

12. Bain, op. cit., p. 97, says that Phan Boi Chau was "literally sold to the French . . . by Ho Chi Minh." Buttinger (*Vietnam: A Political History*), p. 159, says "Ho Chi Minh's intermediary allegedly received 150,000 piasters from the French" but that "some sources question this version of Chau's arrest."

sive drive after Phan Boi Chau's arrest. It was dominated by two main movements. The first was the Vietnam Nationalist Party (Viet Nam Quoc Dan Dang or VNQDD). It was modeled after the Chinese Nationalist Party, the Kuomintang, and was socialist but not communist in its policies. A revolt it organized in 1930 failed and its leader, Nguyen Thai Hoc, was executed. But although weakened it survived, owing to the support of the Kuomintang. The other main revolutionary movement was that of the communists in which at some moments the Trotskyites played an important part. It may be decisive for the future of Vietnam that—even in the opinion of their adversaries—the communists, under some exceptionally dedicated and able leaders, have proved to be the most successful in achieving the nationalist goals. In due course the non-communist nationalists learned the value and the danger of a united front with their communist rivals.

In a subtle and diffused way religion also played a part in the backgound of the nationalist movement. The French tended to favor the Vietnamese Catholics. Roman Catholicism was the religion they had brought to the country and the pretext for their intervention. Its adherents were likely to be more responsive than others to the attitudes and requirements of the colonial power, though this was not always the case. Ngo Dinh Diem, a Catholic, was one of the strongest nationalists. In his case, however, his Catholicism as we shall see lessened his scope and chances as a national leader. Buddhism on the other hand became an element in the nationalist protest, a "safe expression of Vietnamese cultural values," [13] more particularly as there was a general Buddhist renaissance in the twentieth century and the Buddhists did much to spread literacy in the romanized alphabet of the Vietnamese language. Two new cults which emerged in Vietnam in the twentieth century also had nationalist implications. One was Cao Dai, the worship of the universal god, which borrowed from various Western as well as Eastern sources. The other, Hoa Hao, was a much simplified reform Buddhism

13. Bain, op. cit., p. 101.

which also stressed devotion to one's ancestors and the national heroes.

The Communists and the Nationalist Movement

The Indochinese Communist Party (ICP) was founded in 1930 after the Vietnamese Workers Party had amalgamated with the communist groups in Cambodia and Laos. But because of French repression it was led underground the next year by one of its original members who had been a co-founder of the French Communist Party ten years earlier. Born in 1890 in northern Annam near the Tongking border, this man has proved to be perhaps the most experienced and successful communist leader in the world. He was once called Ly Thuy, then he was known by the alias Nguyen Ai Quoc and later by the more famous pseudonym of Ho Chi Minh. A senior American of the Office of Strategic Services (OSS) described him in 1945 as an "awfully sweet guy," and a French naval officer a year later called him an intelligent and charming man and a passionate idealist entirely devoted to his cause. His father, an ardent nationalist, was for a time a minor Imperial official and managed to send his son to an elite school at Hue also attended by the future right-wing leader Ngo Dinh Diem, by the brilliant Northern general Vo Nguyen Giap, and by the later Prime Minister of North Vietnam, Pham Van Dong, a man of good family whose father had been Chief of Cabinet to the Emperor. Ho helped his father in anti-French conspiracy. After leaving school (without a diploma apparently because of his anti-French activity) he learned to be a pastry cook and sailed for Europe around 1911. He worked for a time at his skill in the Carlton Hotel in London, went to America and lived in Harlem, and returned to France to retouch photographs and do other jobs at the end of World War I. He tried to interest the Paris Peace Conference of 1919 in a modest program of reform for Indochina but was ignored. He remained in exile from Vietnam for thirty years and became a marked man in the communist world, attending Comintern conferences in Moscow, organizing the Peasants' International, and doing other services for the cause. He seems to have given to thousands of Vietnamese both nationalist and communist an interpretation of the white man's world which won many converts. A dedicated communist himself, though with a specifically Vietnamese outlook, he has somehow managed to become the leader with the greatest appeal to Vietnamese nationalists in spite of his Marxist affiliations. According to one leading expert, even in the South he has something of the image of the father figure of his country.[14]

From 1924 Ho worked in Canton for Borodin, the Russian-American communist with whom Chiang Kai-shek, now President of Nationalist China, was at that time in close relations. There he helped to lay the groundwork for the Nanyang (South Seas) Communist Party pending the formation of the Indochinese Communist Party and the other anti-French nationalist groups. He sent his Vietnamese communist "cadres" to Chiang's Whampoa Military Academy to be trained by a Soviet general. They were then infiltrated back into Indochina to stir up subversion against the French. This phase lasted until Chiang's split with the Soviets in 1927. When the VNQDD uprisings in 1929–30 failed, Vo Nguyen Giap and Pham Van Dong were imprisoned and Ho took the Communist Party underground. In 1931 Ho was imprisoned by the British in Hong Kong for six months. He had been condemned to death by the French authorities but his extradition was refused by the British on the grounds that he was a political refugee and he was able to leave. In 1935 the Comintern called for "popular fronts" against fascism. The Communist Party then allied itself with liberal non-communist groups to form the Indochinese Democratic Front. The effective

14. See Bernard B. Fall, *Ho Chi Minh—A Profile* (first page) which introduces his *Ho Chi Minh on Revolution*, New York: Praeger, 1967.

leadership, however, was in the hands of the active and ruthless communists Pham Van Dong and Vo Nguyen Giap. Meanwhile a similar alliance in 1936 produced the first Popular Front government of France under the socialist Léon Blum.

IX

INDOCHINA: THE YEARS OF TRIAL

The Impact of the Second World War

As World War II approached, and during its early stages, the course of events in Europe forced on the communists some swift and contradictory changes of front which they made with their usual dexterity. The pact signed by Hitler's Germany and Stalin's Russia in August 1939 put an end to collaboration with non-communist groups in "popular front" governments. During this collaboration Moscow actually sought to restrain the Vietnamese freedom fighters for fear of antagonizing French public opinion. Now the Comintern reverted to an anti-imperialist line hostile to the war and to France's war effort. In November 1939, in accordance with the new directives, the ICP called for the overthrow of the French colonialists. The result was the banning of the communist parties in France and Indochina. The ICP went underground; its top leaders escaped to China but continued to direct operations in Vietnam. From China, Ho Chi Minh appealed for a new kind of popular front, one of all Vietnamese opposed to French rule. With his usual plausibility he claimed for his people the rights and freedoms won in the American and French Revolutions.

Meanwhile Germany had defeated France in June 1940. In anticipation of this, Japan, already in control of most of China, had become Germany's ally. Through German pressure she now secured French agreement to the entry of her troops into Indochina. Yet by arrangement the French authorities continued during most of the occupation to administer the country in effect on Japan's behalf. The Japanese were able to extract from Indochina raw materials of value to their war effort and to close the supply line to the Chinese Nationalists by the Tongking-Yunnan railway. At the same time they raised no objection to French repression of a rising in 1940 by the Phuc Quoc (Vietnamese Restoration Association), disciples of Phan Boi Chau. Yet later they helped these and other pro-Japanese nationalist groups, as well as the Cao Dai and Hoa Hao, releasing many who had been imprisoned by the French, in a bid to undermine the position of the colonial power. The French were also enabled to deal ruthlessly with a communist insurrection in 1940 in the Plain of Reeds west of Saigon, an area which has again become famous during the current struggle for Vietnam as a base for communist guerrillas. Early in 1941 the Japanese forced the French to return the Cambodian and Laotian territory claimed by Thailand in order to reward Thailand for help in connection with the planned Japanese invasion of Malaya and Burma. Owing to the accommodating attitude of the French toward Japan, Indochina suffered less material damage during the occupation than any other part of Southeast Asia except Thailand. Ironically, it is since the war ended that this unhappy land has been rent by destruction which has lasted for a whole generation and of which there is no end in sight.

In May 1941, Ho Chi Minh launched the League for the Independence of Vietnam known ever since as the Vietminh. It was presented as a broad-based nationalist front to attract non-communist nationalist support. A month later Germany invaded the Soviet Union. This imposed on world communism a second change of front which greatly increased the strength and scope of the communist movement in Indochina. From now on the Southeast Asian communists there and elsewhere became comrades-in-arms of the Allies and received their support against the Japanese. From this aspect they were welcomed, with reservations, by the Chinese Nationalists (the Kuomintang), and by the Americans after Pearl Harbor. Hence the warm references to Ho Chi Minh by U.S. officers. In August 1942, however, Ho was arrested by the Kuomintang in circumstances not entirely clear.[1] The Governor of Kwangsi was however concerned to secure a post-war regime in Vietnam which would be loyal to his government and felt that the prospects would be better if the non-communist Vietnamese predominated in the liberation movement. He therefore called a meeting of all Vietnamese independence groups while Ho was still in prison. This set up the Vietnam Revolutionary League, or Dong Minh Hoi, which declared for independence with Kuomintang aid. The Vietminh was just one member among many of this new League. Meanwhile the Dong Minh Hoi proved inadequate for the main objectives of the Allies —to get intelligence from Vietnam and promote guerrilla war against the Japanese—it seems because the communists never put their organization at its disposal. Ho was therefore released from prison in September 1943. In order that these goals should be more effectively pursued, it was at this point that he adopted his present pseudonym (meaning "he who enlightens") with the implication that this ruthless communist leader had emerged with a new and more engaging personality. In fact Ho evidently envisaged future Chinese control of Vietnam as a far bigger danger than the weakened prospects of the French. His reaction was typical of all Vietnamese throughout their history. Meanwhile he used Chinese subventions to strengthen the communists at the expense of the Dong Minh Hoi. The Chinese did not relish this trend. They called another meeting under the leadership of the Vietnam Nationalist Party (VNQDD) in March 1944. This set up a Provisional Republican Government of Vietnam in which Ho was permitted to fill a minor post. In October 1944 he at last returned to Vietnam where

1. Buttinger (*Vietnam: A Political History*), pp. 200, 201, states that Ho was arrested at the end of 1941 and released at the end of 1942. Fall (*The Two Vietnams*), p. 99, says that he was arrested on August 28, 1942, and released on September 16, 1943.

he was able to pursue his struggle against the enemy and his rivals with greater effect.

Ho now made a point of emphasizing his nationalism and cultivating the Americans as a counterpoise to the Chinese. From the standpoint of the United States it seemed a guarantee that Ho had been supported by the Chinese Nationalists. It was therefore the U.S. Office of Strategic Services which gave his men arms and ammunition, backed them with teams of their own, and flew him in to Vietnam. Here the ground had been well prepared for him by his associate Vo Nguyen Giap, the onetime history teacher turned soldier who had learned his trade by studying Napoleon and the precepts of Mao Tse-tung. By 1945 Giap had trained an army of 10,000 men, many recruited in the mountainous border country between China and Tongking, into which it was easy to send agents and arms, remote from the French in Hanoi. The *montagnard* ethnic minorities were won over by promises of local autonomy. More weapons were obtained in the country from abandoned French army depots and even from the Japanese. Six provinces between Hanoi and the frontier were soon firmly in Vietminh hands.[2] By the end of the war Ho Chi Minh had become the most effective leader inside Vietnam of the forces working for independence. Just before Japan's surrender he ordered a general insurrection. Soon afterwards its victory was celebrated in Hanoi where the Vietminh seized public buildings and raised their flag.

Meanwhile, after the liberation of France in 1944, General de Gaulle had begun to organize a resistance movement. He appointed a French Delegate-General to Indochina and the British parachuted arms, ammunition, and French agents into Vietnam. This led the Japanese in March 1945 to round up and intern the French civil and military authorities. At this juncture the Emperor Bao Dai proclaimed the independence of Vietnam with Japanese encourage-

2. See Bain, op. cit., p. 108, and Buttinger, op. cit. (*Vietnam: A Political History*), pp. 202, 203.

ment. Afterwards King Norodom Sihanouk of Cambodia and King Sisavang Vong of Laos similarly declared their countries independent. The French Provisional Government reacted by announcing the formation of a federal Indochina with autonomy within the French Union. When the Japanese surrendered they transferred the administration to a Viceroy who passed it on to a provisional committee of the Vietminh. On August 23, 1945, one week after the surrender, Bao Dai abdicated. By this time the presence of senior U.S. officers at Vietminh functions in Hanoi and the flying of the American flag over their quarters had convinced many that the United States backed the new Hanoi regime. This belief may have contributed to the acceptance of the Vietminh by Bao Dai and his nationalist supporters. To judge, however, by the Emperor's moving declaration at the time, there appears to have been in his case a genuine and patriotic urge to avoid at all costs the division of his people.[3] In September Ho himself proclaimed the independence of the country and established the Democratic Republic of Vietnam. Bao Dai became for a time Ho's "Supreme Adviser." Being weak in Cochinchina the Vietminh came to an agreement there with Bao Dai's United National Front, a coalition of nationalist groups formed to support the fragile, Japanese-sponsored, "independent" regime. The Front then accepted a Provisional Executive Committee of the Vietminh as the authority in the South. By this time there had been friction between the Chinese, the Americans, and the French in regard to the future of Indochina. President Roosevelt maintained his reluctance to see the French resume their former position. Indeed at one point he offered Generalissimo Chiang Kai-shek the whole of Indochina, including Indianized Cambodia and Laos, an offer which China's leader sensibly declined. At another he proposed an international trusteeship.[4] But, President Roosevelt having died, it fell to Presi-

3. See Marvin E. Gettleman, ed. *Vietnam: History, Documents and Opinions on a Major World Crisis*, Greenwich: Fawcett, 1965, pp. 59, 60.
4. See Fall, op. cit. (*The Two Vietnams*), pp. 53, 467.

dent Truman to find, with Stalin and Prime Minister Attlee, some provisional solution at the Potsdam Conference in July and August 1945.

Post-War Dispositions and Conflicts

The Allies decided at Potsdam that the Chinese should take over Indochina down to the 16th parallel while the British occupied the South. This was done in September. The British refused to deal with the Vietminh. Instead General Gracey ordered the release of the French and thus gave them the chance to re-establish their rule. In October the French forces were reinforced by troops from home under one of France's best commanders, General Leclerc. But with nationalist resistance in Saigon and guerrilla attacks in the countryside, not until February 1946 did the French again control the Mekong delta and by then the British had left. Some feel that the Vietnamese war of liberation which will soon have lasted a quarter of a century started with these operations in September 1945.[5] This conflict for which the British were in part responsible was most unwelcome to Lord Mountbatten, the Supreme Allied Commander, who was firmly on the side of the nationalists in other parts of Southeast Asia such as Burma and Indonesia. The British were supposed to disarm the Japanese and not to interfere in internal affairs. Yet they seem to have thought it right to support the French as the only legitimate authority in view of the chaos in which they found Saigon. All that Mountbatten was able to secure from the French government representative was a resumption of French negotiations with the Vietnamese and a temporary truce. Meanwhile General de Gaulle had appointed one of his disciples as French High Commissioner for Indochina. This was Admiral Thierry d'Argenlieu, a naval officer who was also a monk. After de Gaulle's resignation in January 1946 he frequently found himself opposed to the left-wing-influenced governments which followed.

5. Buttinger, op. cit. (*Vietnam: A Political History*), p. 225.

Ostensible moderation was the keynote of the early stages of Ho Chi Minh's regime. The Indochinese Communist Party was dissolved and replaced by an "Association for Marxist Studies." Later a relatively liberal constitution was adopted. The Vietminh included non-communist nationalists and some of these were given posts in the cabinet. Taxation was sweepingly reduced and the much resented opium, alcohol, and salt monopolies revoked. Illiteracy was drastically tackled and famine checked. In order not to antagonize the landlords there was no move toward a general redistribution of land. Only the estates of the French, of traitors and collaborators, and communal lands were taken over and divided among the landless peasants. When Ho realized that he would not get political backing from the United States he decided on temporary co-operation with the French. The Chinese in the North, both soldiers and commanders, had plundered like a conquering army. At the same time their presence had been politically a menace. For the Kuomintang were in a position at any moment to unseat the Vietminh government and substitute one picked by them from their anti-Vietminh nationalist supporters. Negotiations with the French became urgent after France made a pact with China in February 1946. The French relinquished most of their privileges in China and gave the Chinese a free port at Haiphong with duty-free transit of goods on condition that French troops replace the Chinese. Yet the French still needed the goodwill of the Vietminh who could destroy what the French needed when they returned. At this point a glimpse of compromise seemed to promise a future without war. An agreement was reached between Ho and Jean Sainteny, the former head of French intelligence in China and one of the few leading Frenchmen with a personal regard for and understanding of Ho Chi Minh. This was subsequently approved by General Leclerc and by the left-leaning government of France. At the same time the base of the Hanoi government was widened by the inclusion of more non-communist nationalists with the encouragement of the departing Chinese. But control remained effectively with the Vietminh.

By this treaty of March 6, 1946, France officially recognized the Democratic Republic of Vietnam as a free state with its own government, parliament, army, and finances. It would be part of a federation of Indochina and of the French Union. It would cover the whole country, that is, Annam, Tongking, and Cochinchina, subject to a referendum. The 25,000 French troops which would replace the Chinese would be withdrawn in five annual installments by 1952. The Vietnamese undertook to stop their fighting in the south. The implication for Ho Chi Minh and his fellow leaders was that independence would be just as effective for Vietnam as that of Canada or Australia within the British Commonwealth. But some of the French authorities had very different views and Admiral d'Argenlieu in effect sabotaged his government's agreement.

The French had evidently hoped that they would still wield considerable power. The conflicts of interpretation emerged sharply in subsequent negotiations in Vietnam and at Fontainebleau in France. The projected referendum was never held. Around the time Ho left for France, the High Commissioner set up a separate administration for the *montagnards* of central Vietnam and, without authorization from Paris, recognized in his government's name an "autonomous" Republic of Cochinchina, the area of France's most profitable investment. The extent of Cochinchina's autonomy was demonstrated five months later when the President committed suicide, realizing that he had become a tool of the French. In August 1946 Admiral d'Argenlieu held a second conference with Vietnamese to which the Vietminh were not even invited. This deliberate affront to the DRV contributed to the breakdown of the Fontainebleau talks. In any event the fact that d'Argenlieu was not recalled and the modest rank of the French delegation to these talks suggest that the French government had lost interest in implementing its pact. The DRV delegation returned in October with only a temporary modus-vivendi which appeared to buy time by conceding demands which strengthened the French position. Meanwhile non-communist support for the Vietminh diminished during 1946. Diem was invited to join Ho's government but refused and Bao Dai left the country, eventually for Hong Kong. With the prospect of war the Vietminh now sought not a nation-wide consensus but a monopoly of power and the elimination of dissidence. Although they still made some bid for the good opinion of non-communists inside and outside Vietnam, they sought to crush not only the opposition political parties but also the Hoa Hao and Cao Dai religious sects and a basically gangster group which proclaimed nationalism, the Binh Xuyen. Some of these were driven by communist persecution to side with the French. Paradoxically, the French forces during their brief honeymoon with the Vietminh helped them to victimize many nationalists and thus strengthened communist control. Meanwhile Hanoi created a massive single party, which all groups were pressed to join, the Popular National Front, or Lien Viet, incorporating the Vietminh.[6]

In October the French issued a constitution for the French Union without previously consulting the Indochina states. Hanoi countered with a constitution for the DRV, ignoring all French moves and asserting sovereignty over the whole country. This constitution was, as we saw, still relatively liberal in form. It provided for a People's Parliament and all the usual democratic freedoms. It even guaranteed private property. But after an initial session the National Assembly did not meet again for seven years, during which communist control was ensured by a Permanent Committee. This constitution remained in force until 1960 when a new constitution analogous to Peking's was enforced. By the end of 1946 when the all-out conflict started, Giap, switched from the Ministry of the Interior to the Ministry of Defense, had built up a regular army with auxiliaries of around 100,000. The Vietnamese counted on defeating the French quickly before they could outbid them in military strength. The French reckoned with an equally quick victory as a result of their superiority in armor, mechanized equipment, and aircraft. Yet the start of this fateful struggle was basically accidental.

6. Buttinger, op. cit. (*Vietnam: A Political History*), p. 255.

The Indochina War Begins

On November 23, 1946, the French, with the authorization of Paris, launched a naval and military bombardment of Haiphong. This caused a death toll, mostly of civilians, estimated between 6000 and 20,000. A conflict between the Vietnamese and French over the collection of customs duties and the control of imports and exports had led to minor clashes and eventually to a two-hour ultimatum by the French commander to the Vietnamese forces to evacuate the port. When this expired the French attacked with everything available and in five days drove the Vietnamese out. After this deplorable incident Sainteny tried to smooth things over. So did the Socialist leader, Léon Blum, who again became Prime Minister of France on December 17. Last minute peace proposals to him from Ho were held up in Saigon. All failed because it was too late. The bloodshed had put the military on both sides in charge. The French forces took over government buildings in Hanoi and insisted on the disarmament of the Vietminh militia. On the night of December 19 the electricity was cut off and Giap's forces attacked French posts in Hanoi and elsewhere. Ho Chi Minh and other leaders escaped. Soon the French recaptured Hanoi and most of the chief towns in Tongking and Annam. But the DRV controlled the countryside and fought as guerrillas until they were strong enough to resume regular war.

The final break with the Vietminh forced the French to seek cooperation where they could find it. But the field was small since they still could not envisage granting full independence. In January 1947 they started sounding Bao Dai and enlisted the VNQDD, Dong Minh Hoi, Cao Dai, and Hoa Hao. They distrusted the French but were prepared to work with them to create an independent government opposed to the Vietminh. But Bao Dai's advisers objected to proposed French restrictions on the country's freedom and the negotiations dragged on for two years. Then after the communists captured Peking in January 1949 he foresaw American help to the French but hoped that Washington would insist on the French making genuine concessions to the non-communist nationalists. For these and other reasons Bao Dai was eventually maneuvered into acceptance of a specious and qualified promise of independence as a condition of his return. He arrived in Saigon in June 1949 and was installed as Chief of State of a regime with only limited freedom in which many important functions of state remained in French hands and were only gradually and partially relinquished. Once it was clear that he had become an instrument of French policy, the nationalists of highest integrity were ill-disposed to serve him. Nevertheless the new state of Vietnam with authority ostensibly covering the whole country was recognized in February 1950 by the United States and Britain, who at the same time recognized Cambodia and Laos, all as "Associated States within the French Union." Just before this Ho Chi Minh had declared the DRV to be the only lawful government in Vietnam and had been promptly recognized by the People's Republic of China and then by the Soviet Union. In May 1950 Secretary Acheson announced the provision of economic aid and military equipment to the Associated States and France. There thus began an American involvement in Vietnam which will soon have lasted for twenty years. By 1953 the United States was paying 80 per cent of the cost of France's effort to reconquer what had once been hers.

The fortunes of the DRV were much improved by the communist victory in China. For four years it had received no outside help; now it did, although this was not the decisive factor in the French defeat. For most of these years its leaders had concentrated their forces in the Viet Bac, the mountainous region between Hanoi and the Chinese frontier, and had avoided large engagements. The jungle was their ally and they could fight effectively with far fewer troops than the French. They could keep their forces mobile and together, since they held few places of such importance that they could not be readily abandoned. The French, on the other hand, had to garrison the main centers and numerous fortified posts, and this immobilized more than half their forces. Yet they were overconfident, being at first reasonably well entrenched in the rich rice-growing Red River delta which was the main prize of the war. But by October 1950 more than half of Tongking and up to 80 per cent of northern and central Annam was under Vietminh control. In the South, although weaker, the Vietminh had considerable guerrilla strength beyond the Bassac River and in the Plain of Reeds, a situation which was to become painfully familiar to American forces in later years. Furthermore the French, like the Americans later, tended at first to envisage the war too much in purely military terms rather than as essentially a problem of winning mass support. This could have been won only by a program of complete independence. In another form this problem of mass support confronts the Saigon government today.

In 1950, with the help of supplies, training, technicians, and advisers from the communist powers, Giap built up an army of some five divisions. The Vietminh had wisely wooed the *montagnards* and many fought well for them. The price of this aid seems to have been the increasingly hard line taken by the communists of Hanoi. The Indochinese Communist Party was revived as the Vietnam Worker's Party or Dong Lao Dong and the Vietminh and Lien Viet were merged into a United Front, similar bodies being formed in Laos and Cambodia. Thus strengthened militarily and politically, by the end of 1950 Giap had conquered all the posts on the Chinese frontier, including Lao Cai on the Hanoi-Yunnan railway, Cao Bang, and Langson, and had driven the French out of northern Tongking inflicting disastrous losses. The fate of the war seems to have been decided then and some feel it should never have been allowed to drag on for four more years.[7] The DRV's success was achieved through its appeal not to communism but to the national pride and xenophobia of the Vietnamese. It is an awkward fact of history for the Saigon government that their country was liberated from the

7. Fall, op. cit. (*The Two Vietnams*), p. 111.

French not by the moderate nationalists but by the victory of their northern rivals who in spite of being communists were authentic nationalists too.[8]

The Road to Dien Bien Phu

The French were encouraged by brilliant leadership to continue the fight. General de Lattre de Tassigny, a new High Commissioner and Commander-in-Chief, profited by Giap's overconfident attacks on the French in the delta to defeat him three times. De Lattre had brought new vigor and inspired the Americans to believe that the war could still be won. He insisted on building up a Vietnamese National Army to share the burden of the anti-DRV campaign, and this became the nucleus of the later ARVN. Some of these men fought well. Others (like the Burmans in the British forces) lacked zeal so long as command was in the hands of the colonial power. But this Vietnamese army introduced an element of civil war into a conflict which concurrently became more international as the United States with some allies and the communist bloc lent increasing support to the opposing sides. De Lattre also secured a full-fledged agreement on defense and mutual assistance between the United States, France, and the Associate States under which increased American aid was to be channeled through the French. But some of France's leaders were convinced in the early fifties that the war could not be won militarily, that the best they could achieve was a draw. In different circumstances and under self-imposed restrictions other American leaders were to reach much the same conclusion in 1968 about what was still basically the same war.

De Lattre died early in 1952. Soon afterwards the French were forced to evacuate Hoa Binh, the gateway to the hills of northwestern Tongking. Later in the year Giap launched a drive to conquer this area including the highlands where the Thai form Vietnam's

8. Buttinger, op. cit. (*Vietnam: A Political History*), p. 332.

largest ethnic minority. The idea was to draw off and disperse as many French forces as possible. The French countered by invading the Vietminh's home ground, the Viet Bac, hoping to lure back Giap's troops to defend it. Giap managed to force the French to retreat without such withdrawals. In 1953, having built up a center in the Thai highlands ensuring his supplies from China, he turned westward and temporarily overran northern Laos. Here he was rein-forced by the Lao communists, the Pathet Lao, led by Prince Sou-phanouvong, the pro-communist half brother of the neutral Prime Minister of Laos, Prince Souvanna Phouma. American aid to the French was increasing and Giap realized that he had to defeat them before this could become fully effective.

Giap's move into Laos convinced the French that a special effort should be made to hold Laos based on Dien Bien Phu at a road junction just across the Tongking border. The town was in a small plain surrounded by low hills. From there the French counted on being able to check attacks on Laos and on drawing the enemy into battle on the open ground where their mechanized equipment would come into its own. Apart from this, General Navarre pushed a series of other attacks which were ultimately of small avail. In De-cember 1953 Giap's forces cut communications between North and South by a move westward from Vinh in northern Annam to Thak-hek on the Mekong in south-central Laos. By this time Dien Bien Phu was virtually encircled and the Korean armistice had produced a far more generous flow of supplies from China. A later drive by the French to clear the Vietminh from the coastal areas of southern Annam had to be called off at the beginning of March 1954. This same month saw the start of the final battle for Dien Bien Phu. Be-fore it the DRV forces in Laos were brought back to join their troops around the besieged town. The French relied on their sup-posedly superior mechanical equipment, artillery, and aircraft. But with their new Chinese supplies the DRV artillery facing the French fortress was in fact superior to theirs. Through constant bom-bardment Giap's forces held at their mercy the airstrip through which all supplies had to reach the French. Although the siege lasted nearly two months its outcome was inevitable after the first few days. On May 7, 1954, the fortress capitulated with 16,000 men. By the time of this disaster a conference to settle the affairs of Korea and Vietnam had just opened at Geneva.

X

NATION-BUILDING IN POST-WAR INDONESIA AND MALAYSIA

Sukarno and the Indonesian Republic

The Japanese occupation of Indonesia hastened independence through the release of the nationalist leaders and the encouragement they were given by Japan. However harsh and grasping the Japanese regime, it concentrated and developed a somewhat dispersed and fragmented nationalism through mass organization, particularly of youth. In the process it managed to fuse the two Muslim groups, Muhammadijah and Nahdatul Ulama into one body, the Masjumi, which afterwards became a prominent political party. The nationalist leaders who collaborated with the Japanese, such as Sukarno and Hatta, were given valuable opportunities to communicate with the rural masses. The Japanese also established auxiliary armies in Java, Bali, and Sumatra with Indonesian officers and thus gave the nationalists a future source of power. They encouraged the spread of *bahasa indonesia*, an almost identical form of Malay to that of Malaya as a *lingua franca* and national language, transcending the great variety of local tongues.[1] Being ignorant of local conditions, and with the Dutch imprisoned, the Japanese had to employ large numbers of Indonesians in the administration, many of them in responsible jobs. Early in August 1945 an Indonesian Independence Preparatory

1. Feith: Kahin, op. cit., p. 198.

Committee was set to work. Sukarno was summoned to Saigon by the Japanese area commander, Field Marshal Terauchi. A plan was evolved for an independent Republic of Indonesia. After some hesitation the establishment of the Republic was announced just after the Japanese surrender, on August 17, 1945. Sukarno became President of the Republic, with strong powers under the constitution then adopted. Hatta was made Vice-President. There was a regular cabinet and an advisory Central National Committee. The government received wide support from nearly all politically important sectors including those who had opposed the occupation regime. Its forces acquired some weapons from the Japanese.

As the dominant figure of the country for more than twenty years, Sukarno did his best to build and inspire a nation in his own image. It is perhaps fortunate that he largely failed, for in the process some good but much harm was done. An instinctive revolutionary, with a certain passionate Jacobin strain, Sukarno envisaged a role of greatness for Indonesia which was often at variance with reality and common sense. He thought the Indonesian revolution as important as those of America, France, and Russia. He believed that his land had some right to secure both shores of the Strait of Malacca and to dominate Singapore and Malaya as they had been dominated by Indonesian-based empires in the past. Yet through all the vicissitudes of power, and despite many rash and foolish moves, he did succeed in creating out of the disparate peoples of the archipelago a nation with a sense of unity and common destiny. A major step to this end was his vigorous drive to continue the diffusion of one national language. Half Javanese and half Balinese, he saw the nation's focus in these areas of highest traditional culture, and particularly in Java. The Javanese, however, had traditionally displayed qualities of leadership which were not always appreciated by other Indonesians, who had been known to refer to them as "Black Dutchmen." This attitude and the fact that his two principal associates in the early years of the Republic, Hatta and Sjahrir, were both Sumatrans were to lead to trouble later.

The Allied plan was that American forces would reconquer Indonesia. But the sudden surrender of the enemy and the prospective occupation of Japan required a concentration of American forces in that area. Consequently the responsibility for accepting the Japanese surrender in Indonesia, as in southern Indochina, was suddenly assigned to the British. But they were already committed in Burma, and prospectively in Malaya, and found it hard to meet promptly all their Southeast Asian obligations. The occupation forces were not able to arrive until September. By this time the nationalists in Indonesia had had time to gather strength and establish some control. When the British arrived in Surabaya they suffered a damaging attack by the Republican forces.

The Netherlands government had no wish to acknowledge the progress of Indonesian nationalism. The fact that Sukarno had collaborated with the Japanese suggested to them that the whole Republican movement was an artificial Japanese creation of which they could quickly dispose. This attitude changed to some extent after the British had helped the Dutch to return to Djakarta and other parts of Java, as well as to many of the Outer Islands, partly through realization of the nationalist strength and partly through British pressure. They still refused to deal with Sukarno, but they were prepared to talk to Sjahrir, who had resisted the Japanese, after he became head of the government in November 1945. By this time changes had been made in the structure of the Republic. The cabinet was no longer responsible to President Sukarno but to an expanded version of the Central National Committee, the Provisional People's Consultative Congress, which had legislative powers. Four main parties emerged, the Moslem Masjumi; the Nationalist Party (PNI), originally launched by Sukarno; the Socialist Party (PSI), in which Sjahrir led the moderates and Amir Sjarifuddin the pro-communist wing; and the reconstituted Communist Party (PKI). It was a sign of the communists' new strength that in June 1946, under the leadership of Tan Malaka, they tried to overthrow the government by kidnapping Sjahrir, only to release him on the prompt and authoritative intervention of Sukarno. By an agreement negotiated with Sjahrir at Linggadjati under British pressure, the Dutch recognized the Republic as having *de facto* authority in Java, Sumatra, and Madura and undertook to work with it to establish a sovereign federal Indonesia which would be part of a Netherlands-Indonesian Union. But the agreement was provisional in character and was unpopular with the extremists on both sides. The Dutch continued to build up their military forces until they had some 150,000 troops in the country.[2] They also worked in those parts of Indonesia which had again come under their control to encourage the establishment of regimes which reflected their influence.

Then in July 1947 the Dutch launched a major attack on Republican positions in Java and Sumatra alleging that the terms of the Linggadjati Agreement had not been kept. The U.N. Security Council appointed a Good Offices Committee which persuaded both sides to sign a second agreement aboard the U.S.S. *Renville* in January 1948. This was essentially a compromise unfavorable to the Republic since the Dutch were allowed to keep the important plantation and mining areas which they had just taken over. The Renville Agreement was followed by the fall of Sjarifuddin, who had replaced Sjahrir. He was in turn replaced by Hatta with Masjumi and PNI support. But Hatta was faced in September with a dangerous communist revolt at Madiun in Java under a leader called Musso who had returned from the Soviet Union. Although this was suppressed by the Republic, the Dutch again took military action in December 1948 and occupied nearly all of Java and more of Sumatra. They captured Jogjakarta, the republican capital, and arrested the nationalist leaders. In a situation not dissimilar to that of Tongking, the Dutch now controlled most of the larger centers while the nationalists dominated the countryside. But while it seemed as if the clock had been put back the Netherlands had in fact misjudged world opinion. The newly independent Asian and African nations protested strongly in the United Nations while India called a special Asian

2. Feith: Kahin, op. cit., p. 201.

Conference on Indonesia. At the same time the Netherlands action was also condemned by the United States and many of its Western allies. America was deeply perturbed by the progress of communism in China. In Vietnam, Washington had been prepared to support the colonial power in its efforts to defeat a nationalist regime which happened to be communist. But in Indonesia the United States was impressed by the success of the Republic against the communists and therefore condemned the Dutch moves to crush the national revolution. The issue was again brought to the Security Council, this time by the United States and Australia. The Dutch found themselves faced with strong guerrilla resistance in Indonesia and at home with mounting U.S. pressure, including the risk of losing Marshall aid. The result was a fundamental change in policy. A Round Table Conference met at The Hague from August to November 1949 which eventually gave sovereign independence to Indonesia. The Dutch still hoped to maintain their rich economic and financial stake and some political influence. There were two Indonesian delegations at the Conference, one from the Republic and the other from the separate Netherlands-sponsored states. A federal republic of the United States of Indonesia was established from the end of 1949 with Sukarno as President and Hatta as Prime Minister. A Netherlands-Indonesian Union was created but this proved to be a largely impotent body. Guarantees were given to Dutch investors and the Netherlands Indies debt was assumed by the Republic. But no agreement was reached on the future of West New Guinea (West Irian). Both the Republic and the "federal" Indonesians claimed this territory because it had been part of the Dutch colony. Yet ethnically and in other ways it had nothing in common with Indonesia. This issue was to prove a serious stumbling block to Dutch hopes for the preservation of their influence and economic stake. The question was temporarily shelved on the understanding that negotiations would be resumed in the following year. Sukarno and Hatta clearly had mental reservations in consenting to an agreement which embodied so many concessions to the Netherlands standpoint. They knew that once masters in a sovereign country, whatever obligations they had undertaken, they would be able to settle the future as they wished.

Sukarno's Personal Regime

The old leaders of the new nation-wide Republic soon proved that they had no intention of being fettered by the decisions of the Hague Conference. There was a wide demand for a unitary Indonesia and in less than a year the leaders of the separate Dutch-sponsored states were persuaded or maneuvered into accepting the transformation of the federation into a unitary Republic even though this put the country largely under Javanese control. In these circumstances Sukarno retained great influence despite his supposedly ceremonial role under the new Provisional Constitution. The ensuing period of relatively liberal democracy was at first dominated by the Masjumi and Nationalist parties. Until 1953 the successive governments, none of them in office for as much as two years, made some serious effort to stabilize the regime on moderate lines, to check inflation, and promote economic development. Later, tension and division increased and more extreme policies were adopted. The Masjumi and the Socialists gravitated into the opposite camp to the PNI and the PKI, while the Nahdatul Ulama left the Masjumi and became a separate party. The Sastroamidjojo cabinet which held office in 1953–55 was backed by the PNI, the Nahdatul Ulama, and the PKI, an improbable combination of nationalist, Muslim, and communist elements which foreshadowed one of Sukarno's articles of faith. This government strongly stressed neutrality and Afro-Asian solidarity. It held an Afro-Asian Conference at Bandung in 1955 at which Sukarno made one of his first dramatic appearances on the international stage. The government was also narrowly nationalist in economic affairs, replacing foreign experts by less competent Indonesians with consequent inflation, corruption, and disturbance to the vital export industries. Finally, it voiced resentment at the lack of further negotiations over West Irian and categorically claimed the area for Indonesia. Meanwhile Hatta, by now Vice-President, had become identified with the Masjumi and the Socialists, who represented the opposition. Although a new Sastroamidjojo government in 1956 did its best to heal the split between the coalition led by his PNI and the rival groups led by the Masjumi, there was a feeling of disintegration, emphasized by dissension and subversion in the armed forces, and of the need for some strong authoritarian government. In this context President Sukarno urged the introduction of "Guided Democracy" under his leadership. Plans for a military coup were followed in December 1956 by the establishment with army support in parts of Sumatra of regional councils hostile to Djakarta. In 1957 a similar hostile regime was set up in the eastern part of the archipelago. At one point the government's writ hardly ran beyond Java. The leaders of the subversive regional councils were mostly supporters of the Masjumi and the Socialists. They demanded in effect a predominant role in the central government for the Sumatran Hatta. Sukarno countered by the establishment in March 1957 of a National Council representing functional groups and the formation of a basically non-political cabinet of experts. But the breach with the regional councils continued. Toward the end of 1957 the tense mood of the central government was heightened by an attempt to kill Sukarno and a vote on West Irian unfavorable to Indonesia in the United Nations. With this last issue as a pretext, and to distract attention from the country's troubles, Sukarno launched a campaign of confiscation and expulsion against the Dutch. Nearly all Dutch enterprises were nationalized, the Indonesian debt to the Netherlands was repudiated, and diplomatic relations were broken off.

In February 1958, shortly after the anti-Dutch measures were decreed, the Sumatran regional councils established in Padang a revolutionary government of the Republic of Indonesia (PRRI), headed by a Masjumi leader. It was supported by the regional council in North Celebes. The danger to the central government was accentuated by the action of the dissidents in selling some of Sumatra's valuable products direct on world markets, thus depriving the Treasury of badly needed revenue. But under the firm leadership of General Nasution, the Army Chief of Staff, the rebel regime was effectively overthrown by mid-1958 although guerrilla fighting continued until 1961. The United States, then in the Dulles era, had been disturbed by Sukarno's easy relations with the communists. It had shown some initial sympathy with the PRRI and had even sent it some clandestine supplies. After the suppression of the rebellion this inevitably cast a shadow upon Washington's relations with Djakarta.

With the departure of the Dutch the economy had taken a new downward plunge. Despite this, the upshot of these two episodes was a gain in power and prestige for Sukarno and the army. Many of the military had strengthened their hand under martial law and, as in Burma, in the management of some of the newly nationalized firms. Most of the political parties except the PKI were demoralized or discredited. The Masjumi and the Socialists, finally compromised by the rebellion, were eventually dissolved. By late 1958 the President's appeals for "Guided Democracy" had gained new weight. But when he failed to secure parliamentary approval for it he dissolved the Assembly and in July 1959 re-enacted the constitution of 1945 by decree. This meant a reversion to full Presidential power in contrast to a supposedly ceremonial role. He then issued the Political Manifesto of the Republic (Manipol) to mark the "rediscovery" of Indonesia's revolution. A series of slogans were re-emphasized which became the hallmark of Sukarno's rule. The state was supposed to go forward on a basis of "Mutual Aid" (Gotong Rojong), of five abstract principles (Pantja Sila), and five slightly more concrete points (USDEK). The name Gotong Rojong was given to the parliament appointed by the President in 1960. The Pantja Sila were: One God, Nationality, Humanity, People's Sovereignty, and Social Justice. USDEK stressed the 1945 constitution, socialism, guided democracy, guided economy, and Indonesian "identity." The main parties supporting the government were the

Nationalists (PNI), the Muslim Nahdatul Ulama (NU), and the Communists (PKI). This combination was extolled by Sukarno as the proper basis of government under the watchword NASAKOM, standing for Nationalism (NAS), Religion (*Agama:* A), and Communism (KOM). Sukarno retained his dominant role for years by manipulating these divergent elements. Meanwhile, the largely anti-communist armed forces were counterbalanced by the increasing strength of the PKI.

While the country's economy and standards of living declined, President Sukarno pursued with increasing verbal violence and later with armed force, Indonesia's claim to West Irian. As a result of these factors and of the diplomatic intervention of United States Ambassador Ellsworth Bunker and the Secretary-General of the United Nations, the Dutch decided to abandon their costly stake. The territory was transferred to the United Nations and in May 1963 to Indonesia. By this time the President had decided to turn another issue into a national grievance.

Post-War Malaya: Nationalism and Subversion

After the British defeat, the Chinese in Malaya were the chief victims of Japanese hostility. Many who had been known Kuomintang supporters were killed. Some allegedly helped the Japanese in order to secure advantages over their commercial rivals such as the Indian traders in Singapore.[3] Others were dedicated communists who fought for their particular cause as guerrillas in the Malayan Peoples' Anti-Japanese Army. As in the case of Ho Chi Minh, these anti-Japanese communists won the admiration and support of the Allies, who failed to realize, or chose to ignore, the full implication of their political loyalties. They were sent clandestine supplies and weapons and, as in Tongking, they collaborated with Allied military groups or individuals organizing resistance within the country. Meanwhile

3. Allen, op. cit., p. 74 n.

many Chinese in the towns revived a practice of the depression years. To obtain food and evade Japanese regimentation they moved out to the fringes of the jungle and became cultivators of land to which they had no claim. The Japanese made a point here as elsewhere of humiliating Europeans and Eurasians in the eyes of the Asians. They made the usual demands for forced labor from all races, especially for the building of the Burma-Thailand railway. The Indians, and particularly Indian prisoners of war, were encouraged to enter the Indian National Army recruited in the area by the left wing Congress leader, Subhas Chandra Bose, to fight the British. The Japanese also aimed at promoting racial conflict by showing comparative tolerance to the Malays and particularly the sultans. They sought, as in other parts of Southeast Asia, political collaborators from the nationally dominant race. But the pre-conditions for the establishment of another Japanese-sponsored national regime hardly existed in Malaya. The first loyalty of most Malays was to their state and Sultan. The concept of Malaya as a nation was still in embryo and no leaders of the Malay people acceptable to the country as a whole had yet emerged. In Britain's Borneo territories which had shared some administrative personnel and experience with Malaya the occupation was no less harsh. In Sarawak there was little resistance on the part of the local peoples. Accustomed as they were to the safe paternalism of Brooke rule, their mood was one of apathy and disbelief. In North Borneo there was courageous resistance linked with guerrilla activities in the Philippines, under American guidance. This was savagely suppressed. The original Japanese landings in British Borneo had been near the oil installations just to the west of the Brunei border. The Japanese military defeat in Borneo began near-by in Brunei Bay when the Allied forces landed on Labuan Island in June 1945.

In Malaya, however, British forces had not yet landed when Japan surrendered. They could not do so until September in view of the extra tasks suddenly assigned to them in respect of Indonesia and Indochina. Meanwhile the MPAJA had established effective control in some parts and, during the interregnum, sought to establish a communist regime. This further heightened the tension between Malays and non-Malays which the Japanese had fostered. The British military administration officially disbanded these now formidable elements. But many of their arms were not surrendered. They were hidden in the jungle for future use. As might have been expected, the communists did not relax their efforts. They concentrated for the time being on subversion through the trade union movement and the Communist Party, the first having been revived and the second legalized when the regular colonial government was re-established. Other political parties also took shape as the British sought to reform the country.

Singapore with its one and a half million Chinese was excluded from Malaya in order that the Chinese should not become an absolute majority of the population. For the rest of Malaya, including the two former Straits Settlements of Penang and Malacca, a scheme of administrative centralization known as Malayan Union was introduced on a basis of equal rights for all races. This deprived the Malays of their traditionally privileged position and the Sultans lost virtually all political power. There was much in theory to explain the change. Lack of unity had contributed to Japan's victory and the somewhat accommodating attitude of certain Malays to the occupation had deprived them of British sympathy. A more important factor was that the plan envisaged early self-government for the country. But Malayan Union in fact caused strong resentment among the Malays just at the time when Britain needed the friendship of her former dependent peoples, and it was never put fully into force. It sufficed however to produce a strong outburst of Malay nationalism and a nationally accepted leader. This was Dato Onn who had been Chief Minister of Johore and who, in March 1946, founded the United Malays National Organization, henceforth the spearhead of Malay aspirations. Britain had the sense to give way to this agitation. In a new Federation of Malaya covering the whole

country some state autonomy was restored. So was the privileged status of the Malays and the restrictions on the acquisition of citizenship by non-Malays. Although the Chinese objected to it, the Malays found the new system acceptable and a good deal of heat was
taken out of their agitation. Yet the drive for self-government once
launched continued and eventually culminated in a demand for independence supported by all races. But with obvious changes at and
after independence the federal system introduced in 1948 has
broadly survived until today.

By the late 1940's Singapore, which little relished a separate status, had resumed her traditional role as the main port and distribution center of the area. Having been part of a typical British colony
before the war, dominated by officials and nominated non-official advisers, she now moved cautiously forward toward more representative institutions. Some of the Governor's Legislative Council were
now elected by local groups. Meanwhile, Sarawak and North Borneo
had been so damaged by the war that Rajah Vyner Brooke and the
Chartered Company were faced with a huge outlay for rehabilitation. The two territories were therefore taken over by the British
government as Crown Colonies in 1946.

The new federation was introduced against a background of un-
rest. The communists having failed to disrupt the country by peaceful process turned to violence and sabotage and eventually guerrilla
insurrection. This was the work of the old MPAJA leaders and the
outbreaks in Burma, Indonesia, and Malaya seem to have been part
of a co-ordinated plan evolved at a regional communist conference
at Calcutta in February 1948. In June the government declared a
state of emergency but the ringleaders vanished in time. This Emergency, as it was called, lasted for twelve years, from 1948 to 1960.
The insurgents were almost entirely Chinese. They terrorized the
countryside murdering Europeans, particularly the managers of rubber estates. In 1951 they ambushed and killed the British High
Commissioner. They intimidated their countrymen to obtain intelli-

gence and food. They too received a powerful stimulus from the communist victory in China. It needed twelve times their number of troops, police, and home guard to defeat them.[4]

Among those pressed into giving valuable service to the communists were the Chinese cultivators on the fringes of the jungle. One of the most effective measures taken by the authorities was to remove these Chinese "squatters" into "New Villages" in safe areas where they were strictly controlled and the communist elements rooted out. The Strategic Hamlets tried later in Vietnam were based upon this plan but they failed chiefly through lack of country-wide co-ordination and tight control. This was easier in Malaya because the country was under colonial rule for most of the Emergency. Areas where the situation had been controlled were declared "White" and normal life resumed. This normalization was gradually achieved in a slow drive from Johore northward.

By the end of 1951 the communists realized that they could not win a military victory and concentrated as much on political subversion as on fighting. At this point the British government appointed a High Commissioner of exceptional drive and vision, General Templer, who like General de Lattre in Indochina also commanded the military operations. In one respect his task was simpler than that of the French or later the Americans in Vietnam. The British were not facing a national movement of the dominant race which, in spite of its communist leadership, had wide popular support in most parts of the country. In Malaya the enemy was predominantly Chinese and these, despite their strength and numbers in Malaya, were regarded as basically alien by the Malays. Moreover, while the Vietcong can seek aid and comfort beyond the borders of South Vietnam, beyond the frontiers of Malaya the Chinese communists met a conservative

4. The communist-terrorists are reckoned to have reached a maximum of 10,000 at the peak period. Against them were about 20,000 regular troops, 60,000 police and 40,000 home guards. These figures, which are considerably lower than some American estimates, were given to the writer by Sir Robert Thompson, Defense Secretary of Malaya at the time.

and different race, the Thais, with no interest in promoting a communist victory. More important however was Templer's realization that a military victory depended on a political victory and that the struggle could only be won by giving the country a firm prospect of complete and early independence. Some believe that had this been grasped in time by the French—had they, for example, honored the promise implied in their recognition of the DRV in 1946—the long agony of the Vietnam war could have been avoided.

As we saw, independence for Malaya had been demanded by UMNO in 1948 but its leadership soon realized the need to secure the support of the other two principal races. Dato Onn rashly suggested that they should be represented in UMNO, but this was resented by the Malays and led to his downfall. He was replaced in 1951 by the shrewd and patient Tunku (Prince) Abdul Rahman from Kedah who showed a unique gift for winning the trust of all races. Two years later he made an alliance with the national organizations of the moderate Chinese and Indians. Many of the latter, now amounting to nearly 10 per cent of the population, had succeeded in commerce and the liberal professions, in politics and the trade unions. The Alliance, composed of the Malayan Chinese Association, the Malayan Indian Congress and UMNO, first sought responsible self-government like that in pre-war Burma. When this was conceded, it won a sweeping victory at the polls in 1955 and Malayan Ministers took charge of most departments. The Tunku became Chief Minister and has remained the national leader ever since. In this same year Singapore acquired partial self-government under a more advanced constitution, and the leader of the Labor Front, David Marshall, became Chief Minister. The two chief ministers then tried negotiation with the communist leader, Ch'in P'eng, whom they met under flag of truce. They wisely rejected his insistence on the renewed legalization of the Communist Party. The war resumed and also the negotiations with London. Malaya became independent in August 1957 and this at once hastened the end of the Emergency, for the communists could no longer claim that they were fighting to free the people from colonial oppression. The war was declared at an end in 1960, but a hard core of trained communist guerrillas remains to this day on the Thai-Malay border. Should communism spread in other parts of Thailand these could again become a threat. Meanwhile, they serve to keep the authorities constantly alert.

Independent Malaya and Autonomous Singapore

The independent Federation of Malaya, both in its original and later expanded form, could be judged a genuine democracy. Although the parliamentary system was similar to the British, there was a Senate and a House of Representatives. There was an elective monarchy, with the Sultans periodically choosing one of their number to be king of the whole country for five years. The states were given genuine responsibility in fields such as land, agriculture, forestry, and local government, as well as Muslim law and custom. Certain other subjects such as public health and social welfare became, as in India, the concurrent responsibility of the states and the federation. But though there was some real local autonomy, under the strains and stresses of the 1960's Kuala Lumpur became somewhat autocratic in its handling of the states. The Malays retained their privileges, with a guaranteed majority in key government posts, but the conditions for obtaining citizenship were improved for the non-Malays, and the Chinese continued to dominate in the economic field. There was a potential threat to political equilibrium in the fact that the Alliance, like the Indian Congress, became something of a fixture in power. The fragmented opposition, much of it supported by the non-Malays, had perhaps even less chance of assuming office constitutionally than the opposition in India. But a high level of national prosperity, second in Asia only to that of Japan, blunted tension and conflict within the country. In foreign affairs Malaya, with the lesson of the

Emergency, long rejected all contacts with the communist world. British, Australian, and New Zealand forces remained in Malaya and Singapore as a Commonwealth Strategic Reserve under a Defense and Mutual Assistance Agreement. But Malaya declined to join the anti-comumnist Southeast Asia Treaty Organization inspired by Secretary Dulles after the defeat of the French in Vietnam, because it was dominated by non-Asian powers. She did however co-operate in the economic and cultural sphere with its two Southeast Asian members, the Philippines and Thailand, in an Association of Southeast Asia. This had been founded on the initiative of President Garcia in 1961 but Indonesia, by then under the growing influence of the PKI, declined to join.

Singapore acquired internal self-government in 1959. In 1956 differences with Britain over the terms of this advance had led to Marshall's resignation but agreement had been reached with his successor Lim Yew Hock. Britain remained ultimately responsible for the security of Singapore; and Malaya, to whom this was vital, also had a voice. A left-wing group called the People's Action Party won the elections of 1959 under a brilliant and ambitious leader, Lee Kuan Yew. They included communist elements and many feared that Lee might sympathize with, or be a prisoner of, his own extremists. Instead, with great skill and ruthlessness he forced the pro-communists out of the party so that in 1961 they were compelled to form a new organization, the Barisan Sosialis. He subsequently imprisoned a number of their leaders. He also checked the communist drift in a newly founded Nanyang University for the Overseas Chinese. Henceforth his main purpose was to ensure that Singapore should not be taken over by the communists and to seek a renewed association of Singapore with Malaya. In doing this he certainly envisaged a larger role for himself but he successfully convinced conservative Kuala Lumpur that association would guarantee the Federation against having a communist hotbed on its door-step.

The Transition to Malaysia

In May 1961, a month before the communists were excluded from the PAP, the Malayan Prime Minister urged a "closer understanding" between Malaya, Singapore, North Borneo, Brunei, and Sarawak. In this sudden but deliberate reversal of policy he insisted that the association of Chinese-dominated Singapore with Malaya should be balanced by the inclusion of the British territories in northern Borneo where there were many Malays and peoples of indigenous stock and relatively few Chinese. Britain was happy to countenance the scheme in respect to North Borneo and Sarawak after sending out a Commission under Lord Cobbold to check the wishes of the inhabitants. The climate of Asia had changed rapidly since she had acquired these colonies from their former owners. For this and other internal reasons Britain was now in a mood to de-colonize wherever possible. The Commission discovered that about one-third of the people of the two territories approved the plan unconditionally. One-third approved it conditionally, and only one-third opposed it. The opponents included a Chinese party in Sarawak, the Sarawak United People's Party, the left wing of which had communist affiliations. This was to be a source of trouble in the future.

After a preliminary gesture of approval Djakarta turned violently against the Malaysia scheme, partly it seems under the influence of the PKI. The Philippines also objected, though in milder terms, President Macapagal having launched a claim to North Borneo on the grounds that the original cession to Dent and Overbeck by the Sultan of Sulu had been a lease rather than an outright grant. Both Indonesia and the Philippines felt that if ownership of northern Borneo were to change, they as contiguous nations had better rights to it than Malaya, a thousand miles away. It also appears that, the New Guinea conflict having been settled, it suited President Sukarno to distract and arouse his people with this new issue. Meanwhile the

Sultan of Brunei, jealous of his revenues and status, temporized over inclusion in Malaysia. A move inspired by Indonesia helped still further to deter him and in the event he did not join. A Djakarta-trained journalist, Sheikh Azahari, whose People's Party had won all elective seats in the Brunei legislature, launched in December 1962 an insurrection aimed at making the Sultan once again ruler of the whole of northern Borneo. This was defeated by British troops but these events led President Sukarno to accuse Malaya and Britain of "neo-imperialism" and to announce a policy of "Confrontation" against them. Meetings of the protagonists and conciliatory moves by the Philippines President led in July 1963 to a conference at Manila. Here it was decided to send out a fresh United Nations Commission to North Borneo and Sarawak, and this found broadly the same consensus as the British Commission. The conference also endorsed President Macapagal's vision of a Malay confederation under the title Maphilindo from the opening syllables of the names of the three countries concerned. Despite these hopeful signs, when Malaysia was inaugurated in September 1963 both Indonesia and the Philippines alleged irregularities and broke off relations with Kuala Lumpur.

XI

CONFRONTATION
AND THE SEARCH FOR STABILITY

The International Repercussions of Confrontation

Djakarta's rupture with Kuala Lumpur was followed by offences against British persons and property in Indonesia and violation of British and Malaysian diplomatic immunities. There was also some damage to the Indonesian embassy in Kuala Lumpur. The acts in Djakarta were carefully planned and centrally directed and the failure to provide effective protection pointed to the connivance of the authorities. Many saw in them the hand of the left-wing Foreign Minister Dr. Subandrio, suspected by some of being the President's evil genius. British and eventually other foreign firms, including American ones, were placed under government control or otherwise victimized. The operations were similar to but more serious than those to which the Dutch had been exposed in 1957. After the Dutch misfortune the British had replaced them in certain large enterprises in Indonesia. Only humanly the Dutch were by no means distressed to see their rivals suffer in their turn. Indonesia set up a special Operational Command for Crushing Malaysia, and a shooting war began with attacks along the border between Malaysian Borneo and Indonesian Kalimantan. It was to last for three years and to lead later to assaults on the Malay peninsula itself. But it was conducted by the Indonesians alone. The Philippines, in spite of its claim to Sabah (as North Borneo was now called), had, as we saw, favored co-operation between the three countries of Malay race. President Macapagal was distressed at the set-back to his Maphilindo proposals as well as to the Association of Southeast Asia and only followed reluctantly in Sukarno's footsteps. He had proposed to Kuala Lumpur the maintenance of consular relations and this was eventually accepted by Malaysia. Throughout the struggle the Philippine President was indefatigable in trying to promote a settlement.

The Borneo attacks were mostly of the hit and run variety and conducted partly by regular Indonesian forces and partly by "volunteers," some of them Chinese communists from Sarawak who had gone over to Indonesian territory for training. Although Azahari's forces from the Brunei revolt were no longer a real factor, it was Indonesian policy to ascribe most of their attacks to Azahari's "army." In due course the Indonesians set up what purported to be a government in exile, a National Republic of Malaya, in eastern Sumatra, with the help of some minor Malay renegades. They also sought contact with more important pro-Indonesian figures in Malaysia, but most of these were arrested by the authorities before they could do much harm. When the sea and air-borne attacks on Johore occurred in 1964 and 1965 they were no more successful than those in Borneo. Although there were many Indonesians in Johore, and in general many in the Malay states who admired Sukarno as the leading anti-colonial figure in the Malay world, they realized how much they had benefited from Malaysia's wiser economic policies, and when the attacks came they closed their ranks. The invaders had been led to expect a national rising in their favor but they were promptly rounded up and captured.

Indonesia had been liberally supplied with Western arms and many of her troops had been trained at the Commonwealth bases in Singapore and Malaysia. By such aid and by the courtesies paid to the moderate Sumatran Minister for Defense General Nasution, it had been hoped to check the extreme policies of President Sukarno and to stem the influence of the PKI which was increasingly loyal to

Peking. "Confrontation" showed how little these policies had succeeded. The Soviet Union had in any case sent ample military supplies of its own to Indonesia. Under the Defense Agreement the Commonwealth troops were committed to Malaysia's support and these moved into northern Borneo with the Malaysian forces. For the simple people of these countries it was all very puzzling. They had just been told that Britain had ceased to be their master, yet here were the British back. Not only were they in the armed forces, numbers of British were still in the administration at the invitation of Malaysia, as were a few in Kuala Lumpur. Meanwhile, the Sultan of Brunei pursued his own highly individual course. Before finally deciding not to join Malaysia he had discarded most of his British officials and engaged in their place peninsular Malays. But their performance had not impressed him. He also found that some of his own people wanted to reduce him to the role of a constitutional monarch in line with that of the Sultans in Malaya, and this did not appeal to him. All this led him to get rid of his Malay officials and to engage a whole new team of British officers for some of the key posts in his government.[1]

For both sides, Confrontation was a running waste with few concrete results. Battle casualties were light, partly due to the purely defensive strategy imposed for political reasons on the forces defending Malaysia. Economically it was not the defenders who suffered most. The conflict was a disastrous strain on Indonesia's already disordered economy. Wealthy Malaysia and Singapore were far less seriously affected, though the processing of Indonesian tin was diverted from the former to Europe, as were other Indonesian exports from Singapore. At the same time, for the Commonwealth allies of Malaysia, Britain, Australia, and New Zealand, the expense of the fighting was an unwelcome burden, and particularly for the British. At a moment when the United Kingdom was in financial straits the cost of these obligations offset all the profits derived from Britain's investments in Malaysia. This helped to hasten the later British decision to withdraw

1. Allen, op. cit., p. 180.

from these Asian bases. In general Confrontation intensified Indonesia's anti-Western trend. Kuala Lumpur appealed to the United Nations and when in 1965 Malaysia was chosen for a split term on the Security Council, Indonesia left the U.N. She was the first country to do so and her move was vociferously applauded by Peking. During this period there was a certain ambivalence about U.S. attitudes. America felt kindly toward Malaysia because she was anti-communist, economically sound, and friendly to free enterprise. At the same time most Americans knew little about her. Malaysia had been the concern of the British of whose colonial practices they had not always approved. Then the British had a reputation (however little deserved) for being smart and wily and some Americans may well have suspected that there was something in the Indonesian claims that Malaysia was a deal fixed by Britain for her advantage. America had in any case a warm feeling for Indonesia because she had done so much to ensure her final independence. But during Confrontation this feeling was put to considerable strain. In 1964 Attorney-General Robert Kennedy, and in 1965 Ambassador Ellsworth Bunker visited Djakarta on behalf of President Johnson to seek a settlement, but without success. Meanwhile the United States had announced in 1964 that it would give no new aid to Indonesia until the Malaysia dispute was settled. This led President Sukarno to declare in public that the United States could "go to hell" with its aid. Events in the following year fundamentally changed the situation for all concerned.

Separate and Independent Singapore

In August 1965 Singapore was in effect expelled from Malaysia to the bitter disappointment of Lee Kuan Yew and the momentary delight of the Indonesians who believed that this meant a victory for them.[2] With all his brilliance Lee had failed to appreciate the dan-

2. Allen, op. cit., p. 212.

gers of offending the Malay leaders. Some of his public pronouncements about their "feudalism" and race loyalties were irreverent or
frankly discourteous. So was his assertion that the Malays, like the
Chinese, had once been an immigrant race. More seriously, his obvious ambition to play a leading part in the federal government inspired an almost irrational antipathy and fear in the Kuala Lumpur
leaders. Accustomed to being dominated economically by the
Chinese, they were determined not to be dominated politically as
well. Yet this objective was implicit in Lee's insistence on a "Malaysian Malaysia" with equal rights for all races. The Malays also resented his easy popularity with the British to whom this program,
which revived some of the principles of Malayan Union, made a
good deal of sense. Finally they ignored the credit due to him for
having successfully kept communism at bay, a goal which had meant
so much to them when Malaysia was first proposed. The Tunku
called Lee to a secret interview. Legislation was rushed through the
Malaysian parliament and on August 9 the break was made public.
Neither Sabah nor Sarawak, which had joined Malaysia at the same
time, were informed. Nor were the British who had an obvious interest in the partial break-up of the Malaysian federation which they
had helped to create. Lee was so upset that he announced the decision in tears. He stressed that co-operation must continue in the economic field as well as in others like defense. Otherwise the island
would have to make a living by "trading with the devil."

In spite of its Chinese majority Singapore as a sovereign republic
continued to pursue Lee's goal of genuine equality and good conditions for all races. Malay was an official language. The President was
a Malay; so was the Minister for Culture and Social Affairs, and the
Attorney-General. The Minister for Foreign Affairs was Indian, and
a distinguished Eurasian was Minister for Law and National Development. Exceptionally generous social and educational services were
developed. One idea behind all this was that Malays should be attracted to Singapore, that they should find there greater opportunities and higher living standards than in their own country. In this

way the path might be smoothed for renewed association with Malaysia in the future. Taxation inevitably remained heavy, not only to pay for the island's modern social services but also to finance a program of intensive industrialization. Lee realized that Singapore could no longer depend on its traditional role as entrepôt and distributor for the area. In the new conditions this would no longer suffice to pay its way. For there were soon signs of short-sighted nationalism in Malaysia. The peninsula was also developing industry with the help of Japan and seeking to build up port and service facilities making it partly independent of Singapore, thus diminishing the island's trade and income. But while for Malaysia industrialization was just an increment of prosperity, the wealth of the country being assured by plantations and mining, for Singapore it was a matter of survival. Lee's aim was therefore to build an economy similar to that of Hong Kong or even on a miniature scale to that of Japan. To face such a challenge needed great confidence and courage particularly in the light of Britain's later decision to withdraw from her bases in Singapore and Malaysia and elsewhere in Asia by 1971. Australia and New Zealand would still maintain a military presence there and Britain's contribution to the Commonwealth Strategic Reserve would thereafter take the form of a fully prepared force stationed in Britain which could be flown out to deal with any crisis without delay. A gesture of conciliation was the transfer of Britain's great naval dockyard in Singapore as a free gift to the Republic for commercial use. But the bases had been one of the mainstays of Singapore's economy and important reductions in revenue and employment were inevitable. Indeed, the Prime Minister's decision to dissolve the Singapore parliament in February 1968 before the end of its term was understood to be in order to obtain a renewed mandate during the period of the British withdrawal. The results illustrated the remarkable hold which Lee Kuan Yew had managed to obtain upon his small country, an ascendancy which has led his enemies to charge him with establishing a semi-totalitarian regime. For the PAP won all seats and the opposition was totally eliminated. One reason was that his main adversaries, the Barisan Sosialis, had refused to accept the independence of Singapore and had boycotted parliament.

Singapore's program of industrialization has achieved initial success. To compensate for heavy taxation (considerably higher than that in Hong Kong) the government has concentrated on offering superior facilities for investors. It has also equipped a new and highly sophisticated complex for heavy and light industry at Jurong in the western part of the island, with its own port, dockyard, and steel mill. In foreign affairs Singapore is officially neutral between the communist bloc and the capitalist world. Numbers of trade agreements have been signed with the countries of Eastern Europe. On his visits there Lee stressed the need to develop relations with all neighbors, including Communist China. He assured the communists that they need no longer have a false image of Singapore as an anti-communist bastion and armed stronghold of British imperialism. At the same time as a moderate socialist of the Scandinavian or British Labour Party school Lee is on easy terms with most of the Western nations. His brisk, realistic approach to practical problems has strong appeal in such quarters, in contrast to the inert, confused, doctrinaire attitude to achievement of much of the under-developed world. Lee went through an ostensibly anti-American phase although Singapore has been much helped by U.S. orders for Vietnam, and in other ways. He said he did not want U.S. forces in Singapore. The Americans always backed whoever spoke up loudest against communism; therefore they would back the Malays against him. But Lee fully realizes how much the future of Singapore in fact depends upon American strength and enterprise in the economic and military field, and he adopted a much more appreciative attitude on a recent visit to the United States. Relations with Malaysia remain Singapore's most intractable problem. The two countries need each other, yet the antipathy between their leaders tends to persist in spite of occasional rounds of golf between the Tunku and Lee. Kuala Lumpur particularly resented Lee's continued sponsorship of the cause of the non-Malays inside Malaysia. This was marked by the registration of a Democratic Action Party in Malaysia, a group, led by an able Indian, which pursued in effect the policies for which the PAP had stood while Singapore was part of Malaysia. Economically, the most constructive relationship between them would be a common market. But this had not been established during the two years Singapore was in Malaysia, and jealousies and vested interests make it unlikely now. One step backward has been the introduction of customs and immigration controls at the Johore Causeway, another the separation of the two currencies. Meanwhile Singapore has become accustomed to playing an individual role on the international stage and any reassociation with Malaysia is now frankly improbable.

Revolution in Java

On the night of September 30, 1965, dramatic events in Djakarta eclipsed the dissensions in Malaysia. The commander of a battalion of the Presidential Guard made a bid to seize power supported by other units of the armed forces and by some of the PKI. This move was allegedly to prevent certain generals from overthrowing Sukarno "with the connivance of the CIA." A revolutionary council was announced with Dr. Subandrio, the heads of the Navy and Air Force, and some minor communists as members. All the first three afterward denied that they had ever backed the insurgents. Subandrio seems in fact to have been out of Djakarta but the Air Force commander had been heard to broadcast in support of the coup. General Nasution, the Defense Minister and Chief of Staff of the Armed Forces, who, like Hatta, was well known for his anti-communist and anti-Chinese views, was significantly omitted from the Council. On the evening of October 1, it was announced that the coup had been suppressed and order restored. But in the course of it six generals had been murdered, including the Army Chief of Staff, and an attempt had been made to kill General Nasution. It is doubtful whether Aidit, the top PKI leader who had a seat in the cabinet, had taken the initiative as his policy rather envisaged gradual progress toward a communist victory, regarded by many Western observers as an almost certain prospect. But once the outbreak had begun he had no option but to support it and he was said to be behind the communist insurrections which broke out in Central and Eastern Java. When the wounded General Nasution was taken to the hospital the commander of the strategic reserve, General Suharto, seized command of the situation and organized the forces which defeated the rebels in the capital. This virtually unknown officer, who shared General Nasution's views, was afterward made commander of the army. After engaging the rebels in various parts of Java, this virtually established its control over Indonesia. Sukarno's role at the time is obscure. When the coup occurred he had gone to a neighboring airport to be ready to move elsewhere "if anything untoward happened," but on October 3 he announced that he was safe and remained in supreme command. Yet it was soon obvious that his authority had in fact been diminished by the positive part the armed forces under General Nasution had assumed in the making of policy. It became clear that he resented this shift in the balance of power and was determined to reassert himself when he could. Meanwhile the unpopular Dr. Subandrio remained in office as First Deputy Prime Minister and Minister for Foreign Affairs. One consequence of the coup was some slackening of Confrontation. Many of the best Indonesian troops were brought back from Borneo and the areas closest to Malaya to deal with what threatened to be a civil war.

These events unleashed a period of tragic slaughter throughout the country of which the communists were the main victims. As many as 300,000 may have died, including many innocent victims of local grudges. Aidit was killed. This was the third time in forty years that the Indonesian communists had suffered a major defeat. Each time they had rebuilt their strength. No one could predict whether or when they might succeed in doing this again. The PKI having become predominantly the party of Peking, the popular fury with the local communists led to outbursts against Communist China and attacks on local Chinese. In these much injustice again was done, for most of the Chinese in Indonesia, as elsewhere in Southeast Asia, were essentially capitalists. One result of the resentment against their economic success was that trade in the rural centers had recently been restricted to Indonesian citizens and that the Chinese there had been faced with the choice of becoming citizens or returning to China. The Chinese embassy and consulates were attacked as those of the British had been two years earlier. There was also a new though milder hostility toward Russia which had become one of Indonesia's principal suppliers of arms and technical aid. The economic situation continued to plunge downward. The unit of currency had declined from 2¾ to the U.S. dollar to 30–40,000. In December 1965 one new rupiah was substituted for 1000 old ones, but the new currency started almost immediately to lose its value since none of the fundamental ills of the economy had been cured. There were large-scale protest demonstrations particularly by the students. These may have received some encouragement and organizational training from those in or near the government anxious for a change to saner policies, including Adam Malik, the former Minister for Commerce. His Party of the Masses (Murba) had been disbanded by the President and he had been reduced to the nominal duties of Minister for Coordination.[3]

President Sukarno's Decline

In February 1966 Sukarno made a determined bid to regain his old power by dismissing Nasution, but violent reaction by the students caused this to misfire. In fresh demonstrations they surrounded the Presidential Palace insisting on Nasution's return and the dismissal of all ministers suspected of being pro-communist or responsible for Indonesia's economic ills. The Foreign Minister was pilloried as the

3. Allen, op. cit., p. 197.

"Dog of Peking," and "Hang Subandrio" was scrawled and shouted about the town. The troops started to disobey the Presidential orders. In March, Sukarno gave way. General Suharto announced that he had been charged with taking all necessary measures for safety and stability. General Nasution returned for the time being to the cabinet to continue Confrontation, but this was by now a fading prospect. He eventually became chairman of the Provisional People's Consultative Congress which, as we saw, did service for a parliament under the constitution of 1945 and to which even the President was supposed to be subordinate. It became clear that Sukarno had in the last resort been faced with an ultimatum by the armed forces and that Suharto had taken well-planned and forceful action to forestall a similar move by Dr. Subandrio. Despite the President's continued assurances that his authority was still supreme, Indonesia and the rest of Southeast Asia were soon aware that a new course had been set and that major policy decisions in Djakarta now lay in other hands. Subandrio and fifteen ministers, including many of the President's leading supporters, were arrested. Later they were tried and the ex-Foreign Minister and some others were condemned to death. What had been an inner cabinet was reconstituted as a presidium of six which became in effect a triumvirate. The three prime movers of the new regime were given all the vital responsibilities and wielded the real power while three survivors of the former regime, although nominally senior, were relegated to minor tasks. Thus the Sultan of Jogjakarta, a former Minister for Defense and the only hereditary ruler still enjoying influence and respect, was placed in charge of economic, financial, and development matters. Adam Malik became the new Minister for Foreign Affairs and supervised virtually all the ministries of political importance, including Home Affairs, Information, Education, Religion, Justice, Labor, and Health. Finally, General Suharto controlled defense and security. By now Sukarno was for many, and especially for the younger generation, no longer the great revolutionary leader. He had stayed in power too long and his misjudgments had recoiled upon his head.

He had become something of an elderly and mischievous bore and to foreign observers a rather pathetic relic of former greatness. His powers were now largely ceremonial but he showed that he could still be obstructive when the new leaders set about undoing his disastrous enterprise of Confrontation.

The End of Confrontation

Before Ferdinand Marcos succeeded Macapagal as President of the Philippines at the end of 1965 he announced that he would resume diplomatic relations with Kuala Lumpur in the following year. In May 1966 the new Indonesian government advocated a peaceful settlement of the dispute "in accordance with the Manila agreements of 1963." It would "not be upset" if the Borneo states remained in Malaysia so long as the will of the majority there was correctly interpreted. The new approach had not taken the Malaysians by surprise. Through the worst days of Confrontation, confidential contacts had been maintained between certain key figures on each side who hoped to end this feud in the Malay family. At the end of the month, talks between the Indonesian and Malaysian Foreign Ministers in Bangkok were a complete success. Indonesia accepted Malaysia virtually without the latter having to make concessions. The fighting would stop, relations would be "normalized," and diplomatic recognition would follow. Freedom of travel would be restored. Sabah and Sarawak would reaffirm through general elections "their previous decision about their status in Malaysia." Malik indicated that Indonesia, Malaysia, Thailand, and the Philippines had agreed to form a "union of co-operation." In June the Philippines and Malaysia restored diplomatic relations and the Republic of Singapore was recognized by Indonesia. In welcoming the new phase the Philippines made it plain that it had not renounced its claim to Sabah. The two sides would keep in touch for the purpose of "clarifying" the claim and discussing means of settling it to the satisfaction of both parties. They would also co-operate in eradicating smuggling, a constant fact of life between Sabah and the southern Philippine islands. It was hoped that Maphilindo could be revived and perhaps fused with a reactivated ASA and expanded to include other friendly Asian countries. The Philippine Secretary General of SEATO stressed that the resumption of relations with Malaysia strengthened the region against communism. At this point the President of Indonesia elected to make his weight felt.

When the agreement ending Confrontation came before him for ratification Sukarno indicated his disapproval by omitting to sign it. He continued to describe Malaysia as a British neo-colonialist and imperialist (NECOLIM) creation and reminded the world of his plans for a conference of the new emerging anti-imperialist forces (CONEFO). He further antagonized his ministers by planning to dissolve the Provisional People's Consultative Congress. This was promptly vetoed by the new government, though the meeting of the Congress was temporarily postponed. In August, his objections to the Bangkok Agreement were ignored and it was put into force over the signature of the two Foreign Ministers. Despite this the President still managed to delay the resumption of diplomatic relations with Malaysia by not signing the Ambassador's credentials. The agreement invoked the spirit of brotherhood between the two peoples "bound together by history and culture from time immemorial." In it they undertook to pursue economic, cultural, and military co-operation. There would be joint patrols to check piracy in the Strait of Malacca and to suppress communist guerrillas on the Borneo border. The agreement did not mention the British bases and these seemed to be tacitly and temporarily accepted by Djakarta. Indonesia's only worry, said Suharto, was to ensure that they should not be used to threaten her. For all their mutual good will it was not easy for the liaison officers of the two countries to put right all the harm that had been done. During Confrontation Indonesia had trained in subversion volunteers from Malaysia. Among these had been a number of Chinese, including members of the clandestine communist organization in Sarawak. They were by no means ready to give up their struggle for communist control of the region on the lines attempted in the Malayan Emergency. The authorities had to resort again to the New Villages technique, but complete success was hard to achieve in a country with even more jungle than Malaya. A hard core of trained communist guerrillas seems likely to remain indefinitely in Sarawak as in Malaya, ready to take advantage of any weakness favoring subversion.

Tensions Within Malaysia

Relations between Kuala Lumpur and the Borneo states had meanwhile not been easy. When Singapore was dropped the state government leaders were offended that they had not been previously consulted, since their states had joined at the same time and approximately on the same terms as Singapore. It seemed to them that in the light of what had happened their own relations with Kuala Lumpur might need revision. The Tunku and Tun Razak, his Deputy Prime Minister, strongly objected and took authoritative measures to remove the Chief Ministers, first of Sabah and later of Sarawak. This dissension also had some adverse effect upon relations between Malaysia and Britain.[4] Till then these had been remarkably free from the usual frictions between former colony and former ruling power. Moreover Britain had been badly needed since independence first in the Emergency and later during Confrontation. Things were bound to be different when these were a thing of the past, especially with the incipient rise of a new generation of nationalists with little personal knowledge of, or regard for, their colonial rulers. But the main complaint at this juncture was that Sabah and Sarawak had kept on too many British officials who were suspected of having encouraged the leaders in Jesselton and Kuching to resist the federal government. Another later grievance was Britain's inability, through

4. Allen, op. cit., p. 218.

sheer lack of funds, to contribute to the country's First Malaysia Plan. It was partly in consequence of this that Malaysia decided in August 1966 to abolish the preference on Commonwealth goods which had been continued on a basis of reciprocity after independence and, in view of the weakness of Britain's currency, to tie the Malayan dollar to gold instead of sterling.

Malaysia, Singapore, and the United States

As we saw, Malaysia, like Singapore, has sustained a buoyant economy. Both are a welcome exception to the disappointing lack of economic progress in all too many Asian countries.[5] Malaysia was warmly praised for such achievements by President Johnson during his visit to Kuala Lumpur after the Manila Conference on Vietnam, at the end of October 1966. This was followed by the visit of his economic adviser Mr. Eugene R. Black, former President of the World Bank. At this time responsible Malaysians took pride in the fact that their good will toward America, unlike that of many Asians, was in no sense based upon dependence. They were gravely concerned about the war in Vietnam but had no illusions about the consequences of a communist victory. They appreciated the friendship of the richest and most powerful nation in the world but were sufficiently sound and solvent to have no claim on the United States for anything it did not freely choose to give. They were at the same time greatly cheered by a decision of the U.S. authorities which tactfully preceded Mr. Johnson's arrival. This was to limit sales of rubber and tin stockpiled in America and thus avoid depressing the price of Malaysia's two most valuable products. This would mean a considerable increase in the country's revenue, and trade was more important than aid. Nevertheless for the first time Kuala Lumpur re-

5. The discouraging economic record of many of these countries, and its historical, political, social, and cultural causes, is penetratingly analyzed in Gunnar Myrdal, *Asian Drama: An Inquiry into the Poverty of Nations* (3 vols.), New York: Twentieth-Century Fund, 1968.

quested and was promised some American aid. Malaysia's Chinese Finance Minister pointed out with dignity that it was much more profitable to help a nation in good shape like his own than one so insolvent that the investment was liable to be lost. Mr. Black also visited Singapore and discussed financial assistance with the government.

Since these successful visits Malaysia and Singapore have continued to make stimulating progress. Rural development for the benefit of the Malays owes much to the drive and vision of Tun Razak, a vigorous personality still in his forties and the prospective successor of Tunku Abdul Rahman now in his middle sixties. This program was largely designed to minimize communal dissension by narrowing the gap between Malay living standards and those of the Chinese. In September 1967 Malay became the sole official language in West Malaysia. At the same time the government announced that English would continue to be used as a second language in several important fields such as parliament, the law courts, and education, and would be kept officially for another ten years in Eastern (Borneo) Malaysia. The devaluation of the pound sterling in November 1967 justified Kuala Lumpur's decision to tie the Malayan dollar to gold instead of sterling. Nevertheless the impact upon Malaysia was unfortunate. The Malaysian and Singapore governments decided that they would not devalue their new and separate local currencies but that the old Malayan dollar and the old colonial Straits dollar and all the coinage based upon them would be devalued in line with sterling. This produced serious rioting in Penang, Malaysia's predominantly Chinese second city, in protest against the government's decision. In 1968 the Philippine claim to Sabah was revived and led to an almost total rupture of diplomatic relations. After the breakdown of talks on the claim in Bangkok a high level meeting in Tokyo was proposed but abandoned when the Philippines refused to agree that Tun Razak should represent the whole of Malaysia including Sabah. Manila demanded that the dispute should be referred to the International Court of Justice and meanwhile a bill was passed including Sabah within the national boundaries of the Philippine Republic.

The achievements of Kuala Lumpur and Singapore since independence have been a striking victory over adverse circumstances. The former led a state racially divided and born during an armed struggle yet the regime took on the whole a broad view of the need for interracial understanding. At the same time the Malays showed a real capacity for government, as they had in the fifteenth-century Sultanate of Malacca. The Chinese and Indians—even those supporting the Alliance—may feel no great emotional loyalty to a state dominated politically by another race. But for them the existing nation is a convenient and highly effective framework in which to pursue their personal objectives. There is some analogy here with the former Austro-Hungarian Empire.[6] The present pattern of rule could perhaps be described as parliamentary democracy with some autocratic trends. These are implicit in the entrenched position of the Malays in the administration, in the apparent determination of the Alliance government to remain in power, and in its prompt action to bring firmly into line elements such as the Borneo states which have displayed a mind of their own. One disturbing feature, masked for the present by prosperity, is that the stability of the country is based upon a skillful and delicate equilibrium at the mercy of any intensification of racial antipathies. The situation is broadly similar in Singapore with one dominant party, the PAP, and equally firm leadership, but with a theoretical absence of racial discrimination. The Singapore government has also been more sharply authoritarian in dealing with opponents formerly of considerable strength, and with a constant menace of subversion.

6. R. S. Milne, *Government and Politics in Malaysia*, Boston: Houghton Mifflin, 1967, p. 245.

Sukarno Deposed

In March 1967 the People's Consultative Congress in Djakarta revoked Sukarno's mandate and appointed General Suharto Acting President in his place. The scene was darkened, however, by the intensification of the Vietnam conflict and the slow pace of Indonesia's economic recovery. The latter was due to the depth of the evil and the hesitation of the former sources of aid to come forward, after all their set-backs, with the massive and urgent rescue operations required. Yet the risk of a communist comeback obviously increased the longer recovery was delayed. The United States sought to avoid any revival of the resentments caused, here and elsewhere, by its somewhat massive and ponderous pattern of direct bilateral aid. Instead it pressed for reform through international bodies such as a Western-oriented consortium known as the Tokyo Club comprising, in addition to Japan and America, Britain, West Germany, Italy, France, the Netherlands, Switzerland, Canada, Australia, and New Zealand. This was facilitated by Indonesia's resumption of membership in the United Nations and other international bodies. The new approach achieved some success and the International Monetary Fund and the World Bank, in co-operation with the General Agreement on Trade and Tariffs (GATT), undertook an Indonesian economic stabilization program, development planning, and trade promotion. The United States also secured for its investors specific guarantees against inconvertibility, nationalization, and internal upheavals. There was international agreement to defer the repayment of Indonesia's formidable debts, pending a period of recovery. Even the Soviet Union, one of Djakarta's largest creditors, for all its obvious reluctance to help a regime to which it was now ideologically opposed, felt obliged to agree to this concession and to envisage a resumption of aid. It no longer had the power to influence the policies of the Indonesian government and risked losing all it had already invested if it stood out. It was a notable sign of the at least temporary phasing-out of the cold war that America had actually come round to stipulating that the Soviet Union should join in the aid operation to Indonesia.

Even in 1966 there were those in America who believed there was an ironic paradox in the Vietnam war waged in part on the basis of the domino theory, that is, of the belief that a compromise in Vietnam would lead to a communist victory in most other parts of southern Asia. By September 1965 Washington had largely given up Indonesia as a lost cause. Yet communism there had been defeated without U.S. help, save to the extent that American command of the sea and air guaranteed the islands against communist assault. When Indonesia and her Malay neighbors resumed friendly co-operation they envisaged broadening this new area of stability by the inclusion of parts of Indochina. In these circumstances some could argue that a continuing Vietnam war fought ostensibly for the stabilization of Southeast Asia might prove an obstacle to the achievement of stability by the efforts of the Asians themselves.[7]

When Suharto replaced Sukarno and became Acting President the fallen leader was still treated with great consideration. He was permitted the continued use of the presidential residences. When some clamored for his trial, his successor took the line that he had been misled and exploited by the PKI. From one aspect this chivalrous treatment reflected a humane tolerance characteristic of the Malay races at their best; indeed Sukarno himself had shown reluctance to order the killing even of those who had tried to take his life. From another, it was a shrewd and cautious move. Sukarno's figure still inspired many simple people in the remoter parts of the country. To have publicly humiliated or destroyed a man who for a generation had been the symbol of the nation's unity might have risked at best a damaging clash of loyalties, at worst another insurrection. It was not without value even for those who had rendered

7. This was the view taken by the *New York Times*, in an editorial of February 17, 1966, entitled "The Indonesian Irony."

CONFRONTATION AND THE SEARCH FOR STABILITY   181

him impotent that his visible presence remained. In 1967 Djakarta's anti-communist trend was further marked by the invitation of a trade mission from Taiwan and the suspension of diplomatic relations with Peking. March 1968 saw Sukarno's definitive eclipse. In that month General Suharto was sworn in for five years as Indonesia's second President with full presidential powers. After twenty-three dramatic years of partial or total freedom the 3000 islands spread over 3000 miles of sea which make up the Republic of Indonesia were beginning to find that Unity in Diversity, the banner and purpose of the nation, which had so long eluded the greatest country of Southeast Asia.[8]

8. See Legge, op. cit., p. 3.

XII

INDOCHINA: WASHINGTON AND THE COMMUNIST THREAT

The Geneva Agreements

The conference to settle the affairs of Korea and Indochina opened at Geneva on April 26, 1954, just eleven days before the fall of Dien Bien Phu. The day after the French disaster it started to discuss a settlement for Indochina. No real progress could be made on Korea and these discussions broke down in June. The conference had been sponsored by France, Britain, Russia, and the United States. Early in May it was agreed that, apart from them, the countries taking part in the talks on Indochina should be the three Associated States of Vietnam, Cambodia, and Laos, who were invited by the French; and the Vietminh regime, which was invited by the Soviet Union. Bao Dai agreed to the participation of the Vietminh on condition that this would not imply recognition of the Hanoi government. Pham Van Dong, then Ho Chi Minh's Vice-President and Foreign Minister, arrived in Geneva on May 4 and on that day Secretary of State Dulles, the principal U.S. representative, departed, leaving the American delegation in charge of Mr. Bedell Smith. The People's Republic of China was represented by Chou En Lai, Prime Minister and Foreign Minister of the Peking government. The French were represented by M. Bidault and later, in June, by M. Mendès-France. All participants agreed that the Indochina sessions should be presided over alternately by the British and Soviet Foreign Ministers, Mr. Eden and Mr. Molotov. The French, Vietnamese, and Vietminh delegations presented detailed proposals for a cease-fire and a political settlement in Indochina. Then after prolonged debate a British plan was accepted for direct negotiations between the military commands of France and the Associated States, and of the Vietminh authorities. This was the final phase of any French rule in Indochina. In the previous July, and already in a desperate military situation, the French had at last agreed to "complete the independence and sovereignty of the Associated States by transferring to their governments the various functions which had remained under French control." But there was no swift, sweeping, and categorical transfer of power such as had occurred in India. The French clung while they could to the details of their "presence," the chances of making their weight felt. Not until April 1956 did the last French soldiers leave.

In the course of the debates at Geneva, Pham Van Dong asserted that the Indochina war had begun with French "aggression" in Saigon in 1945 and that the Vietminh had been anxious to negotiate even after full-scale fighting had broken out a year later. But the French had offered terms amounting to complete surrender and had set up an alternative government when these had been rejected by the Vietminh. He alleged that the United States aimed at ousting France from Indochina, at turning that region into an American colony, and making it a base for the conquest of Southeast Asia. For the re-establishment of peace it was necessary to stop deliveries of U.S. arms and ammunition, to recall American military missions, advisers, and instructors, and to end any U.S. intervention in Indochina. These were remarkably pointed and far-reaching accusations at a time when actual U.S. involvement in the area was so modest and hesitant compared with what it became fifteen years later. According to one leading American authority, Britain, once again under Winston Churchill's leadership, was the only Western power working wholeheartedly for the success of the conference. Because

Britain, unlike France, did not have to pay the price of compromise, and because it did not share the American obsession with the danger of communism in Asia, it possessed the necessary freedom of action to match the tactical flexibility of the communist delegations.[1] There was in fact a depressing degree of Western disunity at the time and according to this same authority the diplomacy of the Eisenhower administration was "wildly incoherent." In December 1953 Vice-President Nixon had declared that were it not for Communist China there would have been no Indochina war, ignoring the fact that France had been fighting the Vietminh for four years before China went communist. Mr. Nixon had also indicated that the United States would if necessary replace the French in Indochina to prevent a communist conquest of Southeast Asia. In the light of such remarks, Pham Van Dong's statements could hardly cause surprise. In April 1954 President Eisenhower asserted that the loss of Indochina would cause Southeast Asia to fall like a set of dominoes, yet in the following month he and Secretary Dulles conceded that the retention of Indochina was not essential for the defense of Southeast Asia. A remarkable feature of the settlement eventually reached in July was that Peking and Moscow evidently compelled a reluctant Hanoi to accept terms a good deal less favorable than those which the Vietminh thought they should secure. They did not obtain, as they had hoped, the representation at the conference of the pro-communist groups from Cambodia and Laos, the Khmer Issarak and the Pathet Lao, nor any official agreement to the retention of Vietminh forces in these two countries. Finally they had counted on early elections which would give them the chance of taking the whole country over. These were relegated to the future. When partition became inevitable they had also hoped to obtain a dividing line at the 13th parallel, leaving most of the country in their hands. Over this too they had to yield. Meanwhile, considerable strain had been placed on Anglo-American relations. Secretary Dulles was also highly displeased with the shape of

1. Buttinger, op. cit. (*Vietnam: A Political History*), p. 370.

things to come and not least with the willingness to compromise of the communist great powers. But as the result of a meeting in June between Prime Minister Churchill and President Eisenhower and their respective foreign advisers, Washington agreed to accept the partition of Vietnam. Mr. Dulles insisted, however, that the part of Vietnam preserved from the Vietminh, as well as Cambodia and Laos, should be permitted to arm against internal and external aggression, and that no elections should be held as long as a communist victory seemed certain.

Under the cease-fire agreements, Vietnam was to be partitioned for the time being into two zones by a demarcation line drawn near the 17th parallel, the northern zone being controlled by the DRV, the southern by Saigon. The French and Vietminh forces would be regrouped in the southern and northern zones respectively. International Commissions of Control, with representatives from Canada, India, and Poland, would supervise the armistice arrangements in Vietnam, Cambodia, and Laos. Other important political and military provisions were contained in a Final Declaration which was not signed but was orally accepted and regarded as binding by France, Laos, the People's Republic of China, the DRV, Britain, the Soviet Union, and (with certain reservations) Cambodia. This prohibited the introduction into Vietnam of foreign troops and military personnel as well as arms and munitions. No military base at the disposal of a foreign state was to be established in either zone. Moreover, neither zone was to form part of any military alliance, nor was it to be used for the resumption of hostilities. The military demarcation line was not in any way to be interpreted as constituting a political or territorial boundary. General elections to decide the future of the whole country would be held two years later, that is in July 1956, under the supervision of another international commission of similar composition to that of the International Commissions of Control. It would have Canadian, Indian, and Polish members representing the Western, neutral, and communist standpoints respectively. There would be consultations about these elections between representatives of the two zones from April 1955. There would be no reprisals for collaboration with either of the opposing sides. All members of the conference undertook to respect the sovereignty, independence, unity, and territorial integrity of the Indochina states and to refrain from any interference in their internal affairs.

Washington Rejects the Settlement

The French government urged that the agreements should be guaranteed by all the participating powers. The United States however declined to accept the settlement, but stated that it would refrain from using force to disturb it. Washington would "view with concern any renewed aggression" and "favored the reunification of involuntarily divided nations through free elections supervised by the United Nations." The bid for U.N. supervision was a deliberate and arbitrary departure from the arrangements for supervision laid down in the Geneva settlement. These somewhat inconsistent declarations masked an implicit rejection of this compromise deal. The Saigon leaders were also strongly opposed to the terms which had been accepted. It seemed to them that the French, who had backed the anti-Vietminh nationalists as a prop for their continued "presence" in the country, had now sacrificed them without hesitation as soon as it became militarily and politically expedient to do so. A month before the end of the conference the government, headed by a cousin of Bao Dai, resigned on the grounds that "its mission had been fulfilled by the conclusion of the treaties of independence and association between Vietnam and France." Bao Dai at once invited Ngo Dinh Diem, the staunch Roman Catholic nationalist of distinguished family who had already been his Minister for the Interior before the war, to become Prime Minister. Diem had a fine record of independent patriotism. Before the war he had dropped his association with Bao Dai as soon as it became clear that no genuinely effective reform could be accomplished. He had refused to collaborate with the French or the Japanese or the Vietminh after being released by the latter from confinement in Tongking. Although, like many Vietnamese Catholics, he had long refused to be drawn into aggressive opposition to the Vietminh, he had been in America in 1950 to appeal for support for an anti-French, anti-communist Vietnam. Unfortunately, with all his qualities of character, his religion was a distinct handicap for national leadership in a country of predominantly Confucian and Buddhist traditions. Catholicism was after all the religion of the colonial conqueror. One brother was a bishop. Another, Ngo Dinh Nhu, was a political organizer who had been a trade union leader. He was married to a formidable lady of striking beauty who became the official hostess of the bachelor Diem. Nhu and his wife between them developed increasingly authoritarian views. These came to infect the whole regime and some think that Diem's evil genius was his family. In any event, with his religion and family connections Diem was by no means an obvious choice as head of the government. But he was highly regarded by conservative elements in America, and notably by Cardinal Spellman. Moreover, on the analogy of the China "lobby," a Vietnam "lobby" had been organized in the United States even before the Geneva conference.[2] It has therefore been alleged that Diem was in effect picked by the United States. According to one extreme opponent of America's involvement in the Vietnam war whose views must be judged with reserve, Secretary Dulles urged the French authorities while they still had some influence to bring pressure on Bao Dai to appoint Diem.[3]

2. Marcus G. Raskin and Bernard B. Fall eds., *Vietnam Reader*, New York: Random House (Vintage Books), 1967, pp. 66–81. The account of the Vietnam lobby given in this by Robert Scheer and Warren Hinckle suggests that Buttinger was one of its principal promoters. It also indicates that President Eisenhower "recognized Ho Chi Minh's popularity and was opposed to the effort to install an 'alternative' as both undemocratic and of dubious success." Buttinger's works give in any event an admirably careful and well-balanced account of the rise, decline, and fall of the Diem regime.
3. Felix Greene: *Vietnam, Vietnam!*, Palo Alto: Fulton Publishing Company, 1966, p. 131. Buttinger (*Vietnam: A Dragon Embattled*, Vol. II, p. 848) contests this allegation on the grounds that there was no need for American pres-

The Southeast Asia Treaty Organization

Before the end of the conference Bao Dai and Diem strongly protested against the proposals eventually embodied in the Geneva Agreements. They declared that the regrouping of forces proposed would amount in practice to a partition of Vietnam. The projected elections would be held in an atmosphere of terrorism and disorder. They would have no value because the final aim was to make Vietnam an impersonal satellite of the Vietminh. Could France be renouncing her ideals at a time when other great nations were meeting in Washington to study a general defensive system for Southeast Asia? A situation, they said, which threatened to cost the free world the key position in Southeast Asia had been caused by France's obstinate sidetracking of the country's desire for independence. In words which were to ring hollow a few years later Diem promised to work for a lasting peace, for "complete democracy and direct participation of the people in the affairs of state," for social reforms to improve the conditions of the peasantry and working class, for the suppression of corruption, and for complete independence and national unity. He later declared that the Geneva Agreements had been "signed against the will of the Vietnamese people" and that his government did not consider itself bound by them. Meanwhile Ho, whose forces might have overrun much of the country after Dien Bien Phu, saw a situation taking shape in which he was cheated of the fruits of a seven-year struggle conducted with outstanding courage, skill, and persistence. This was the result of having agreed to negotiate and of being forced to accept concessions im-

sure to bring about Diem's nomination. The French disliked Diem as an opponent of colonial rule but were indifferent about his appointment at a moment when they were giving up. Bao Dai also disliked him but realized that someone was needed who had an anti-French record and was firmly anticommunist. Finally his many enemies were maliciously convinced that his assumption of responsibility at that juncture would lead him to his doom—as it ultimately did.

posed upon him by his communist allies. This helps to explain the long reluctance of the North to negotiate again and their stubborn and devious tactics once the negotiations did reopen many years later.

Meanwhile the United States continued for some time to speak with two voices. Ambassador Bedell Smith said that the Geneva settlement was the best which could possibly have been obtained in the circumstances. Winston Churchill spoke of it as a try for peaceful co-existence between the communist and Western worlds. This was another prophetic insight into the kind of situation which developed fifteen years later. At the time this same idea was endorsed by President Eisenhower who spoke of it as a search for a *modus vivendi*, a way of living with communism, in place of the previous U.S. policy of massive retaliation. Secretary Dulles, however, remained loyal to certain strongly held views. He said that the important thing was to prevent the loss of North Vietnam from leading to the extension of communism throughout Southeast Asia and the Southwestern Pacific. After the preliminary talks in Washington on a general defense system, a conference was held in Manila which resulted in the signing on September 8, 1954, of a Southeast Asia Collective Defense Treaty. This is usually known, by analogy with NATO, as the Southeast Asia Treaty Organization or SEATO. Yet its title was somewhat unreal since it embraced six nations outside Southeast Asia, the United States, Britain, France, Australia, New Zealand, and Pakistan, and only two Southeast Asian countries, the Philippines and Thailand, both of them in effect clients of the United States. It was a group dominated by the Western powers and by the only great power of Southern Asia which at that time was aligned with the West in its own national interest. It was for this reason that Malaya and Indonesia and Burma would have nothing to do with SEATO. In October, Senator Mansfield presented a report to the Senate Foreign Relations Committee proposing that the United States should support Diem's government. In November, General Collins arrived in Saigon as the Special Representative of the United

States with a promise of $100 million in aid, to be given thenceforward not to the French but to the Saigon government direct. In later years the corrupt or improper use of much of this very generous American aid to South Vietnam has been sharply criticized in Washington.

The Rise of Diem

Diem took over a country politically fragmented, severely war-damaged, and in economic chaos after what one writer has called "the longest and most senseless attempt of this century to defeat an anti-colonial movement of national liberation by military means." [4] The North and South were complementary to each other in normal times. Now the North had to achieve economic survival and industrial progress on its own. There could thus be no relaxation of the severe communist regimentation necessary to achieve victory in the French war. The South also needed autocratic rule to cope with subversion and civil war. Yet only to a limited degree did it succeed over fifteen years in achieving administrative efficiency and military strength. In spite of his initial promises, Diem seemed to think it too risky to initiate real democracy lest this might benefit his communist enemies. But his other adversaries were also formidable and most people prophesied his early downfall. Nevertheless in the initial phase of his regime Diem with great skill and courage ruthlessly outmaneuvered the army, and the sects with their gangster-racketeers. The Binh Xuyen controlled the police. They joined with the Army Chief of Staff General Nguyen Van Hinh, who surrounded Diem's residence with his forces, and with the Cao Dai and the Hoa Hao in a bid to oust Diem with the help of Bao Dai. Diem was able to split this alliance with U.S. financial support. A number of his ministers having resigned, he brought some of the Hoa Hao and Cao Dai leaders into the government, their transition being sweetened by

4. Buttinger, op. cit. (*Vietnam: A Political History*), p. 382.

American contributions to both sects. At this juncture Diem's hand was decisively strengthened. It had been decided that the French military would be withdrawn, and that the training of the Vietnamese Army would be a U.S. responsibility. The future of South Vietnam lay in American hands and Washington at that stage wanted Diem to stay. General Hinh was summoned by Bao Dai to France and then dismissed. A letter to Diem from President Eisenhower in October 1954, accompanying an offer of aid, stated that the U.S. purpose was to help South Vietnam in "developing and maintaining a strong, viable state, capable of resisting attempted subversion or aggression through military means." This somewhat ambiguous document has been used by the Democrats to claim that it was the Republicans who initiated U.S. military intervention in Vietnam in the 1950's. President Eisenhower denied any such commitment. He had only envisaged economic aid.

Meanwhile Diem in his first years, with the support and encouragement of the United States, became progressively more intransigent toward the North. Conditions in the DRV, he said, ruled out the possibility of free elections. There could be no question of negotiations with Hanoi. The goals of the United States and the Saigon government were "the peaceful reunification of Vietnam in freedom in accordance with the U.N. Charter." At the same time the British and Soviet governments, regarded as co-chairmen of the Geneva settlement, continued vainly to urge its implementation. By now the British government's position had become somewhat equivocal. As one of the co-chairmen it had some obligation to speak up for the Geneva Agreements and indeed to concern itself with certain details of that settlement so far as it had been put into operation. For some years London and Moscow urged Saigon and Hanoi to hold consultations about the elections foreshadowed at Geneva. Yet Britain was America's closest associate. She had continued to recognize the Saigon regime even after it had rejected the Geneva terms and had increasingly become a national state separate from the North despite the provision that the demarcation line was not to be interpreted as a political or territorial boundary. A few years later, in 1961, Britain even sent an advisory mission to Saigon headed by Sir Robert Thompson, the former Defense Secretary in Malaya, to share Britain's experience in the Malayan Emergency with Diem's government and in effect to help it win its war against the North.

Diem had won the first round in the fight to maintain himself in power. He was also strengthened by the fact that with the shift of U.S. aid to his government the National Army came to depend on him rather than on the French. But a renewed struggle with the sects, whose power in politics he was determined to eliminate, occupied much of 1955, and in this he narrowly escaped defeat. He was saved mainly by their dissensions. He closed the gambling establishments of the Binh Xuyen and stopped the subsidies to the Cao Dai and Hoa Hao. The three groups formed a United Front against him in February 1955 and the sect representatives resigned from the government. In March the Front demanded a "national government." Diem temporized and managed to secure a few defections. But when he attacked the Binh Xuyen headquarters in Saigon he was stopped by the commander of the French forces who still regarded himself as responsible for security. The French set out to discredit Diem and for a time his setback made him seem unacceptable even to the Americans. General Collins advised Washington to drop him. Bao Dai urged Diem, from France, to co-operate with the sects, replaced his nominee as head of the Army, and at the end of April summoned him to Paris. Diem refused to go or accept defeat. He again attacked the Binh Xuyen and managed to drive them from Saigon. He also announced that elections would be held in a few months. In June he started military operations against the Hoa Hao and drove their main forces and leaders into Cambodia. These resolute moves renewed Washington's determination to support Diem. His war against the sects was later concluded between October 1955 and February 1956. He eliminated the Cao Dai leadership, including their "Pope," and put an end to their military resistance.

Meanwhile Diem's brother Nhu had built up a grouping called

the National Revolutionary Movement, largely directed by officials, and also a Civil Servant's League. The former derived some of its ideas from a French Catholic movement known as Personalism and sought a synthesis between Marxism and capitalism with emphasis on Vietnamese traditions and beliefs. Later Nhu evolved a Revolutionary Personalist Workers' Party, the Can Lao, a kind of inner group of trusted officials whose membership was secret and which kept watch on other parties by infiltration and by supplying the government with intelligence about them. When Diem decided that the time had come to replace Bao Dai the methods he chose were characteristic of the family pattern of closely woven power. A General Assembly of Democratic and Revolutionary Forces of the Nation was organized in Saigon to demand that Bao Dai should go, and to give evidence of popular support for Diem. They elected and operated through a Revolutionary Committee but the Committee was discarded by Diem when it had served its purpose. With all this vigilant planning the popular vote for Diem was overwhelming. A referendum in October 1955 showed 98.2 per cent of the voters in his favor. He was then installed as President of the Republic of Vietnam.

The DRV Resumes Command of the North

On October 10, 1954, Hanoi was restored to the Vietminh after nearly eight years. In December the Peking government agreed to provide equipment to repair road and rail communications and water works throughout North Vietnam. A further Chinese aid agreement and a similar Soviet agreement followed in 1955. The return of the regime had been a muted affair in view of the appalling problems it faced. Yet in one way Ho's task was easier than Diem's; there was no argument about who was in command. In another, it was far harder. Destruction in the North had been greater than in the South, as it was again to be ten years later when American bombing sought to destroy the physical basis of the North's war effort. Meanwhile there was a gigantic task of reconstruction to be undertaken without skilled technicians and with quite inadequate supplies. While the Saigon government still had some say in the North all equipment it judged to be of value had been dismantled and shipped to the South. Although Sainteny, the French representative closest to Ho, had returned to Hanoi to try to safeguard French interests, French firms and industries soon realized that they would be faced with the usual communist pressures. Their people withdrew what they could and most of their skilled operators departed, having been handled with the usual rigid insensitiveness of communist bureaucracy. French companies were nationalized before the end of 1955, mostly without compensation. By 1960 practically all private industry, commerce, and transport were under state control and three-quarters of the craftsmen and small traders were organized into co-operatives.[5] Until the first group of local Vietnamese engineers graduated from the Hanoi Polytechnical Institute in December 1961 such complex enterprises as textile factories and coal mines were run with virtually no technicians at all.[6] It was hard for Russia or China to spare such people except for demands of the highest priority. It is all the more credit to a land so backward, and fighting one of the longest wars in history, that it should somehow have managed to become one of the most industrialized countries of Southeast Asia. Yet this was of course achieved only through the strictest regimentation and by imposing human privations of the harshest kind. There was also a wholesale exodus to the South of some 900,000 people, most of them Catholics, who became one of the mainstays of Diem's regime. Yet this exodus had advantages for Hanoi. It removed some of the worst enemies of the Vietminh. And in a land suffering from rural overpopulation it made available some half million acres of good rice land for redistribution. The credit thus earned by the government was, however, soon lost by ill-judged measures which at-

5. Bain, op. cit., p. 150.
6. See Fall, op. cit. (*The Two Vietnams*), p. 139.

tempted to collectivize agriculture on a pattern similar to that of the Soviet Union.

One of the first tasks was to set up again a properly organized administration. The rough and ready methods which had sufficed during the guerrilla war were quite inadequate. Some waste, corruption, and inefficiency had to be rooted out before the Vietminh could embark upon the goal of turning their country into a full-fledged communist state. The mood had changed since 1946. A few years after their return, an embittered and embattled Vietminh, cheated, as they saw it, of the fruits of Geneva, dropped all pretence of enthusiasm for the ideals of Western democracy quoted in their first constitution. On January 1, 1960, a new constitution was promulgated which, like that of Diem's Republic, declared Vietnam to be one nation from north to south. The preamble was a "hate-filled doctrinaire indictment of the West," [7] denouncing French and American imperialists and their henchmen. The state was "an alliance between workers and peasants under the leadership of the working class." The Lao Dong, the Workers' Party, would lead the government and the people in "building socialism" and struggling for national reunification. The means of production would be state-owned. Private property was still acknowledged but subject to state "guidance." The Constitution provided for a strong President, with powers resembling those of General de Gaulle, as well as a Vice-President and a Prime Minister. The constitution marked the multi-racial character of Vietnam, thus tactfully conceding that *montagnards* of Malayo-Polynesian origin should not be treated like the Vietnamese of the plains. One-seventh of all seats in the National Assembly were reserved for these minorities. The greater ostensible care shown by Hanoi for the susceptibilities of the mountain tribes gave the DRV a certain competitive advantage over its neighbors.[8] The functions of the National Assembly were in practice carried out by a Standing Committee resembling the Soviet Presidium. A significant factor

7. Fall, op. cit. (*The Two Vietnams*), p. 131.
8. Ibid., p. 141.

was that the electoral system assigned heavier representation to the cities than to the rural areas. This appeared to reflect a distrust of the peasants similar to that shown in the Soviet constitution. This distrust was already manifest in the land reform. The drive for collectivization had been tentatively launched in the later stages of the French war but it was intensified in 1955. Anyone regarded as a "rich" landlord was liable to be victimized, but most landholdings in the North were so tiny that even the owners of a few acres might be classified and dealt with as "exploiters." In the latter part of 1956 the campaign was called off, the Party leaders having realized how rash it had been. Even Party members and Vietminh fighters had suffered, some 10–15,000 people may have been killed, and a serious provincial rebellion had to be sternly suppressed. The hatred engendered was liable to wreck the regime's goals, the most vital being the reunification of the country. The North needed the rice and rubber from the South. The gap in the North's food supply had to be filled and the export of both products would help to finance Hanoi's essential program of industrialization. Of greater moment was the conviction of the North's leaders that they, more than anyone, deserved the chance to lead the whole country. Who after all, they could argue, had finally freed the Vietnamese from colonial rule after years of the hardest fighting, while many of those behind and around the Saigon government had collaborated with the French? And who but Saigon had invited the United States to begin what soon became a new and massive foreign intervention in their nation?

Post-War Cambodia and Laos

In contrast to Vietnam there was remarkably little bitterness and hostility about the transition of Cambodia and Laos to freedom from the French. Despite the Japanese-sponsored declarations of independence which they made in March and April 1945, in 1946 the

French returned and both countries were declared to be "autonomous states within the French Union." Freedom groups in each, the
Khmer Issarak and the Lao Issara, rebelled in protest against the
continued French "presence," while Vietminh forces supported subversion and used the area, as we saw, in their campaign against the
French. Also in 1946 the two countries recovered through a Franco-
Thai agreement the territory they had been compelled by the Japanese to surrender to Thailand. The French confirmed the unification
of the various regions of Laos under the sovereignty of the King at
Luang Prabang. A left-wing member of the royal family, Prince Souphanouvong, was expelled from the Lao Issara in 1949 and became
an associate of the Vietminh. He afterward headed the pro-communist Pathet Lao. Later, in 1950, Cambodia and Laos were recognized
by the United States on the same footing as Vietnam, as "independent states within the French Union." By now the rulers seem to
have decided that in view of the smallness and weakness of both
countries there was more to be gained by patient negotiation with
the French than by encouraging rebellion. In 1955, after subversion
had attained considerable proportions and his proposed reforms were
blocked, King Norodom Sihanouk of Cambodia abdicated. He put
his parents for the time being back upon the throne and concentrated thereafter with marked success on being the political leader of
his country. Prince Sihanouk, as he then became, launched the People's Socialist Community through which he has ruled Cambodia
with a genial brand of popular autocracy ever since.

At the Geneva Conference Cambodia insisted stubbornly and
with some success on obtaining genuine sovereignty; hence her reservations over part of the settlement. Later, however, the Laotian and
Cambodian situations took on aspects of alternate gravity and farce.
Under the Geneva Agreements it had been conceded that the communist Laotian forces, the Pathet Lao, should move into the two
Laotian provinces of Phong Saly and Sam Neua next to North Vietnam. General elections were to be held in 1955 after which the

Pathet Lao would be represented in the central Laotian government. The Pathet Lao claimed, however, that these provisions gave them exclusive control of the two provinces and would not allow normal administration to be restored there or the presence of troops of the Royal Laotian Army. In 1955 U.S. aid to Laos and Cambodia began as it had to Vietnam. Early in 1956 Prince Sihanouk started a dispute with Thailand over a temple on their border which was characteristic of Cambodia's feelings of resentment toward her former suzerain. This led to two ruptures of diplomatic relations, and was finally settled by the International Court of Justice in favor of Cambodia. On many later occasions Prince Sihanouk complained of violations of his frontier with Vietnam as the fighting developed there, and for these he held the United States responsible. He visited Communist China and declared that both countries had agreed to "abide by the principles of peaceful coexistence." He made an aid agreement with Peking and visited Moscow. Despite all this flirtation with the communist powers, Secretary Dulles "undertook to respect Cambodia's neutrality." In 1956 Prince Souvanna Phouma, a middle-of-the-road neutralist leader, became Prime Minister of Laos. He then agreed with his pro-communist half-brother Prince Souphanouvong, leader of the Pathet Lao, that the Laotian government would be neutral and that the Pathet Lao would be represented as a political party in a Government of National Union. In return the Pathet Lao would hand over the two northeastern provinces to the government and place its troops under government orders. The Government of National Union was formed in November 1957 and Souphanouvong became Minister for Town Planning and Reconstruction. But in 1958 only 1500 Pathet Lao troops were integrated into the Royal Army. The remaining 7500 were ostensibly demobilized but were used against the government in the following year when the internal situation had deteriorated. In 1958 U.S. financial aid was suspended because there had been abuses, and Souvanna Phouma resigned as Prime Minister.

Diem: Dominance and Decline

In 1956 Diem's popularity reached its peak while the hold of Hanoi over its people was severely shaken by the land reform. Yet the constitution promulgated in that year was hardly less autocratic than that in the North. There was no Prime Minister, as in Hanoi. The President was the head of the government as well as head of state, on the American pattern. But his powers and the way in which they were exercised were highly significant. He could suspend laws in an emergency, rule by decree when the legislature was not in session, and make quarterly appropriations when it failed to pass the budget. The constituent assembly became the first National Assembly.[9] The administration was highly centralized, the lives of the people minutely watched and regimented. Officials nominated by the central government dominated even local administration and the traditional village councils were sacrificed. Government-directed mass organizations sought to mobilize opinion and personal activities. Madame Nhu recruited women's brigades and even had dancing and contraception banned under a portentous moral code which brought ridicule on this tightly knit family autocracy. The exodus from the North had eased the situation for Hanoi. For Saigon it was an enormous complication. Nearly a million people had to be resettled, some 600,000 of them farmers for whom land and equipment had to be found. Resentment was bred when some land was taken from the *montagnards* without compensation. More was made available by measures of land reform intended to benefit all landless peasants. The Mekong delta was on the whole a region of large estates and had a high proportion of tenant cultivators. Instead of rents as high as half the crop, Diem in 1955 reduced rents to 15 per cent and 25

9. For a detailed analysis of the 1956 constitution of South Vietnam, since superseded, see Fall, *The Two Vietnams*, pp. 259–268. The full text of the 1960 DRV constitution will be found at pp. 417–434.

per cent according to the productivity of the land. Another measure in the following year limited holdings of rice land to 100 hectares (247 acres) with provision for the purchase of the excess on what were meant to be easy terms. The trouble was that the Vietminh operators in the South (later known as the Vietcong) had expelled a number of the larger landlords. They had lowered rents or cancelled them and "given" the land to the peasants, who were then ill-disposed to pay either rent or purchase price. The communists were determined to prevent the land reform program from working and to some extent they succeeded. Many of the landowners were government officials, some of whom were alleged to have acquired improperly land meant for redistribution. Moreover for some peasants the prices were too high and the periods of payment too short. Only one-tenth of the tenant farmers seem to have received land.[10]

One of the many complexities in a grave and baffling situation was that Saigon, which had rejected the Geneva Agreements, gave facilities to the International Control Commissions established at Geneva, while Hanoi, which was a party to the Agreements but saw small hope of the settlement ever being implemented, was unco-operative. In July 1957 Pham Van Dong, then DRV Prime Minister, wrote directly to Diem proposing consultations regarding the elections contemplated at Geneva. He was told that free elections were impossible under the conditions prevailing in the North. This categorical closing of the door three years afterward on the prospects offered to the Vietminh by the Geneva settlement may well have been a decisive factor in the formidable increase in communist guerrilla attacks and terrorist murders in the South during 1957. The Vietminh had been able to retain a relatively firm base in certain areas. When their main units were withdrawn to the North they left behind hidden stores of arms as well as agents and guerrilla units. The government's civic action teams tended to have only limited success in rallying the population, and the local defense units were often ineffective. Some attempt was made as we saw to apply Brit-

10. Bain, op. cit., p. 121.

ain's experience in Malaya, first by concentrating the peasants into fortified rural cities (*agrovilles*) and later into "strategic hamlets" nearer the peasants' land. Both failed through lack of tight discipline, co-ordination, and official integrity. Another weakness was that the Vietnamese Army had been trained by the French for conventional warfare. They were at a disadvantage, as the French had been, against the kind of attacks the communists had perfected. Strangely enough the Americans encouraged this conventional approach on the basis of their experience in the Korean War, and to a large extent followed it themselves when they became directly involved. The Vietminh, on the other hand, followed basically guerrilla methods, tested by the communists in China and elsewhere, even when attacking regular units in force. According to one experienced expert this was a main reason why only qualified success was achieved in the 1960's against an enemy with highly flexible tactics who seemed constantly able to score through the element of surprise.[11] One of his effective methods was the infiltration of Southern communists who had been retrained in the North. As the fight to discredit and overthrow the Saigon government continued, Hanoi set up an apparatus to justify and prosecute its campaign. In 1956 the Lao Dong established a Central Reunification Department. The South Vietnam National Liberation Front was formed in January 1961, one of its main activities being clandestine broadcasts. In December 1961 the People's Revolutionary Party emerged in the South. It was in effect the Southern branch of the Lao Dong.

By the latter date Diem's popularity and prestige had disastrously declined although government-influenced elections, in 1959 for the Assembly and in 1961 for the Presidency, had gone in his favor. He had not checked the Vietcong insurrection and his controls were harsher than ever. In April 1960 a letter from eighteen of Vietnam's most prominent citizens protested with moderation and dignity

11. This was the general opinion expressed to the writer by Sir Robert Thompson, head of the British Advisory Mission to Vietnam, whose *Defeating Communist Insurgency*, London: Chatto & Windus, 1966, based on his experiences in Malaya and Vietnam, is something of a recent classic in this field.

against the dictatorship of the regime, its inefficiency and corruption, and urged reform before it was too late. This only led to their
arrest. In November 1960 the military mounted a coup which failed.
A year later a national emergency was proclaimed and Diem received
powers to make laws by decree on all matters of public security. Yet
in February 1962 his palace was bombed by dissidents. By this time
he was widely condemned in the foreign press. But the American
government, while itself urging reform, felt obliged to continue support for South Vietnam in a process of disturbing escalation which
was to continue for years to come. By mid-1962 there were 12,000
Americans in Vietnam, still theoretically in the position of advisers,
against less than 700 the year before. In spite of all these hostile
moves the final crisis for Diem's regime was caused, not by the politicians or the military, but by a clash between the Catholic-led regime and the Buddhist hierarchy.

XIII

INDOCHINA: AMERICA'S
ENHANCED ROLE

Laos, Cambodia, and the Vietnam Drama

The war in Indochina has been called a quicksand. As tension mounted in South Vietnam, Laos was threatened with disintegration. In 1958 and 1959 the Pathet Lao, supported by North Vietnam and Peking, accused the Laos government of victimizing former Pathet Lao adherents contrary to the Geneva Agreements. In the latter year one part of the Pathet Lao forces refused further integration into the National Army, deserted to the hills with their arms and started a civil war. The Laotian government accused the Pathet Lao of intimidation and terrorism and of receiving support from North Vietnam whose forces had encroached on Laotian territory. It also appealed to the U.N. Security Council which confirmed this last accusation. In June 1960 a right-wing government was formed with General Phoumi Nosavan, its strong man, as Minister for Defense. Two months later a paratroop officer, Captain Kong Lae, took over Vientiane in protest against these rightist policies and the acceptance of U.S. aid, and demanded a neutral government. This was later formed by Prince Souvanna Phouma. General Phoumi and Prince Boun Oum then set up a right-wing counter-revolutionary committee supported by troops in Luang Prabang which in effect forced Prince Souvanna Phouma out of office. The United States

was understood to have been behind this second elimination of Souvanna Phouma because they disliked his neutralist policies. Prince
Boun Oum became Prime Minister with U.S. support and with
Phoumi as Minister for Defense. In February 1961 the Pathet Lao
set up an administration of its own at Xieng Khouang conveniently
near to North Vietnam and by the end of March the communists
controlled six provinces of Laos. At this juncture President Kennedy
"strongly supported the goal of a neutral and independent Laos." In
May a cease-fire was arranged between representatives of Souvanna
Phouma, Phoumi, and the Pathet Lao. This was followed by another Geneva Conference concerned this time with Laos alone. In
the course of 1961 the three princes, Boun Oum, Souphanouvong,
and Souvanna Phouma, representatives respectively of the right
wing, left wing, and neutral center, met various times and decided
on a coalition government. In February 1962 the generous aid which
America had once again been giving, this time to the right wing in
Laos, was suspended. In June 1962 a new and neutral Provisional
Government of National Union was established in Vientiane with
Prince Souvanna Phouma as Prime Minister. Despite all the vicissitudes through which his country subsequently passed he managed to
retain this post through most of the 1960's. Phoumi and Souphanouvong became Vice-Premiers in this new Government of National
Union. These arrangements, together with an undertaking to respect
the neutrality, sovereignty, and independence of Laos, were confirmed by the Geneva conference when it ended in July. The final
withdrawal date for all foreign troops was to be October 1962. Earlier in the year, however, the Pathet Lao had managed to move into
northwestern Laos and thus outflank Luang Prabang and Vientiane.
This in turn had led to President Kennedy ordering additional U.S.
troops to Thailand in May 1962, in effect to keep an eye on the situation in Laos. In December 1962 Laos moved toward neutrality by
agreeing to aid from the communist countries as well as from the
United States, but American aid continued to form the mainstay of
the economy. Unfortunately, like so much else in Laos, the new deal

seemed beset by unreality. Of the 10,000 North Vietnamese troops estimated to be there at the time of the cease-fire only forty passed through the checkpoints established by the International Commission of Control to verify their withdrawal. Furthermore Prince Souphanouvong and a Pathet Lao colleague, supposed to form part of the National Government, withdrew from Vientiane early in 1963 and took no further part in its work.

Meanwhile Prince Sihanouk of Cambodia, determined not to be taken for granted, claimed that there should be another major conference to guarantee Cambodia's independence, neutrality, and integrity. When this was ignored he insisted in 1963 that the United States stop its aid to Cambodia. As elsewhere, America had been uninhibited in her generosity. She had built a Cambodian-American Friendship Highway from the capital to Sihanoukville, the port named after the national leader. This cavalier treatment of America's generosity seems to have been encouraged by the President of France who had worked hard to re-establish French influence in this former dependency.

The Fall of Diem and After

The Buddhist majority in Vietnam, most of them represented in the General Buddhist Association formed in 1954, were bound to be suspicious of a government depending so extensively on Catholic support. They particularly resented the favored position of Catholics in government posts and the special legal advantages they enjoyed. Yet no major clash need have occurred had the government shown greater flexibility and tact in handling Buddhist susceptibilities. In May 1963 the jubilee of the consecration of Diem's elder brother as a bishop was celebrated by the flying of Catholic flags. On the Buddha's birthday in the same month the Buddhists were forbidden to do anything similar by a government order which forbade the flying of any but the national flag. This led to a protest demonstration at

Hue, the nation's religious as well as dynastic capital, in which eight people were killed. Subsequent demonstrations were handled too severely by the authorities and culminated in tragic acts of self-immolation when monks and nuns burned themselves in the streets. A compromise agreement reached by Diem with the Buddhists in June was in effect rejected by Nhu. In August, Nhu organized attacks on the pagodas by the government's Special Forces which had been diverted from anti-communist operations to guarding the Presidential palace. Martial law was proclaimed. Students then joined the anti-government demonstrations. At this juncture President de Gaulle declared that Vietnam and the other parts of Indochina should be neutralized. His policy seemed to envisage an extension of the Geneva settlement along the lines successfully implemented in Europe in the case of Austria after long negotiations between the Western and communist powers. Whatever the constructive possibilities of this suggestion there was small chance of its evoking a response in Washington at a time when the French President's general policy toward the United States was so provocative. The prospect of French support and help in the event of the government adopting neutrality allegedly led Nhu to start secret negotiations with the communists. But according to one French authority this was basically to blackmail the Americans into continuing their support.[1] If so, the move failed. In September President Kennedy delivered a public admonition to Diem. This was followed by the suspension of U.S. subsidies for Vietnamese imports and for the government's Special Forces until they returned to their military duties. By October the impression had gained ground in Saigon that Washington would not object to a coup to remove Diem.[2] The coup was

1. Jean Lacouture, *Vietnam Between Two Truces*, New York: Random House (Vintage Books), 1966, pp. 82–85.
2. Felix Greene, op. cit., p. 131, says characteristically . . . "When, after eight long and terrible years, the U.S. finally withdrew its support, Diem was immediately hounded down and shot and the people went wild with rejoicing. . ." Buttinger in his measured and cautious account of the tragedy does not deny

mounted by two groups of military officers, who eventually managed to work smoothly together. Two crucial factors were winning over the general most trusted by Diem and forestalling Nhu's plans to stage a faked coup so that the government could uncover and destroy its enemies. In both they succeeded. After the rebels had surrounded the palace and occupied the government buildings, the brothers escaped by a tunnel and eventually took refuge in a Catholic church in Cholon. From there Diem telephoned to surrender. After they were picked up and on the way to Saigon both were murdered, allegedly with the approval of General Duong Van Minh.[3] This officer then became head of state and government as Chairman of a Military Revolutionary Council in which the generals took charge of the key ministries. The special groups and movements supporting the Diem regime were disbanded. Elections and a return to civilian rule were promised within a year. In practice the numerous successor administrations in South Vietnam have been mostly dominated by the armed forces despite civilian participation and, later, a constitution on democratic principles. They have been regularly recognized by the United States, by Britain in America's wake, and by various other Western nations.

Two months after the coup, on January 30, 1964, General Minh was displaced as Chairman of the Council by a triumvirate headed by General Nguyen Khanh, but remained for the time being as head of state. Some distinguished civilians were included in the government. An impressive government program included the mobilization

---

the main contention that the withdrawal of U.S. support was in effect decisive, since the stopping of U.S. imports and other measures convinced the Vietnamese that Diem was being dropped by Washington. He speaks of the "passive but exceedingly effective promotion of the coup by Washington," once it had "reached the conclusion that Diem had to be replaced if South Vietnam were to survive. . ." He incidentally rejects the view that, "if Diem had remained . . . the military situation would not have deteriorated to the point where only U.S. military intervention could contain the Vietcong. . ." (*Vietnam: A Dragon Embattled*, Vol. II, pp. 1001, 1002, 1009.)
3. Buttinger, op. cit. (*Vietnam: A Political History*), p. 474.

of all fit citizens to combat the grave increase in communist insurgency which had followed the removal of Diem's stern hand. The Strategic Hamlets were renamed Rural New Life Hamlets. These were to be so well run that security and order would spread outward from them. The land reform was to be made more genuine. Khanh, himself a Buddhist, annulled the legal privileges of Catholics and recognized the United Buddhist Association formed in January. But the monks still complained of repression. When the political leaders proposed to organize an all-civilian cabinet parallel to the Military Council, they were told that the Army was the only disciplined force capable of leading the country. The Vietcong inevitably profited by these dissensions and by the purging of administrative personnel. Their mounting attacks led the United States to increase their forces in Vietnam to 22,000 in 1964 under the orders of a U.S. Military Assistance Command established two years earlier. American concern was also marked by the appointment of a General, Maxwell Taylor, as ambassador to Saigon.

Direct Intervention of U.S. Forces

The year 1964 was a fateful one for the future of the Saigon regime and of the United States and its allies. In the course of it a fear gained ground that the South Vietnamese forces, sustained merely by American advisers, might be defeated. United States aid was again stepped up and in August American forces were sent officially into battle on behalf of South Vietnam, the first occasion being the bombing of patrol boat bases and oil depots in the North. This was the first direct military involvement of the United States in Asia since the Korean War. The change in American policy was ostensibly brought about by attacks on U.S. naval vessels in the Gulf of Tongking, the details of which are still obscure. Many take the view that these comparatively minor incidents were regarded in Washington as a convenient pretext for a direct military intervention which had become necessary if the South were to be saved from collapse. President Johnson declared that America would stay in Southeast Asia as long as the struggle required. General Khanh seems to have been encouraged by these developments to have a new provisional constitution introduced, making him President with more or less unlimited powers. Faced with agitation by students, Buddhists, and communists, Khanh resigned after a couple of weeks but returned to power as part of a triumvirate with General Minh, which promised a civilian government and a national congress. In September a coup against them was defeated with the help of a young Air Force officer, Nguyen Cao Ky, who started to emerge as a public figure at this time.

By approving the President's policy and adopting the so-called Gulf of Tongking Resolution, Congress in effect gave the administration a blank check to pursue the war by escalation or otherwise as it saw fit. There thus passed in 1964 the third decisive moment when the United States might have been able to avoid assuming the heavy commitment it has undertaken in this remote area. The first was in 1946 after the French authorities in Vietnam had sabotaged their government's agreement with Ho Chi Minh. At this point America decided to support France in her efforts to resume control over her former colonial territories, this curious reversal of the policies of President Roosevelt being dictated by a determination to stop what seemed the greater evil of communism. The second was in 1954 when Washington supported Diem in rejecting the Geneva settlement, despite its endorsement by Churchill and other familiar and respected figures. The third occasion was when this risk of a collapse in the South occurred in 1964. However painful, it might still then have been possible to point out to the Saigon leaders that the predicament which they had failed to solve with their own forces was essentially one to be settled between Asians, that in the 1960's with colonialism dead and discredited the time was past when the white man could seek to impose his will on Asians or to fight their battles for them.

Saigon, Washington, and the Communist Campaign

From September 1964 politics in South Vietnam were increasingly influenced by the young officers of the armed forces. This in part explains the inconclusive efforts to install civilian rule. In November a civilian government was set up under a former Mayor of Saigon. But in the face of Catholic and Buddhist demonstrations this was dismissed in January by an Armed Forces Council headed by General Khanh. In February another largely civilian government was formed under a former Foreign Minister, Dr. Phan Huy Quat, which lasted somewhat precariously until June when a group of young generals took over. While in office Quat had been faced with a Catholic coup which removed Khanh, and a Buddhist peace drive which proposed a Reconciliation Committee to reunify and neutralize Vietnam. Foreign troops and advisers would be withdrawn and the NLF abolished. This led some to suspect that the Buddhists were responsive to communist influence. Quat had, however, succeeded in holding ostensibly fair provincial and municipal elections despite communist efforts at disruption. After the military resumed power in June 1965 new provisional constitutional arrangements were announced. The Armed Forces Council would temporarily be the sovereign power. It set up a ten-man all-military National Leadership Committee. The Buddhist Nguyen Cao Ky, now air marshal, became Prime Minister, the Catholic General Nguyen Van Thieu, chief of state. The former, a gifted officer, remained a major government figure for many years. Meanwhile in the first half of 1965 the communists went over to the kind of general offensive contemplated in Mao's precepts on revolutionary war now that they seemed to be acquiring the advantage in the "equilibrium of forces." They scored some striking successes and the National Liberation Front launched a diatribe against the United States. Prime Minister Ky responded with some measures to increase the military effectiveness of South

Vietnam. He put the country on a war footing and formally declared war on North Vietnam. He also broke off diplomatic relations with France as a gesture of rejection of General de Gaulle's appeal for neutralization. President Johnson's response was far more significant. Faced with a gravely deteriorating military situation in the country to which America had pledged her support he judged that occasional bombings of the North coupled with U.S. military advice was no longer enough. He took the crucial decision to send the full weight of U.S. forces into battle for the defense of South Vietnam. One consequence was a formidable escalation in the numbers of these forces and of the burden to the American taxpayer. In the seven years from 1961 to 1968 the number multiplied some seventy times, from seven hundred to half a million.

The Smaller Neighbors: Crisis, Clamor, and Unrest

The situation in Laos remained fragile. It was punctuated by fighting, some of it heavy, in 1964–66. This led to Kong Lae and his neutralist forces losing control of the central strategic area of the Plain of Jars to the Pathet Lao, supported by the North Vietnamese, and to advances in other areas by the communists. By July 1965 there were estimated to be some 24,000 North Vietnamese troops in Laos. The United States was a party to the Geneva Agreement on Laos of 1962 although it had not accepted the earlier Geneva Agreements of 1954 dealing with the whole of Indochina. It therefore had ostensibly no military commitment in Laos. Nevertheless U.S. aircraft carried out numerous raids on areas controlled by the Pathet Lao and on the Ho Chi Minh Trail, many of them from their bases in Thailand. Privately owned American planes also carried food, arms, and medical supplies to the pro-government Meo hill tribes in the communist-occupied northeastern provinces of Phong Saly and Sam Neua. In dealing with the communist threat the Laos government forces were weakened by struggles for power between their military leaders. Thus there was an attempted right wing coup with heavy fighting in Vientiane early in 1965 followed by the flight of General Phoumi to Thailand.

Meanwhile Prince Sihanouk had raised himself by plebiscite to the post of permanent Chief of State. In 1964 his displeasure with the United States and Britain mounted, chiefly because of the delayed response to his proposal to convene a conference on Cambodia. The U.S. and British embassies were attacked and the Prince issued a statement in conjunction with Peking condemning U.S. actions in Indochina. In 1965 he broke off diplomatic relations with Washington.

National elections in July 1965 did not notably regenerate Laotian political life. The Pathet Lao refused to participate. The fortunes of the desultory struggle between the government forces and the Pathet Lao helped by the North Vietnamese continued to sway back and forth with some over-all advantage to the latter despite the fact that the government troops were fighting a good deal better than they had when there was a significant American military presence in Laos some years earlier. In late 1965 and early 1966 the situation became temporarily critical in the southern areas of Thakhek and Savannakhet and the Plateau des Bolovens. Hanoi denied that their troops had intervened in Laos and alleged that this rumor was "just to prepare world opinion for American intervention." In mid-1966 U.S. intelligence put the number of North Vietnamese in Laos, including construction workers and coolies as well as soldiers, as high as 70,000, many of them manning the Ho Chi Minh Trail.

France Elaborates Her Proposals for a Settlement

At the end of August 1966 President de Gaulle paid a state visit to Cambodia and met there a representative of Hanoi. He praised Cambodia's neutrality and called on the U.S. forces to leave South Vietnam as France had left Algeria. While an American military defeat was, he said, unthinkable, there was no chance that "the peoples of Asia would bow to the law of a foreigner who came from the other side of the Pacific." There could thus be no military solution. Only a political agreement could avert ever-growing misfortunes. He then restated the policies he had earlier proposed. There could be an agreement like the Geneva settlement of 1954 aimed at establishing and guaranteeing the neutrality of Indochina, leaving each part full responsibility for its affairs. The opening of such negotiations would depend on a prior commitment of the United States to repatriate its forces within a given time. Meanwhile the powers concerned should accept or renew a commitment to observe the Geneva Agreements.

An example of France's disapproval of U.S. policy in Indochina had been the curious role of the French military mission retained in Laos to help train the Laotian forces. The mission had been markedly inactive apparently to avoid "helping the American cause." Americans, as we saw, keenly resented such attitudes. They were disposed to ignore the pronouncements of President de Gaulle despite his unquestionable qualities of character and intelligence and the courage and statesmanship he had shown in taking France out of Algeria, which had for so long been counted as an integral part of his country. The suggestion that America might do likewise in the case of Vietnam was unwelcome although this could in no sense signify a sacrifice of comparable proportions for the United States.

Laos and Cambodia in the Orbit of the Vietnam Struggle

In October 1966 confusion in Laos deepened when a government Air Force commander bombed the capital apparently out of spite against his military colleagues and subsequently fled to Thailand with other officers who took with them the entire Laotian Air Force consisting of twelve aircraft. In the same month parliament was dissolved because it refused to pass the budget. Soon afterwards Kong

Lae resigned command of his 8000 neutral troops supporting the government and complained that he had been forced out by the Americans for the benefit of the right wing.

Early in 1967 Prince Sihanouk accused the CIA of plotting against him and trying to kill his parents. Newsmen from western countries were then banned from Cambodia. Subsequently all foreign newsmen were excluded.

At this juncture the Laos war seemed a kind of draw. It could not be regarded as a success for either side. At the same time U.S. troops were fortunately not involved. There was no well-organized terrorist movement in Laos comparable to that of the Vietcong, and the Pathet Lao were not a very formidable military force. One incidental advantage for the Laotian government was that the Vietnamese stood out as a different race whom the Laotians tended to dislike, having suffered under them in the past. Another was the support of the Meo guerrillas. These were fighting the communists in the mountain areas held by the latter with the help of supplies dropped by U.S. planes. In general, moreover, the areas dominated by the communists had only been occupied militarily. They had not been won over politically and 200,000 people had fled from them to the South where the main centers down the Mekong valley were held by the government. On the other hand the communists effectively dominated the Ho Chi Minh Trail. They also threatened Luang Prabang and seemed at times in a position to occupy the whole country. They held the Plain of Jars and a thick belt of territory along the China and North Vietnam borders. They also controlled Routes 6 and 7 from North Vietnam and its prolongation from their junction to the Plain of Jars. Finally Hanoi claimed as part of North Vietnam the communist-controlled northern province of Sam Neua. Yet in the atmosphere of inconsequent unreality which in Laos seemed to infect even the communist adversary the threat of a total take-over, without disappearing, constantly receded into the future. The communists could be judged to control about 40 per cent of the area of Laos and a quarter of the population. But there were important pockets of government territory inside the communist areas. In April 1967 Prime Minister Souvanna Phouma said how much he regretted that the Laotian government could not halt the passage of North Vietnamese troops through its territory on their way to South Vietnam. He nevertheless urged that there should be no U.S. military intervention in Laos. Once Laos could get rid of the North Vietnamese as the result of a settlement in Vietnam the Pathet Lao would cease to be important.

In 1967 and 1968 Prince Sihanouk of Cambodia continued his act of delicate suspension between East and West. In 1967 he installed a new cabinet under a middle-of-the-road Prime Minister which included leftist as well as moderate elements. He accused the communists in the province of Battambang of subversive activity but emphasized that this did not mean that he was "moving closer to the United States." To drive his point home he established diplomatic relations with Hanoi, arguing that the National Liberation Front had pledged itself to respect Cambodia's frontier with South Vietnam. He could now therefore feel assured that this area would no longer be used for attacks by the Vietcong against their American and South Vietnamese adversaries.

Thailand: From Second World War to Second Vietnam War

Thailand, like many of America's smaller allies, had become inexorably involved in the Vietnam crisis. She had sided with the Western allies in the first World War and had joined their enemies in the second, yet had managed to avoid fighting on her own soil. As always, her keen instinct for self-preservation taught her to seek the winning side. Indeed Prime Minister Pibun had said candidly in 1942 that whichever side would be defeated was the enemy.[4] It long looked as if Japan might be the winner and, after the sudden de-

4. Wilson, op. cit., p. 20.

scent of the Japanese on her southern territory in December 1941, Thailand had virtually no alternative but to acquiesce in the free passage of these troops on their way to attack Burma and Malaya. She was already obligated to the Japanese who had, as we saw, forced the French to give back to her some ceded parts of Laos and Cambodia. Up to this point, Pibun and Pridi had worked together for the prestige and expansion of their country. Now their ways parted. Immediately after the Japanese invasion Pridi left the government to become Regent for the young king. He also became with Prince Seni Pramoj, the Thai Ambassador in Washington, the moving spirit of the Free Thai movement opposed to the Japanese and secretly in touch with the Western Allies. Thailand having declared war on Britain and the United States, Prince Seni refused to deliver the declaration to the U.S. government. This proved to be valuable after the Japanese surrender. Washington did not consider itself to have been at war with Bangkok as had Britain, and persuaded London to moderate its post-war demands on the Thais. Pibun had been eliminated in 1944 and Pridi dominated or led the government for some two years after the war. His position was, however, severely shaken when in May 1946 young King Ananda was found shot in bed in circumstances which have never been cleared up. Pridi resigned as Prime Minister soon afterward in favor of a supporter, Admiral Thamrong. But in November he was forced to flee the country and eventually took refuge in Communist China. After a short conservative caretaker government Pibun resumed power, this time by force, in April 1948. For over nine years, until September 1957, he survived a number of crises, including three changes of constitution and attempts by ambitious rivals to unseat him. He was even kidnapped for a time in an abortive naval coup in 1951. After this two younger officers, Generals Phao Siyanon and Sarit Thanarat, emerged as powerful figures, the first as Director-General of Police, the second as commander of the Bangkok Army. This strong triumvirate with conflicting ambitions adopted a firmly anti-communist policy in line with that of the United States. This again was a course which seemed clearly in accord with Thai traditions and interests. Chinese communism was an obvious danger to a country with some three million incompletely assimilated Chinese and an entrenched elite of essentially capitalist outlook with a keen appreciation of the personal advantages of money. Moreover the United States was by now looked up to as the hoped for triumphant bastion of non-communist Asia. It was thus that Thailand became, with the Philippines, a founding member of the Southeast Asia Treaty Organization, that later America sent increasing numbers of troops and aircraft to Thailand, and that both these smaller allies eventually sent forces to serve in South Vietnam.

After a repressive period Pibun decided in 1955 to encourage free speech, following visits to America and Britain. This appears to have been a bid for popular support, which General Phao sought likewise. Both, however, were outmaneuvered by Sarit, who denounced the elections held in 1957 and in September mounted a coup against his former patron. He then replaced Pibun, who fled the country. Phao went into exile. Sarit temporarily installed his deputy, General Thanom Kittikachorn, as Prime Minister. A year later, having returned from treatment abroad, he assumed dictatorial powers, abrogating the constitution of the moment. During his rule some economic progress was made. Investment was encouraged and industry developed, helped by substantial financial aid, not least from the United States, the presence of whose forces also brought considerable funds into the country. Sarit was ostensibly dedicated to cleaning up abuses, including graft. It was therefore a windfall for the cynics that after his death it was found that he and his family had acquired a fortune of over a hundred million dollars. The political kaleidoscope in Thailand has been critically judged. "The succession of constitutions operating in Thailand from 1932 . . . amounted to little more than a façade designed to impress Western observers. Governmental coups . . . on the average of three or four times per decade invariably saw one element of the political elite supplanting another in a game of musical chairs . . . Since the Army constituted the best-organized political clique, its representatives managed to exercise control." [5] At the same time there was a surprising degree of administrative stability. Another stabilizing element was the popular young King Bhumibol, who, as symbol and inspiration of the nation, retained a traditional prestige despite all constitutional restrictions.

During the past twenty years Thailand has had on the whole uneasy relations with her neighbors, except for Malaysia, and the Vietnam conflict has had disturbing repercussions inside and outside her borders. There have been minor mutual grievances between her and Burma, such as the Kuomintang refugees and Karen rebels. More important is Burma's jaundiced view of Thailand's client-relationship with the United States. She fears that this might create a dangerous Vietnam-type of cold war confrontation nearer to her borders, into which hitherto neutral parts of Southeast Asia could be dragged. There have been armed clashes with the Cambodians, some originating in incursions from Thailand of right-wing Khmer groups allegedly trained by the U.S. and Thai forces to avert a communist takeover in Cambodia. The situation facing Thailand in Laos has been far more serious. Although the conservative generals in Thailand have been on close terms with similar right-wing leaders in Laos, such as General Phoumi, they have been increasingly disturbed by the fragility and fragmentation of the Laotian state and by the large-scale activities of the communist forces, both North Vietnamese and Pathet Lao, inside the country. This has been brought home to them by increasing communist-fomented guerrilla subversion in the poverty-stricken Khorat plateau across the Mekong River border in the northeastern part of their country, led by the so-called Thailand Patriotic Front. The Thai authorities have reason to suspect links between this Front and the communists in Laos and in 1967 the communists complained that Thai forces were fighting with the Laotian Army against the Pathet Lao. Unfortunately, foreign observers judged that the Thai Army had devoted itself so long

5. Cady, op. cit. (*Thailand, Burma, Laos and Cambodia*), p. 15.

to making revolutions and running the government that it was far from being formidable in combat.

Thailand's somewhat cloudy future depends on two great powers, the United States and China. Pridi has become a protégé of Peking, which has encouraged him to revive the Free Thai movement for a purpose very different from that which it served during World War II. It is almost certainly correct, as one American authority suggests, that should Bangkok judge that Washington was wavering in its determination to check communist expansion in Southeast Asia, Thailand would probably seek some accommodation with China, as Burma has.[6] This possibility acquires disturbing significance in the light of the policy forecast by President Nixon of an eventual withdrawal of U.S. forces from Vietnam. This could mean that, failing special precautions, a statesman to whom Thailand owes much but who is now dedicated to the communist cause, might change decisively the destiny of his people.

6. Cady, op. cit. (*Thailand, Burma, Laos and Cambodia*), p. 14.

XIV

THE SEARCH FOR PEACE: INITIAL MOVES

Deadlock with Hanoi

There were fresh bids for a settlement in 1965 and 1966, some conciliatory, some pugnacious and uncompromising. In March 1965 the National Liberation Front declared in a five-point statement that the Americans had sabotaged the Geneva Agreements, that the Front would drive them out and liberate South Vietnam as a step towards reunification with the North, that the United States must withdraw not only its troops but its support of the Saigon government, that the NLF must have the decisive voice in negotiation, that the Front would stand by the Laotian and Cambodian peoples in their struggle against the common enemy, the United States and its allies, and that the Front had the right to receive aid from abroad while the United States had troops in South Vietnam and would continue the fight until complete victory. In April the DRV Prime Minister Pham Van Dong put forward four points which were in effect a gloss upon the NLF manifesto. The first insisted on complete withdrawal of U.S. forces, the dismantling of American bases, the abolition of the alliance with Saigon, and cessation of U.S. attacks on the North "in accordance with the Geneva Agreements." The second said that the division of Vietnam would continue temporarily but strictly in accordance with the military provisions agreed upon at Geneva; the third that the internal affairs of South Vietnam must be settled by the South Vietnamese people in accordance with the NLF program and without foreign interference. Finally, the peaceful reunification of Vietnam would be settled by the Vietnamese of both sides, again without foreign interference.

When in the same month seventeen non-aligned nations called for negotiations without pre-conditions, President Johnson in a speech at Baltimore offered almost exactly that. In a significant variant on the Geneva provisions he declared that the United States "sought the independence of South Vietnam without outside interference, alliances, or military bases." He offered one billion dollars for the co-operative development of Southeast Asia. As might have been expected, Hanoi had other ideas. This did not deter the U.S. government from issuing a fourteen-point peace program in January 1966.[1] Rather curiously this accepted the 1954 and 1962 Geneva Agreements "as a good enough basis for negotiations." America's rejection of the 1954 settlement had in fact had fateful consequences which could not readily be undone by its qualified acceptance twelve years later. Furthermore Washington was formally a party to the 1962 Agreement on Laos and could not therefore very well accept it merely as a basis for negotiations. Most of the other fourteen points were more obviously constructive. There could be unconditional negotiations anywhere in Asia. A cease-fire could be the first order of business or a preliminary to a conference. The United States was ready to "discuss" Hanoi's four points. America desired no military bases nor a continuing military presence in Southeast Asia, nor did she seek any new allies. The generous offer of aid was repeated. The Vietcong could be represented at the negotiations. The bombing would be stopped if it was known what would happen next. This conciliatory package deal, like other offers, was rejected by Hanoi. Ho Chi Minh insisted on the acceptance of his government's four points and on the recognition of the National Liberation Front as

1. *Department of State Publication* 8050, Far Eastern Series 144, released March 1966.

the sole genuine representative of the people of South Vietnam for the purpose of negotiations. The American move was nevertheless accompanied by a large-scale "peace offensive" in which Washington sent representatives to some thirty countries to explain its views on the Vietnam situation. One motive for this appears to have been a pessimistic bi-partisan report to the Senate Foreign Relations Committee after a Senate team led by Senator Mansfield had visited Vietnam in December 1965. This suggested that the only alternatives were a cease-fire, leaving South Vietnam largely in NLF hands, or the possible extension of the war to the whole of Southeast Asia.

In February 1966 President Johnson met the leaders of South Vietnam in Honolulu. American opinion suggested that this was in part to divert attention from the Mansfield report and the subsequent debate in the Foreign Relations Committee and to reassure Saigon which feared that the "peace offensive" might result in the formation of a coalition government including representatives of the NLF. The conference noted a "total absence of present interest in peace on the part of the government of North Vietnam." Nevertheless peace efforts would continue. So would efforts to combat inflation and promote "rural construction" emphasizing the attempt to build democracy in rural areas and to meet the people's needs in agriculture, handicrafts, and light industry, and in health and education. There was also agreement on a "policy of growing military effectiveness" and closer co-operation between American and ARVN forces. In a Declaration of Honolulu by both governments the United States mainly recalled the points in its peace proposals, while the Saigon leaders spoke of defeating the Vietcong illegally fighting on their soil in a so-called war of national liberation which was part of a communist plan for the conquest of all Southeast Asia. They also emphasized their dedication to the eradication of social injustice. More concretely they promised to set up a democratic constitution and an elected government. This was to have substantial civilian participation and in June, ten civilians were elected to the National Leadership Committee. Saigon continued to emphasize that it would not negotiate with or recognize the NLF. Meanwhile appeals to end the fighting continued to be received from other quarters. In July 1966 Mrs. Gandhi, the Prime Minister of India, produced a peace plan calling on Britain and the Soviet Union to reconvene the Geneva Conference and urging the withdrawal of all foreign forces from Vietnam. The British Prime Minister failed, however, to make headway with the Soviet government, which insisted that British and Russian views were diametrically opposed since Britain "supported United States aggression." In August there followed President de Gaulle's proposals already noted.

The Manila Conference

In September South Vietnam elected its Constituent Assembly. The large popular vote was alleged by some to be due to government orders. In the same month a Philippines Expeditionary Corps left for Vietnam, thus joining the forces of America's other allies, Australia, New Zealand and Korea, and later Thailand.

In October 1966 President Johnson attended the Manila Conference. He had previously established a precedent by being the first American President to visit Australia and New Zealand, both of whom sent delegates. The other participants, apart from the Philippines, were South Korea, Thailand, and South Vietnam. Just before the conference a cabinet crisis broke out in Saigon due to rivalries between the North Vietnamese ministers (including Ky and most of the Junta) and the South Vietnamese, and to the civilian ministers' resentment of the military's high-handed methods. At the Manila meeting the allies of South Vietnam pledged themselves to withdraw their forces within six months if the North would do the same but declared that, while seeking a just peace, they would go on fighting as long as necessary to meet any communist challenge. The rest of the decisions of the conference were basically designed to keep the South Vietnamese up to the mark. The Saigon government must provide a "substantial share" of the forces needed to regain territory from the Vietcong and to win the loyalty of the population. It must fight inflation and plan its post-war economy. It must accelerate the introduction of the new constitution and install a representative national government by September 1967. It must expand social welfare, improve education and health, reform agriculture, and train refugees. The Conference also issued a high-minded but somewhat unrealistic declaration on Goals of Freedom. Among these Goals, some of which were reiterated in the next Presidential Message, were the following: building a region of security, order, and progress; checking aggression; breaking the bonds of poverty, illiteracy, and disease; and strengthening economic, social, and cultural co-operation in Asia and the Pacific. Following the Conference the President went to Southeast Asia and, as we saw, established a fresh precedent by visiting Malaysia.

State of the Union Message, 1967

In his State of the Union Message in January 1967 the President reviewed the sacrifices demanded of the American people and set forth the classical arguments of those convinced that the war was right and necessary. He said that the United States was in Vietnam because an international agreement signed by it, by North Vietnam, and others was being systematically violated by the communists.[2] America, said Mr. Johnson, had decided to fight this war in order to prevent a larger one which was almost certain to follow if the communists succeeded in taking Vietnam over. If they were not checked now the world could expect to pay a far higher price later. Thus the United States had checked communism in Europe twenty years ear-

2. *State of the Union: Address of the President of the United States, January 10, 1967.* House of Representatives Document 1, Serial 12765-1. The President referred to the agreement as being signed in 1962. Yet the only agreement signed in 1962 was that relating to Laos. On the other hand the United States was not, as we saw, a party to the 1954 Geneva agreements relating to Vietnam.

lier and again in Korea more recently. The Asia of tomorrow would be different because the United States had said in Vietnam "thus far and no farther." The President stressed that the United States faced more cost, more loss, and more agony but that General Westmoreland, the U.S. commander-in-chief in the field, had assured him that the enemy could no longer succeed on the battlefield.

The U.S. stand in Vietnam had shown the peoples of Asia that "the door to independence would not be slammed shut" and that they could choose their national destinies without coercion. The efforts of the United States on behalf of humanity need not be restricted by any boundary. It would help all the peoples of Vietnam when peace came. America continued to hope for a reconciliation between mainland China and the world community and would be the first to welcome a China which respected her neighbors' rights and concentrated on improving the welfare of her people. The United States would continue to probe for peace but until the infiltration of the South ceased it must firmly persist in its present course. American boys in Vietnam must be given nothing less than full support.

Tensions and Changes in Saigon

Also in January 1967 the Deputy Prime Minister in Saigon was dismissed on allegations of corruption and Premier Ky, during his own visit to Australia and New Zealand, declared that the military situation had improved since the Vietcong were no longer able to launch big attacks. One day, he said, South Vietnam would defeat the aggressors and unify the country. The leader of the Australian Labour Party struck a discordant note by publicly describing Australia's guest as a "murderer and gangster Quisling." A year later Ky's words about the decline in enemy capacity for aggression were startlingly disproved by a major communist offensive launched during the Tet (Lunar New Year) period at the end of January 1968. Meanwhile elections had been held in August 1967 under the new constitution promulgated in April. In September Lieutenant-General Nguyen Van Thieu was elected President. Former Prime Minister Ky, who was rumored to be on indifferent terms with Thieu, became Vice-President.

The Reckoning

By 1968 the Vietnam war had become the fifth costliest in the history of the United States. It was also, from the time of the first American deaths, becoming the longest. The participation of U.S. forces in this distant struggle had risen as we saw from a few hundred in 1961 to about 550,000 in the latter part of 1968. Soon more than 30,000 American lives would have been lost. These and other casualties, with enormous losses of aircraft, equipment, and material, were producing in the American people a widespread mood of impatience and resentment and a keen wish to end the war. This was the kind of discouragement on which the communist leaders had been counting. It was small consolation that Vo Nguyen Giap, the Northern commander, had reportedly admitted that from first to last the people of his small country had lost in their various struggles some half a million men.

The Vietnam Debate

By the later 1960's the Vietnam controversy had become acute. Had America's decision to intervene on an ever expanding scale been wise, far-seeing and constructive, a timely preventive of far greater evils, or a gigantic blunder? While the debate raged in America two authoritative British sources took exactly opposite views. One, in November 1966, declared that the Johnson doctrine for Asia was starting to pay off. What was happening in and around Southeast

Asia in 1966 was exactly what had happened in and around south-eastern Europe in 1947. When President Truman had committed the United States to the defense of Greece and Turkey he had given the non-communist forces in the region a center of power to rally round and had started an argument in the communist camp between those who wanted to pull back and those who wanted to fight to a finish. It took two and a half years for the Greek communists to accept the fact that they could not take over by armed force, but they did accept this in the end. A similar process was now visible in Asia's crisis. On the non-communist side President Johnson was building up a Pacific consensus and a security system for the Western Pacific through such meetings as the Manila Conference, while the gap between China and Russia was getting wider. Many of the countries bordering on the Pacific were pleased to have an American umbrella over them, even if they did not say so. But Japan, India, and, one day, Indonesia must play their part in a future Asian security system, for a permanent American military presence in Asia was not desirable. The Asian governments must in the end stand on their own feet. Ho Chi Minh was being invited by American intervention to give up the hope of putting the communists into power in South Vietnam in return for the prospect that the area would not be garrisoned by U.S. troops. He was asked to choose between South Vietnam being another Greece or another South Korea.[3] This line of argument appealed to some Americans but it ignored one fundamental factor. Greece had no well-entrenched communist state with a veteran army established in part of the country. Today, if the Hanoi government should agree to any Western proposals involving the departure of U.S. forces it knows that in the long run, being more tightly and ruthlessly organized, it could impose what terms it pleased on a Saigon regime already undermined by a subversive movement inspired by the North.

The contrary view on America's intervention was expressed in January 1968. It called Vietnam the greatest tragedy to befall the coun-

3. *The Economist*, London, November 13, 1966.

try since the Civil War. Apart from all the cost and loss, America's sharp image in the world had been obscured, that of a people which used power with purpose and restraint and with motives generally more trustworthy and disinterested than those of the European nations. The cruel foe had become transformed in the eyes of many into a "brave little country." Moreover, years of falsified predictions about the outcome of the war had undermined Washington's credibility, while the flaws in Washington's policy-making process had raised serious doubts about the United States as leader of an international system such as the Western Alliance. The war had also helped to destroy the confidence of the American people in their vision of law and order and international justice. Although President Kennedy seemed to have realized that insurgency was the real problem, the influence of others such as Secretaries McNamara and Rusk committed America to seeking an essentially military solution. Consequently the U.S. forces had been organized for conventional rather than guerrilla war. The British and French experience in Malaya and Algeria was ignored. This had shown that such subversion could only be countered by a wide range of civil action, particularly in the fields of welfare, justice, and communications, and by efficient police rather than military force. But by 1963, with the immense influence acquired by the Pentagon, there was little hope of modifying the military emphasis. Admittedly the Americans were not dealing, as the British had been, with a colonial territory where they were in over-all control. But when there proved to be no competent Saigon leader after Diem, they should have temporarily assumed full civil and military power (as some Vietnamese had wished them to do) and appointed one person to command in all spheres. Meanwhile because of the war anti-Americanism had made quick strides in Europe and Japan. It had fortified President de Gaulle, strengthened the Russians, and convinced the Germans that the United States was losing interest in Europe. It had emasculated the foreign aid program which was the basis of U.S. influence in India and many

African and Latin American countries. By giving a superb diplomatic advantage to the communist powers it had weakened America's capacity to check their moves. Internally too the war threatened grave consequences. A political and social revolution even more extensive than the New Deal was fermenting in America. It would attract enormous intellectual and economic resources. But the cold war and the Vietnam war had held it up. One danger was that some Americans, instead of just blaming their government's blunders, might assume that America's power could not underwrite stability and security in other parts of the world, that Americans were unwanted overseas and might just as well wash their hands of it all and revert to isolationism. An overriding factor was that no power with universal interests such as the United States could afford to become so deeply committed in one corner of the globe that it lost ability to influence events elsewhere. That was a mistake the Soviet Union had never made.[4]

American voices on the issue have been equally opposed and have pursued broadly similar lines of argument. Some have examined in greater detail one fundamental aspect, namely the legitimacy and effectiveness of the Saigon regime. Here the contrast seems particularly sharp. Thus one writer asserts that the elections for the Constituent Assembly held in September 1966 were a "phenomenal victory" for the government. Foreign diplomats and newsmen, he says, found no significant evidence of government manipulation or coercion of voters or of malpractice in ballot counting. The proportion of those who voted was remarkably high even in provinces where the Vietcong were strongest. The results were humiliating to both the Vietcong and the militant Buddhists, supporting some pre-election estimates that each had a following of no more than 10 per cent of the population. The voters clearly defied communist terrorism. The new Constituent Assembly represented all walks of life. Much

4. Alastair Buchan, Director of the Institute for Strategic Studies, London, in *Encounter*, London, January 1968.

young blood enlivened Saigon's war-weary political scene. The Ky government promised to return to military duties after elections under the new constitution.[5]

A less cheerful comment on these last elections said that the "harsh reality of a Saigon military dictatorship determined to achieve a military victory was always politically embarrassing to Washington because it conflicted with the claim that the struggle for Vietnam was one between dictatorship and freedom." This writer suggested that the elections for President and Senate in September 1967, on the basis of a constitution tailored to the needs of the ruling military clique, were to camouflage the existing dictatorship so as to contain the upsurge of "neutralist" and "peace" sentiments among the vast majority of the people. The elections, he said, were not an exercise in, but a denial of, political freedom. The popular General Minh was barred from running because he was suspected of "neutralism"; the Buddhist slate was rejected. After the election the defeated civilian candidates produced proof of shocking election frauds, and popular demonstrations demanded that the result be annulled. This demand was accepted by a large majority of a commission of the Constituent Assembly; then the Assembly itself, faced with a strong police force, accepted the result by a narrow margin. The new government remained the old Thieu-Ky military regime although these two candidates received only 35 per cent of the votes. Measured by the propaganda requirements of Washington this was an evident fiasco. But the regime could not be dropped since Washington was not prepared to heed the South Vietnamese forces which desired peace.[6]

5. Bain, op. cit., p. 144.
6. Buttinger, op. cit. (*Vietnam: A Political History*), pp. 479, 480.

XV

PARIS AND THE FUTURE

President Johnson's New Course

Against this background came the moves for peace so dramatically initiated by President Johnson at the end of March 1968 coupled with the announcement that he would no longer run for office and followed by the meetings in Paris in May between representatives of Hanoi and the United States.[1] The impression conveyed was that Washington had by then decided that the war could not be won militarily or at least only by two unacceptable alternatives. One would have been an invasion of the North which would almost certainly have brought the Chinese communist forces into battle, since China would have felt her security threatened as she did when United States troops approached the Yalu River during the Korean war. The alternative would have been the use of nuclear weapons. Apart from any moral issue this would have invited direct retaliation upon the cities of America, till then in no way threatened by the Vietnam war, because both the main communist powers now had a nuclear capacity.

The decision of the United States to make a special bid for a settlement at this juncture could be interpreted by some as a weak

1. *Department of State Publication* 8376, East Asian and Pacific Series 173, released April 1968.

concession to a faltering public opinion. Thus Washington unilaterally reduced the bombing of the North without the preliminary assurance it had previously demanded that there would be reciprocal de-escalation by Hanoi. Yet this was not an act of weakness since Hanoi too had made a significant concession by departing from its earlier standpoint that there could be no talks until "all acts of war by the American imperialists" had ceased. Ho Chi Minh obviously had the shrewd thought that he could do a good deal to improve his military position while the talks were going on. But so of course could the Allies. It was clear that the communists had also come to realize that they could not win militarily as they had done against the French. Indeed by comparison with the French the United States had won at least a partial victory.

Weaknesses in Washington's Bargaining Position

Nevertheless the position of the United States at the talks was in one way weaker than Hanoi's. Ho Chi Minh had counted, as we saw, on the growing distaste for the war in America, especially among the young people who faced the draft. These were by no means convinced that the existence of their country was at stake and had little relish for becoming potential cannon-fodder in a land which seemed divorced from all the realities of American life. At the same time many Americans were disturbed by the appalling waste of national resources which the country could ill afford. This had already endangered the dollar and prevented the government from spending much that was needed in other vital fields such as poverty and education. There was also the moral dilemma that the "small" Vietnamese in the South had suffered so appallingly for more than twenty years from victimization first by one side and then the other that some would, it seemed, have given almost anything for the war to end even if it meant accepting communist control. If this interpretation were correct, was America justified in prolonging the war when many of those for whom it was being fought would rather settle it on their own terms? Finally, the visible relief of most Americans at the prospect of an end to the fighting meant that it would be extraordinarily difficult for Washington to re-escalate the war to an even more destructive and expensive scale.

The Chances of a Settlement

The talks lasted for over a year with virtually no progress toward agreement. It became clear that they might be as tough and frustrating as other long wrangles with the communists, some of which ultimately achieved a settlement, such as those over Korea and Austria. President Johnson had said on March 31 that as a move toward peace he had taken the first step to de-escalate the conflict by ordering American aircraft and naval vessels to make no attacks on North Vietnam "except in the area north of the demilitarized zone where the continuing enemy build-up directly threatened Allied forward positions . . . an area including almost 98 per cent of North Vietnam's population and most of its territory." The DRV for its part, after reciting its grievances against the United States, declared its readiness to meet U.S. representatives "with a view to determining with the American side the unconditional cessation of U.S. bombing raids and all other acts of war . . . so that talks might start." This was subsequently elaborated in similar terms by Xuan Thuy, a member of the Hanoi cabinet and former Foreign Minister, who led its delegation in Paris. He said that the object of the talks was to agree on the unconditional cessation of the bombing and of all acts of war, and afterwards to hold conversations on other problems of interest to the two sides. The Hanoi delegation taxed the United States with non-observance of the Geneva Agreements of 1954 (to which America had never formally acceded) and denied that Washington had any right to demand reciprocal action from the DRV in response to its measures of de-escalation. Hanoi's four points were the correct interpretation of the Geneva Agreements and only after the internal affairs of South Vietnam had been settled in accordance with the program of the NLF could they "move towards the peaceful re-unification of the country." From this clear-cut posture the DRV never departed. However infuriating their attitude, it could hardly be called deceptive.

There was, however, some initial ambiguity about the American position. It had been widely assumed from Mr. Johnson's statement that American bombing would be limited to areas near the DMZ. When it was subsequently explained in Washington that bombing would continue up to the 20th parallel (or the edge of the Red River delta some 225 miles further north) this caused sharp criticism in the United States. It handed the communists a gratuitous propaganda point. The U.S. team was led by Mr. Averell Harriman and subsequently, after the inauguration of President Nixon, by Mr. Henry Cabot Lodge, Washington's former Ambassador in Saigon. Both had Mr. Cyrus Vance as their deputy. The main U.S. arguments were that between 1955 and 1960 there had been such improvement in the lives of the South Vietnamese that they were outdoing the North in peaceful competition. Therefore the Hanoi leaders had turned in the late 1950's to terror and violence to destroy this progress. The introduction of regular units of the North Vietnamese Army into the South had preceded that of U.S. combat forces. Despite America's original refusal to accept the Geneva settlement, the U.S. negotiators did not hesitate to invoke it. They stated that it forbade aggression by either North or South Vietnam and that it had been violated by the North's invasion of the South. They proposed that both sides should start by restoring to the DMZ its original and proper status, that the 1962 Agreements on Laos, and also Cambodian territorial integrity, should be respected, and that coercion of, and attacks upon, the South should be stopped. Furthermore the DRV must recognize the role of the government of the Republic of Vietnam in a settlement of the conflict. Mr. Xuan Thuy pointed out that according to the Geneva Agreements the demilitarized zone was linked with the military demarcation

line, both being only temporary, and that the Saigon "puppet" regime had only a provisional right of administration pending the elections for the reunification of Vietnam. He also admitted by implication the presence of DRV troops in the South by saying that Vietnam was one country and the Vietnamese one people. The South
Vietnamese had the right to receive total aid from their compatriots
in the North. Any Vietnamese had the right to fight anywhere in
their country against the Americans, who must stop their aggression
without asking for "reciprocity," "restraint" or "mutual de-escalation." The DRV should discuss with the United States problems
connected with the fundamental principles of the Geneva Agreements and with Vietnam as a whole, while the NLF should take
part in discussions on purely Southern affairs.

On October 31, 1968, after calling home for urgent consultations
the Commander of the U.S. forces, President Johnson announced
another significant step in the de-escalation of the war by the United
States. As of November 1 all air, naval, and artillery bombardment
of North Vietnam would cease. Furthermore from early November
representatives of the Saigon government as well as representatives
of the NLF would participate in the talks. This, however, in no way
implied U.S. recognition of the NLF. In justifying this decision, the
President pointed out that the Saigon government had grown steadily stronger. The effectiveness of its armed forces, which now had a
million men under arms, had steadily improved. Meanwhile the superb performance of the U.S. forces under Generals Westmoreland
and Abrams had produced truly remarkable results. Due to this,
enemy attempts to mount a so-called third offensive at the end of
August had not materialized, more enemy troops had been withdrawn from the battle area than after previous offensives, and there
were fewer enemy-initiated attacks or engagements than at any time
since 1965. Washington officials pointed out that although there
was no "contract" with the DRV on the military restraint it must
show, there was "good reason to believe that Hanoi fully understood
that it must respect the DMZ and cease attacks on South Viet-

namese cities if productive talks were to go forward in Paris."
Should the DRV not observe these conditions the U.S. forces were
under orders to retaliate. After some months of four-party round
table talks it became clear that this second conciliatory step by the
United States was evoking no notable response from Hanoi. Yet the
bombing of the North was not resumed. The Northern leaders, who
chose to take this unilateral de-escalation as nothing more than their
due, clearly perceived the fundamental weakness in the U.S. position, namely that the state of opinion in America would prevent the
resumption of the bombing in virtually any circumstances. The indi-
cations given in the first months of the Nixon administration, of
Washington's desire to get out of Vietnam whenever the South
could assume the full burden of its defense, inevitably encouraged
Hanoi to stand firm in the hope of further unilateral concessions by
the United States.

In spite of all the tension and frustration, in mid-1969 there was
still some prospect that the talks would achieve eventual success.
For all its insolence and bluster the North was likely to see little
point in fighting indefinitely a war which it now knew it could not
win. There was also the strong presumption that Russia wanted a
settlement, and this might be a main factor in guaranteeing that
agreement would one day be achieved. In spite of her intervention
in Czechoslovakia in 1968, Russia's communism had evolved to a
maturer phase since the death of Stalin as had that of Yugoslavia,
Romania, and other countries of eastern Europe. Even after disci-
plining its communist satellite in Prague, Moscow had made it plain
to Washington that it still desired to pursue the path of co-existence
between East and West which it had sought to follow for some
years and in the context of which the Vietnam war was a frustrating
obstacle.

Peking had, it was true, indicated its disapproval of the negotiations but it was encouraging that Hanoi had ignored these rum-
blings and that Peking had not in the event done anything to block
the talks. At the root of China's objections lay, of course, the fact

that she had not yet reached the maturer phase of communist evolution but was still in the vituperatively revolutionary stage and strongly resentful of America's exclusion of her from the comity of nations. Some mending of fences by Washington in that quarter was clearly going to be an important factor in bringing about a more constructive attitude of Peking toward a Vietnam settlement.

Peking's Obsessions and Objectives

One possible interpretation of China's embittered attitude could be that she was chiefly motivated by fear for her own security, a fear not unnatural in a country which had been brutally abused by the advanced nations through most of the nineteenth and twentieth centuries. There was, after all, no conclusive evidence that China was working to take over Southern and Eastern Asia by force. In recent years there had been easy chances for her to do just this in certain areas, chances which she seemed deliberately to have discarded. One was in 1962 after Chinese troops had defeated the Indian forces in India's Northeast Frontier Agency. The Chinese had actually reached the edge of the Brahmaputra-Ganges plain and, had they continued, could have held northern India at their mercy. Instead they suddenly withdrew, having occupied approximately what they regarded as the proper India-China border. Another relevant factor could be that America had half a million troops on China's doorstep while China was in no position to offer a comparable threat to the United States. It seemed possible that China's main objective was to emulate what Russia had achieved in eastern and northern Europe, by ensuring that she was surrounded by a ring of strictly neutral or harmless or sympathetic near-by countries which offered no threat of hostile military bases. These countries did not have to be communist. In Europe neither Finland nor Austria (which used to be partly in the Soviet sphere) were in this category nor, among China's neighbors, was Burma. Moreover while China sought to match and outdo the position of Russia in the communist world both she and the Southeast Asian countries might well be moving into a traditional orbit now that they had thrown off Western rule. The history of these peoples, to which in one scholar's view America had paid too little heed, had affected their indigenous points of view and conditioned their reactions to each other and to external interference. The Southeast Asian countries had a long established custom of paying political deference to China's suzerainty while resisting actual Chinese control.[2] There was no evidence that Ho Chi Minh intended to depart from a tradition more deeply ingrained in his own country than anywhere else.

What Kind of Settlement Might Be Possible?

Because of the military stalemate, in mid-1968 the best obtainable settlement seemed to be one which might eventually be based on the two main Western policy declarations of 1966, those of Presidents Johnson and De Gaulle. Though there had been no positive response to them at the time, both offered points which might well be ultimately reconcilable with the dogmas of Hanoi and the anxieties of Peking. Both took their stand on the Geneva settlement of 1954 and both envisaged possible neutrality for the area with no foreign presence there. The French President's plea was ignored at the time partly, as we saw, because of the almost irrational antipathy he inspired in Washington but partly also because he had proposed a repatriation of American forces as a concession to get negotiations started. But this last hurdle had been surmounted, since the talks had started on the basis of a mere reduction in the bombing. It was incidentally significant that Paris had become the scene of the talks. Saigon having broken off diplomatic relations with France in 1965 President de Gaulle had promptly established diplomatic contact with Hanoi. He had shown a keen and natural interest in these for-

2. Cady, op. cit. (*Thailand, Burma, Laos and Cambodia*), p. 27.

mer French dependencies and in rescuing what could still be saved of France's impressive economic and cultural stake in Indochina. It looked as if his influence had contributed to bringing Hanoi to the conference table and to the choice of sites being so presented that the selection would ultimately fall on Paris. It could also be presumed from his utterances that he anticipated the possibility of France playing some role in the achievement of a general settlement. Even after his departure the French government, being exceptionally familiar with the area and closer to Hanoi than Washington, might be in a position to offer some compromise solution to a prolonged deadlock. A positive American response could go far to ease relations between two countries which had been sadly clouded by insensitiveness and misunderstanding during the De Gaulle regime.

Could Neutralization Work?

In any event, in the difficult circumstances of 1969 a strict neutralization of Laos, Cambodia, and Vietnam on the lines recommended by President de Gaulle was a practical possibility which deserved to be explored. The neutrality of these countries could be guaranteed by all the powers concerned, communist and non-communist, on the pattern of the neutralization of Austria in 1955. It seemed likely that the communist powers, even Peking, would eventually accept and abide by this as they had stood by the Austrian settlement and indeed other pacts once they had laboriously convinced themselves that they were in their interest. But to achieve any such settlement another general conference on the lines of the first Geneva Conference might well be necessary. This could help to ensure Soviet support for a stable settlement as well as the eventual acquiescence of Peking. The necessary participation of Communist China could indeed be a useful step toward better relations between Washington and Peking, particularly if the United States were able by that stage to change its attitude with regard to the latter's seating at the United Nations. Such a conference could be held in Paris as an extension of the initial bi-lateral, and subsequent four-party talks.

No Ideal Solution

It was clear that by now no ideal solution was attainable. After 1954 America had sought to ensure that communism should not spread beyond the borders of North Vietnam. This could no longer be firmly guaranteed for the rest of Indochina. But a widely based international arrangement of the kind contemplated could perhaps ensure that communism did not spread to the rest of Southeast Asia outside Indochina.

After fourteen more years of costly war since his victory over the French, it was unlikely that Ho Chi Minh would settle for anything less than what was offered him in 1954, namely, the prospect of the reunification of all Vietnam. He was also certain to require the withdrawal of foreign troops. It was his life's ambition to be the leader of all Vietnamese. He believed that his struggle of nearly forty years against the subordination of his country gave him the best credentials for this role.[3] A number of his non-communist countrymen seemed to believe this too. The North was war-weary, like the rest of the country. It had suffered very high military casualties and material damage. Due to constant troop requirements it was short of labor for agriculture, and for its hastily developed industries which had been widely dispersed in caves and tunnels to protect them from the bombing. Much war equipment still moved on bicycles, mostly made at home and carrying five hundred pounds apiece.

3. Ho's death on September 3, 1969, betokens no change. His ambitions and objectives have all along been shared by his outstanding associates in the long revolutionary struggle and in the present Hanoi leadership, on whom the main burden seems to have fallen for some time. From what was nominally a supporting role—although much power lay in their hands—these men have now stepped forward formally to assume the guidance of their cause.

There was disorganization and mismanagement, yet in many new institutions of higher learning great steps had been taken to bridge the technological gap. There were conflicts of dogma and personality and external loyalties in the leadership of the ruling party. Yet the determination to end the foreign intervention which had succeeded French rule had never flagged. Despite all outside pressures, and the international ramifications of the communist creed, it could be said of the men of Hanoi that their strength was to have remained dedicated to one widely appealing proposition rooted in the traditions of their country, namely, that the affairs of Vietnam should be settled by the Vietnamese alone.

Now approaching eighty, Ho retained his prestige and power of inspiration as the most durable and perhaps the most skillful and flexible of the "old" communists—those of the years immediately after the Bolshevik revolution—however diminished his active role. He now made few public appearances and these seemed to be stage-managed by his Prime Minister and heir apparent Pham Van Dong. Meanwhile General Giap took pride in having "shaken" the largest country in the world.[4] These three leaders of the Lao Dong were generally considered supporters of the Soviet Union in contrast to a pro-Peking group led by Truong Chinh, Chairman of the Standing Committee of the National Assembly, chief party theoretician, and third in the Lao Dong hierarchy after Ho Chi Minh and the present General Secretary, Le Duan. Truong Chinh, a hard line Stalinist, was replaced as General Secretary in 1956 after his disastrous farm collectivization policy had led, as we saw, to peasant revolts. Le Duan, the party's leading spokesman on major issues in recent years, was also reportedly a supporter of Peking and was long dubious about negotiations with the United States. But during his period in office the party spokesmen have on the whole managed to remain impartial between the two great communist powers. The Ho Chi Minh regime has continued to draw help from both and has so far

4. Gereon Zimmermann and Marc Riboud, "Communist North Vietnam," *Look*, January 21, 1969, pp. 19–30.

deftly avoided falling out with either. This did not prevent it from supporting the Soviet invasion of Czechoslovakia and from ignoring dark warnings from Peking about a deal between Soviet revisionism and U.S. imperialism.

Early in 1968 Truong Chinh produced a major report which was adopted by the Politburo. This criticized the policy favored by Le Duan of the all-out offensive such as the Tet attacks in January and February of that year, the political preparation for which had been "inadequate." It was suggested that the North should be the "great rear" to the "front" in the South but that the Northern communist revolution had been impeded by over concentration on intensifying the war. Hanoi should revert to the policy of a "protracted" war of small-unit, guerrilla techniques, supported by a strong political base in the South. Strict discipline must be established there over the non-communists in the NLF and the newly formed Alliance of National Democratic and Peace Forces (VANDPF) through which the rural based NLF was trying to mobilize urban support. Meanwhile the political and diplomatic struggle should take precedence over the armed struggle. Truong Chinh particularly condemned the "reformism" of eastern Europe. He also complained of agricultural co-operatives being insufficiently collectivized. Private plot production accounted for some 40 per cent of the income of all co-operative members and these people had been allowed to regain lost ground. He apparently resented as "revisionism" the fact that the decentralization of industry, though originally necessary, had been pursued for its own sake by technocrats interested in economic efficiency rather than ideological correctness (which required centralization). Despite the report's adoption, it is hardly surprising that Hanoi Radio spoke of "heated debate." For many of Truong Chinh's views ran counter to those of other more pragmatic leaders such as Le Duan, who urged, for example, the adoption of material incentives for the workers. While the broad implications of Truong Chinh's report may be acceptable to the Politburo this may be a case of formal acquiescence in the pontifications of their most ortho-

dox spokesman rather than of literally following all his recommenda-
tions. The launching of another major, though less successful, offensive at the Tet period in 1969 would seem to bear this out.

The slow pace of the Paris talks may have been due to a communist belief that the longer they lasted the more concessions they
might win from an increasingly war-weary United States. But March
1969 seemed to open a new phase. By now Hanoi and the NLF
knew that Washington would not re-escalate the war, and they had
gained one further point. They had rejected the U.S. proposals for
restoring the DMZ to its proper status on the basis of mutual withdrawals of troops (although they had in fact withdrawn a number of
their own forces to the North). They alleged that these proposals
would perpetuate the division of Vietnam but in reality they had no
intention of giving up the fruits of years of armed struggle in the
South. Yet, despite this rejection, in March the U.S. representative,
Mr. Henry Cabot Lodge, temporarily shelved the DMZ and troop
withdrawal issues and agreed to discuss the NLF's five points, which
Hanoi chose to regard as one indispensable basis for a deal.[5] An
impression gained ground that the real horse-trading was beginning,
on a basis, of course, of secret contacts and explorations rather than
of public exchanges. One other significant development was that
since the start of the four-party talks Peking had suddenly ceased its
propaganda campaign against the negotiations. China may well have
decided not to forgo all chance of influencing events should agreement be reached. This might also be a sign of the possibility already
foreshadowed that she might wish to participate, as at Geneva, in
any general negotiations for a final settlement. But in mid-1969 no
one could do more than guess at the kind of compromise solution
which might permit America to withdraw and shape the future of
the country in which she had been so long and fatefully involved.

5. *Far Eastern Economic Review*, Hong Kong, March 20, 1969, p. 517.

Elections and the Destiny of Indochina

It was virtually sure that, apart from foreign troop withdrawals and a cease-fire, Hanoi would demand that elections should be held after a given period to decide if, when, and how reunification should take place. But it would be hard to persuade the communists to have them under United Nations auspices, as Washington would prefer, so long as China was excluded from that body. Indeed it might be necessary to accept the Canadian, Indian, and Polish membership of the supervisory body laid down in 1954, or possibly an all-neutral team. In any case with a balanced system of checks and control, and if the South were again given something like two years to recover from the stress and chaos of war, it was by no means certain that such elections would lead to a general triumph of the communists, though admittedly the chances of this were greater than when the South was in Diem's firm hands. While the communists claim to control some ten million people in the South, it was reckoned in 1968 that they in fact dominated hardly one-third of the Southern population. Among them, apart from supporters of the unpopular Thieu-Ky regime and the NLF, there is evidently an important sector of opinion which supports neither the extreme right nor the extreme left. Such people argue that the Saigon government needs the war to stay in power and that even a limited U.S. disengagement would bring about its collapse. They suggest that the United States should propose at Paris a neutral post-war South Vietnam. This would accord with the long-term interests of the United States as well as with President Johnson's earlier terms for peace and, they say, it should appeal to the Soviet Union and other Asian and European countries. It might well be opposed by the present Saigon leaders who have repressed or imprisoned non-aligned, non-communist, anti-government persons. This "third force" claims to represent a majority of the war-tired South Vietnamese. Its members believe